Cognitive Behaviour Therapy
Case Studies

Cognitive Behaviour Therapy Case Studies

Mike Thomas and Mandy Drake

Los Angeles | London | New Delhi
Singapore | Washington DC

SAGE Publications Ltd
1 Oliver's Yard
55 City Road
London EC1Y 1SP

SAGE Publications Inc.
2455 Teller Road
Thousand Oaks, California 91320

SAGE Publications India Pvt Ltd
B 1/I 1 Mohan Cooperative Industrial Area
Mathura Road
New Delhi 110 044

SAGE Publications Asia-Pacific Pte Ltd
3 Church Street
#10-04 Samsung Hub
Singapore 049483

Library of Congress Control Number: 2044929629

British Library Cataloguing in Publication data

A catalogue record for this book is available from the British Library

ISBN 978–0–85702–075–8
ISBN 978–0–85702–076–5 (pbk)

Typeset by C&M Digitals (P) Ltd, Chennai, India
Printed and bound by CPI Group (UK) Ltd, Croydon, CR0 4YY
Printed on paper from sustainable resources

Contents

About the Editors and Contributors

Matt Bowen is a senior lecturer in mental health at the University of Chester. After qualifying as a mental health nurse in 1999 he worked primarily in the field of personality disorders, initially at Guys Hospital and then as a Clinical Specialist at the Henderson Hospital, a specialist therapeutic community for people with a diagnosis of personality disorder. He has a keen interest in psychological approaches to treatment, particularly group based, and the application of psychotherapy across cultures. He leads a Masters programme exploring an intercultural approach to psychotherapies and teaches on postgraduate CBT programmes. Matt's current research interest is media representation of personality disorder.

Mandy Drake is a senior lecturer in mental health at the University of Chester. She qualified as a mental health nurse 20 years ago and the majority of her career has been spent in the community, working primarily with people experiencing common mental health problems. She has worked in the field of CBT for the last 12 years, the more recent of which have been dedicated specifically to brief and minimal interventions. Mandy has an interest in increasing the accessibility of psychotherapeutic interventions to both those wishing to train in the field and to those wishing to engage with the therapy, and this has led her to develop a Masters programme in multi-method therapy. Mandy maintains her clinical practice as an associate practitioner within the university counselling service where she provides a CBT clinic.

Janice Lamb is a principal psychotherapist and a sexual and relationship psychotherapist accredited by both the UKCP and COSRT. She has also completed a PG Dip in forensic sexology and is a COSRT accredited supervisor. Janice currently works in psychology services within an acute NHS hospital trust but she has had a varied career since qualifying as a mental health nurse in 1984. For the past 15 years, however, her clinical practice has drawn heavily on CBT, particularly within her psychosexual work. Janice has a particular interest in working with women experiencing sexual dysfunctions, including those with a history of gynaecological problems.

Ian W. Ross is a qualified psychologist, counsellor, clinical supervisor and cognitive behavioural therapist, accredited by the BABCP. He has extensive experience as a lecturer at the University of Chester and the Open University, with both undergraduate and postgraduate students. Ian is a strong proponent of an integrated approach to psychotherapy and has worked with a range of clients in the NHS, GP settings, occupational health and private healthcare. He also manages an independent CBT clinic in North Wales.

Mike Thomas is Professor of Eating Disorders at the University of Chester. He has spent nearly 30 years in clinical practice and academic life and has worked with clients experiencing eating disorders since 1990. As a consultant psychotherapist he currently runs two separate clinics, one specialising in severe and enduring conditions and the other in differential diagnoses. His current research interests are the impact of family therapy for adults experiencing eating disorders and in exploring physiological aspects which influence chronicity of mental health conditions. He also works with clients diagnosed with personality disorders and PTSD and is a clinical supervisor for CBT therapists working in both the NHS and the independent sector. Mike acts as a consultant/adviser for clinical provision and is actively engaged with ex-Forces personnel, supporting medically discharged servicemen and women to gain new careers in civilian life.

Dennis Turner is a senior lecturer in mental health nursing at the University of Chester. He has more than 38 years' experience of working in the NHS and higher education. His current interests include mental health care within BME communities and cognitive behavioural interventions with this client group. He maintains links with clinical practice by spending time with the local Primary Care Mental Health Team where he is involved in working with clients with mild to moderate mental disorders using cognitive behavioural approaches. Dennis is also an associate practitioner within the university counselling service where he provides a CBT clinic with Mandy.

Preface

There are several textbooks available covering the subject of cognitive behavioural therapy (CBT) and it is no revelation to discover that the reason is because CBT is the dominant approach to psychotherapeutic interventions in most clinical services. In fact the approach has gained such popularity that many cognitive behavioural principles are now applied in areas outside its normal practice environments of health and education. Proponents can be found in areas such as sports and executive coaching, and similarly many commercial and public organisations use CBT principles in their management and leadership programmes. In our everyday lives we can see CBT influences around us, in business, marketing, advertising and the media; it has even gained the interest of politicians and economists. We can see its application as consumers; for example, when we are influenced by cognitive techniques in marketing to develop product loyalty, which forms conditional responses through repeated purchasing and generalises our good-will so we go on to buy different products from the same source – an adaption of positive maintenance principles. Modern politics is beginning to understand that people don't significantly change by being hectored or through crude propaganda; there are better and arguably more honest techniques to modify or strengthen underlying assumptions or core beliefs for the benefit of the community.

Yet this social application of clinical application and the popularity of cognitive behavioural principles has not occurred suddenly, even though it may appear to have done so. It has taken nearly 60 years for CBT to reach its current status and it has its beginnings in psychoanalysis and educational learning approaches as well as advancements in early cognitive and behavioural techniques. Many people perhaps forget that Aaron Beck, one of the most significant figures in the development of CBT, was trained as a psychoanalyst, and it was his attempts to include analytical theories in his behavioural treatment clinic that acted as a catalyst for what became his theories of cognitive behavioural therapy.

CBT is, however, criticised for its instrumental, almost mechanical approach to clinical conditions and it has difficulty shaking off a reputation for being aloof and a bit cold. This may be because it has been the subject of more clinical research studies than other forms of psychotherapy, and the constraints of research paradigms, particularly relating to objectiveness and applying validated measuring instruments, does it no favours in this regard. Yet from early proponents such as Beck, Ellis, Gelder and others, to more modern practitioners, there has been an emphasis on developing trust and empathy within CBT and there is a growing view with developments such as compassionate and mindfulness-based CBT that practitioners could do more to highlight these aspects of therapy.

It is no surprise either that CBT has grown significantly from its earlier clinical and educational roots; research studies repeatedly demonstrate that the approach is efficient and effective. In other words it is good value for the use of time, resources and money, and produces results which are consistent, repeated and measurable across a range of different presenting conditions and services. CBT is a very adaptable therapy; it can be applied in community settings, residential and in-patient services or in the home through guided self-help, psycho-educational approaches and computerised CBT (c-CBT). Therapeutic interventions can be as brief as 6–12 one-hour sessions or last longer for chronic and severe conditions, and individuals can have 'top-up' sessions to prevent relapse. This has led to another debate amongst CBT practitioners: some suggest that the values underpinning CBT are more than just reductionist economic applications and that the quality of therapy is being compromised by utilitarianism; others argue that it is a professional and even ethical responsibility to offer the best quality at the lowest cost.

Nevertheless such efficiency and effectiveness has ensured that the National Institute for Clinical Excellence (NICE) suggests the use of cognitive behavioural therapy as a clinical intervention across a wide range of clinical presentations. This has led to a debate amongst CBT practitioners regarding the application of clinical methods such as conceptualisation and formulations. As the increase in protocol-driven formulation and treatment models for specific clinical conditions continues some practitioners argue that they should displace the case and individualised formulation planning approach; others suggest there is room for all three to be accommodated in practice.

CBT is also flexible; it has no school of theoretical rigidity, although there may be a number of orthodox CBT practitioners who would like to establish such a school, and it has grown to encompass more traditional humanistic approaches such as mindfulness-based CBT. The current 'third wave' of cognitive behavioural psychotherapies also includes couples and family therapy as well as trans-cognitive and multi-modal principles and early research findings suggest that CBT is continuing to develop and adapt new applications.

All this has ensured that CBT is often the most common therapeutic option offered by service providers and the chances of a mental healthcare professional not encountering CBT provision today is unusual. More practitioners are also engaging with CBT practices in their own professional fields, such as general mental health practice, nursing, psychology, psychiatry, social work, occupational therapy, dietetics and physiotherapy, to name just a few. Yet out of the many books available regarding cognitive behavioural therapy there are fewer covering case studies than there are theories or principles, and unfortunately feedback and evaluation from our own students, clients and fellow-practitioners suggest that sometimes the presentation of CBT principles applied to practice is too dense, jargon-filled, aimed at the specialist, or all a bit confusing.

This is therefore a general textbook aimed at the individual specifically interested in the application of CBT in practice and covering some of the most commonly encountered clinical conditions. Its aim is to further the understanding of theory-application and can be used by students, practitioners, service-users, carers and lecturers to support and develop their interest in cognitive-behavioural therapy. It is not a specialist text covering theory in great detail or a diagnostic manual – there are no 'exemplar' treatment interventions based on hypothetical clients – but a book highlighting individuals with clinical presentations and the realities of clinical life when applying cognitive behavioural psychotherapy. For example, some of the case studies demonstrate good progress through treatment interventions; others show clients struggling with the dilemmas faced when developing counter-conditioning strategies or with behavioural experiments that challenge their normal avoidance-strategies to disconfirm their negative beliefs. Such varied and different case studies hopefully reflect the individuality of clients and therefore the cognitive behavioural therapy best suited to their individual needs.

Mandy Drake and Mike Thomas

1
Principles of Cognitive Behavioural Therapy

Mandy Drake and Mike Thomas

Learning objectives

By the end of this chapter you should be able to:

Discuss the historic development of CBT
Describe the Stepped Care model
Explain the principles of CBT
Outline the therapeutic process

This chapter will cover some of the background to cognitive behavioural therapy (CBT) principles using the device of common questions and answers. Perhaps one view that needs to be challenged right at the beginning of the text is the invidious belief that CBT is an instrumental approach lacking the degree of human contact and empathy which are often highlighted in other therapeutic approaches. This is not a new criticism and this continuing negative perception of CBT may, in part, be due to the protocol-driven case formulations which are increasingly used in practice. These are tested formulations with proven effectiveness which are applied to specific conditions or problems and have pre-set guidance, even down to a specific session's content, and can be observed in the Improving Access to Psychological Therapies (IAPT) programmes currently in vogue. This text demonstrates the application of some protocol-driven formulations, particularly when engaging in maintenance therapy, but we have also attempted to present generic and idiosyncratic case formulations (idiosyncratic referring to bespoke and more appropriate formulations based on clients' multi-problem or complex presentations).

CBT exponents have had to constantly emphasise the compassionate and humanistic elements of the therapy. As far back as 1989, Gelder noted that CBT was concerned with the thoughts and feelings of the individual and was therefore an important bridge between the then more dominant behavioural approaches and the dynamic therapies. In 1995 Judith Beck emphasised the empathetic skills required of the CBT practitioner and the need for them to be authentic and genuine in their commitment and interest towards the client as an individual. By 1996 Salkovskis had argued against the mechanical application of CBT whilst Padesky (1996) had highlighted the need for skilled psychotherapeutic application to prevent a prescriptive approach. More recently, Thomas (2008) pointed out that the founder of CBT, Aaron Beck, originated from a psychoanalytical background and that it was his attempt in the late 1950s and early 1960s to bring psychoanalytical principles into behavioural approaches that first gave him the origins of what became CBT. More recently Westbrook, Kennerley and Kirk (2011) have acknowledged that, despite repeated refutation, CBT still has the reputation of being a mechanical application of techniques and as such they have argued that CBT is in fact a therapy of understanding (see below). This approach supports the work of Leahy (2008), who argues that the therapist who demonstrates understanding of the clients' suffering increases the chances of a successful therapeutic outcome.

This book continues to argue that CBT has a humanistic aspect in that therapeutic interaction cannot be adequately practised without a good, sound level of communication skills, empathy and understanding for, and of, the client. It also demonstrates that case formulation and assessment require the establishment of trust and confidence in both the therapy and the therapist and that this cannot occur without sound and skilful interpersonal interaction. In fact one could posit a view that CBT treatment interventions without the necessary understanding and empathy are not actually CBT but an artificial application of CBT principles, often based on an economic model of cost effectiveness rather than a genuine, authentic interest in the plight of those seeking support. That is perhaps where the mechanistic, instrumental approach lies; with those practitioners who claim to practise CBT but do not grasp the level of interpersonal techniques and skills required to support clients through difficulties.

This constant drive to retain and highlight the compassionate elements of CBT as a reaction to those who promote the recipe models may explain the 'third wave' of CBT techniques now gaining popularity with more emphasis on mindfulness-based cognitive therapy, integrated meta-cognitive approaches, schema-focused therapy and the assimilation of brief, group and family therapy techniques into CBT practices.

One of the aims of this book is to demonstrate through case studies the reality of practising CBT with clients who have myriad difficulties and who seek compassion, trust and skilful intervention to support them as they deal with the intricacies of their daily lives. Thus, the reader will not find exemplars here, as clients with simple, single-issue presentations may well be suited to the theoretical application of CBT but unfortunately tend not to exist in the realities of practice. Instead we have attempted to demonstrate the application of CBT to cases that are reflective of the real issues found in clinical practice, thus better representing the complex clinical world experienced by many CBT practitioners.

Some background reading may be useful, and certainly having access to the *Diagnostic and Statistical Manual of Mental Disorders*, 4th edn – *Text Revision* (DSM-IV-TR; APA, 2000) and the *International Statistical Classification of Diseases and Related Health Problems, 10th Revision* (ICD-10; WHO, 2007), would enhance understanding of the diagnostic criteria for each presented clinical problem. There are also several excellent CBT texts available which provide ample background knowledge of theory and principles in more depth than we go into, and it is our assumption that readers will draw on these to complement the case-study approach taken here.

Yet a text on CBT cannot be presented without some acknowledgement of the principles of CBT and this chapter begins with one of the most common queries.

Why CBT?

CBT appears to meet three conditions which have helped it to gain popularity as a treatment of choice in many clinical environments and more recently within the wider social world. These include the strong evidence base for its effectiveness, its cost benefits in terms of resource use, particularly with the advent of guided self-help, psycho-educational and e-CBT approaches, and its flexibility in application in relation to the number and duration of sessions, the level at which treatment can be aimed and the growing number of conditions to which it can be applied.

Gelder (1989) noted that it was during the 1970s and 1980s that CBT gained popularity, stating that this is when it was found to be more amenable to clinical trials and was thus considered to be more scientific in its approaches than the other approaches of that era. The range of conditions to which it could be applied was demonstrated by Hawton and colleagues (1989), who listed panic, generalised anxiety, phobias, obsessions, eating disorders, sexual dysfunctions, relationship problems, somatic problems and depression among those where CBT was effective.

Beck, Freeman and Associates (1990) went on to apply CBT with individuals presenting with personality disorders and not many years later Haddock and Slade (1997) demonstrated CBT to be effective with individuals experiencing psychosis. Since then Murray and Cartwright-Hatton (2006) have looked at CBT interventions in the field of child and adolescent mental health, Free (2000) has used it in group settings and Crane (2010) has applied it in a mindfulness context. Lazarus (1997) and Curwen, Palmer and Ruddell (2008), have emphasised its use in a brief therapy setting and Robinson (2009) has observed that CBT is being incorporated into family therapy interventions. Westbrook et al. (2011) suggests that CBT has increased in popularity over the last 30 years because its roots lie in scientific psychology and therefore it has taken an empirical approach which allows practitioners and researchers to provide more evidence for its use more rapidly than other therapies. Alongside such efficacy studies it has also consistently demonstrated an improved economic model compared to other therapies, particularly with its emphasis on 6–12 sessions.

CBT has been shown to be effective in many evidence-based studies, with reduced negative symptoms for clients and more positive health outcomes and changes in their daily living. For the health economist, the service managers and the politicians this indicates less need for health intervention and therefore less utilisation of health resources; for as well as demonstrating effectiveness CBT also demonstrates efficiency. This makes it a treatment of choice for the independent sector, the privately funded single-practitioner therapist and the NHS, particularly if there are time-limited sessions of around 6–12 sessions. Its effectiveness and efficiency has gained CBT the attention of the National Institute of Clinical excellence (NICE) which has produced a series of guidelines specifying CBT as the recommended treatment therapy. CBT therefore meets government objectives (of whatever political persuasion) of managing public funds (Thomas, 2008).

CBT also has the flexibility to be included in the Pathways to Care (Stepped Care model) widely implemented in mental health settings in the United Kingdom. In this model there are a number of steps representing different intensities of treatments and interventions. Each step therefore provides an increasing level of support and the client can be referred out of the Pathway or upwards or downwards as their condition deteriorates or improves. Clients can also access a step without necessarily completing lower steps, depending on their level of need and severity of presenting symptoms.

Step 1, Watchful Waiting, is used when clients do not want any health interventions or when the practitioner believes that they may recover without any interventions, and is generally viewed as a sub-clinical situation. Step 2 is aimed at individuals presenting with mild to moderate conditions and involves guided self-help, CBT utilising psycho-educational interventions, e-CBT and exercise-on-prescription or sign-posting towards local voluntary or self-help groups. Step 3 is for clients presenting with moderate conditions and this is where CBT becomes more intensive. The emphasis, however, is on briefer therapies where possible, sometimes coupled with psycho-pharmaceutical interventions. Step 4 is for individuals experiencing moderate to severe conditions, involves chronic or severe disorder management and may involve assigning a case manager to work alongside the client. The case manager in turn, usually supported by a specialist mental health worker liaises with the client's general practitioner and other significant carers, co-ordinates case conferences, and maintains contact with the client on a regular basis. Interventions may involve brief CBT, psycho-pharmaceutical input or longer-term CBT for up to 16 to 20 sessions. The final stage of the Care Pathway, step 5, is for clients experiencing chronic, severe or enduring problems, is offered by specialist mental health services and aims to support clients who have failed to improve in the previous steps or who have such severe problems that those interventions in steps 1–4 are inappropriate. Treatment usually means inpatient care providing complex psychological and psycho-pharmaceutical interventions.

In summary, CBT has spread widely over the last four decades. It has demonstrated its effectiveness and efficiency in two ways: across different clinical services and clinical conditions using evidence-based studies; and in its cost effectiveness in terms of resource allocation. It is therefore recommended by NICE as a treatment intervention in many clinical conditions, and as such has become the most advocated intervention in the Stepped Care model which is integral to current mental health service delivery.

What is the aim of CBT?

CBT heralds primarily from the work of Aaron Beck who first published in this area in the 1960s and 1970s. It aims to provide a problem-orientated framework within which a cognitive-behavioural assessment and resulting case formulation can be conducted and compiled (Hawton et al., 1989).

Originally the aims of the assessment and formulation were to provide an individualised treatment programme for clients presenting with a variety of clinical problems, but CBT has developed so that it is now applied in a variety of non-clinical settings, including education, sport, business, politics and the media.

This book, however, focuses on its application in the clinical setting. Persons (1989) stated that the aim of therapy was to differentiate between the client's overt difficulties, in other words the real problems presented by a client, and the underlying psychological mechanisms which underpin or cause the overt problem, often based on irrational beliefs about the self. The therapist should therefore support the client in exploring the overt problem and the relationship with underlying psychological mechanisms in order to alleviate the underlying causative factors.

However, CBT has never been a 'school' of therapy and there are many different philosophical and practical views regarding its theoretical basis and implementation. As mentioned above, Westbrook, Kennerley and Kirk (2011) suggest that the aim of CBT is to gain understanding: understanding of the clients' own individual situation and problems and understanding of CBT principles, the aim being that the two together would provide the most appropriate clinical treatment. Trower, Casey and Dryden (1996) give a slightly different view by pointing out that CBT teaches clients to recognise their own maladaptive thinking and to become aware of those thoughts, feelings and situations that trigger negative automatic thoughts (NATs). Once this has been accomplished, CBT aims to clarify whether the client actually wants to change their current problems, which is an interesting perspective and perhaps one that is often forgotten in the 'rescuing' principles found in many therapies. Only when the client wants to change is the next aim of CBT instigated; namely for the client to learn how to modify maladaptive thoughts. This is reflected in Thomas's (2008), view which states that CBT is a structural therapy which aims to modify dysfunctional thinking, behaviour or assumptions. Therapy is focused on the client learning to recognise their own NATs, and by subsequently identifying the triggers for such thoughts and evaluating their impact on their life the client can then modify their responses, thus preventing unwelcome symptoms and gaining a better quality of life. Kinsella and Garland (2008) add that another aim of CBT is to achieve agreed outcomes or goals which will improve the clients' emotional state, and they propose that decreasing negative thoughts and behaviours should be undertaken within a time-limited structure using evidence-based interventions.

What are the theoretical bases of CBT?

CBT is based on a series of principles starting perhaps with Beck's Cognitive Triad (1976) which states that an individual may be prone to negative thinking about the self, the world and the future. The model has been elaborated many times since his early work, but Beck basically suggested that thinking is underpinned by attitudes (termed assumptions) which are based in early childhood experiences and later life events. For many people such assumptions support adaptation to the world around them and motivate activity to develop and maintain wellness. Everyone has a predisposition to react in certain ways in certain situations and this is based on genetics, environment, early upbringing and life events.

Some life events can, however, be traumatic or at the very least disappointing and can precipitate negative thinking and lower mood states. Low mood in turn heightens the probability of more negative thinking, which reinforces the mood state and in time forms a negative circle which begins to influence day-to-day living. This generalisation of negative thinking is sometimes referred to as cognitive distortion. The person therefore develops a negative view of *themselves*, their current experiences in *the world* and about their *future*; hence the cognitive triad.

One of the problems for the individual with the development of the cognitive triad is that they develop selective attention to only those incidences which confirm their negative view of themselves, the world or their future and this can be difficult to alter. For example they may avoid any situation which may cause a different way of thinking, especially if they think that any attempts at change are doomed to failure anyway. Their mood or cognitive condition may worsen as change begins to happen, causing the individual to think the treatment is not working and reinforcing the sense of failure. Physical symptoms may worsen (an area often neglected in therapy generally) and maintenance strategies may be disturbed such as the family dynamics or relations at work. These negative effects may cause the individual to take avoidance measures such as not attending therapy sessions, not participating in out-of-session activities or leaving therapy altogether. Changing the way that the individual sees the triad from a negative to a more positive position is not always easy and the process is sometimes referred to as the process of cognitive restructuring or cognitive reframing.

Cognition itself was viewed by earlier Beckian CBT practitioners as having three levels, and all three were influenced by two other factors, mood and behaviour. The deepest level of thinking or cognition is often referred as the Core Belief level. These beliefs are supported with a structure which helps link together thoughts, past events and current experiences and additionally assimilates new experiences into existing beliefs. This structure is referred to as the schema although many practitioners and theorists use the terms schemas and core beliefs interchangeably.

Core beliefs support a second, intermediate level of thinking, originally called attitudes but over many years the term assumptions has become the preferred word. In turn these assumptions (both functional and dysfunctional) support automatic thoughts which are immediate, sometimes sub-conscious,

responses to events or issues in a person's life. Beck took the view that disturbances in a person's core beliefs caused dysfunctional underlying assumptions
and supported negative automatic thoughts, known commonly as NATs.

In CBT the therapist works with the client to identify which level of cognition is viewed as the main problem and therapy focuses on interventions at
that level. Because NATs are normally immediate problems they can be the
quickest to respond to treatment and consequently there is a greater interest
in CBT working at this level, as sessions may produce results within 6–12
sessions. Working at the intermediate level takes longer whilst working at
core level can be complex and will often take many sessions. A similar view is
taken within the Stepped Care model where intervention at the NATs level
can usually be carried out at steps 2/3, intermediate interventions at steps
3/4 and core level interventions at steps 4/5. Although core level work takes
longer there is benefit, as interventions at NATs and intermediate level tend
to occur when working at core level as a reframing of core beliefs' impact on
dysfunctional assumptions and NATs in a positive way. Similarly, work aimed
at NATs can undermine an individual's assumptions and core beliefs but the
effect is less immediate.

Both the cognitive triad model and the three levels of cognition have been
the mainstay of CBT principles, but other models do exist and Beck's early
work has been elaborated since the 1970s. One of the most popular models is
one espoused by Padesky and Mooney (1990) which incorporates the three
levels of thinking in Beck's work and in addition places import on the areas of
physiological state, mood, and behavioural and environmental aspects of the
person. This model is known as the five aspects of life experience, and assessment takes into account all five areas of a person's life with equal scrutiny,
recognising how the thinking at either NATs, intermediate or core level inter-
connects with mood, behaviour, physical well-being and the environment.
Therapeutic intervention may be at NATs level, intermediate or core, and
simultaneously work may be done with problems identified in one or more of
the other four areas of physical reactions, behaviour, mood and environment.

Other models have developed alongside Beck's original triad. Meichenbaum
(1975), for example, developed a form of self-help approach to stress management which focused on core beliefs, dysfunctional assumptions and the
physiological aspects of stress as areas where interventions could provide good
outcomes. Ellis (1977), with his rational-emotive therapy model has been an
important influence on the development of CBT as he emphasised the ABC
model. In this approach A refers to an activating event, B to the beliefs associated with the event, and C to the thinking, emotional and behavioural consequences. Ellis himself was interested in the way predisposing and precipitating
factors influenced a person's responses. Persons (1989), preferred cognition,

mood and behaviour, with an additional modality of the problem itself, as the basis for a case formulation approach, whilst Lazarus (1997) practises a form of multi-modal brief therapy underpinned by seven modalities rather than the five popularised by Padesky and Mooney (1990).

How is CBT applied in practice?

CBT interventions can best be described as occurring in phases starting with socialisation, assessment and case formulation, moving into treatment interventions and ending with evaluation.

Socialisation is important yet is often an aspect of CBT which is taken for granted. It refers to the early phase of the therapeutic process in which the CBT approach is explored by the client. In our view the role of the therapist in socialisation is to explain the principles of CBT, its evidence-based findings, how and why assessments are important, the method by which the case formulation model is contextualised and the potential interventions available to the client. In other words explain in a suitable manner the therapy itself and emphasise the elements of choice and control available to the client. It is akin to gaining informed consent for the therapy to continue and it seems entirely reasonable therefore that the potential client should be in a position to decide whether it is the right type of therapy for them at that particular time.

Some therapists talk through the socialisation aspects, others employ educational materials to assist information-giving and others provide demonstrations during therapy sessions to highlight the links between the cognitive triad or to show how thoughts, feelings, behaviour, physical symptoms and the environment interact. Some practitioners incorporate the socialisation phase with the formulation presentation itself; for example Wells (1997) and then later Cooper, Todd and Wells (2009: 96) state that socialisation involves 'selling the model' and includes educating the client about CBT, discussing the patient's role in treatment and presenting the formulation. Many therapists also use this phase to provide information to the client on the clinical diagnosis itself. It remains surprising how many clients know that they have a diagnosis and the name given to their symptoms but lack any details about the condition itself.

Therapy takes a certain amount of courage, the client is being asked to open up with some of their closest thoughts and feelings, within a short time of meeting, to someone who, at first, is a stranger. There is not much time to gauge each other's attitudes or reactions before therapy sessions concentrate on the problems. Achieving the trust of the client is a major aspect of the therapist's responsibility and involves skilled interpersonal awareness. Therapy is also hard work; one hears and reads about the therapeutic effects on the therapists but little regarding the therapeutic effects on the client; yet if therapy is to be successful it requires time, effort and commitment from the client while they struggle with the problems that first brought them to therapy, as well as seeing to all the other tasks that must be accomplished on a daily basis. Beck (1976) discussed the draining effects when change is being attempted, and the therapist plays an important role in ensuring that clients have enough strength to continue the change process. In our experience future therapy is made more difficult when past therapy has been abandoned.

Socialisation is therefore a good point to discuss therapeutic agreements, sometimes referred to as therapeutic contracts, which involves discussing issues such as confidentiality, trust, boundaries for the therapy and the role the therapist may play in a multi-disciplinary team or in liaising with other healthcare professionals. The collaborative aspect of CBT can also be explored with discussions focusing on the client's input regarding activities, assessments, feedback and evaluation.

Despite the different approaches to socialisation there is a general agreement amongst CBT practitioners that socialisation increases the likely benefits of therapy (Roos and Wearden, 2009). For instance, the therapeutic alliance formed in socialisation can have a demonstrable effect on treatment outcome. Daniels and Wearden (2011) found that outcomes had higher success rates if socialisation led to the client and the therapist having agreed treatment goals. Additionally, where there was higher understanding of treatment, there was improved collaboration, which supports the earlier findings of Martin, Garske and Davis (2000), who concluded from a meta-analysis of the literature that a collaborative approach to treatment increased the success of the therapeutic relationship.

Assessment is the process used to gather data in order to develop ideas regarding the presenting problems. The information derived from assessment is used to inform treatment, one example of which is whether the problems experienced are at the immediate, intermediate or core level. Assessment data also provide information about the severity of the problems; whether they are mild, moderate, severe, complicated by comorbidity and so on. It is from the assessment data that clients start to gain an understanding of the CBT principles such as the cognitive triad and the interaction between the modalities of thoughts, feelings, behaviour, physical sensations and environmental influences. The initial assessment can take up to two hours, either in one session or two, but in the new briefer therapies the time available may be one hour or less, whereas for clients with severe or complex problems this could be extended to three or four.

Assessment gives a structure to information gathering and thereby develops conceptualisation and thereafter the presentation of findings in the formulation itself. Assessment is an ongoing process and certainly where measures are used re-assessment is undertaken at set times throughout treatment, usually the beginning, middle and end of therapy to monitor progress and demonstrate outcomes. This is particularly useful if standardised instruments or tools are used, as the results can provide a before-and-after comparison.

For ease of explanation we propose that assessments can take two forms: comparative – matching the results against validated pre-set data scores; or exploratory – gaining further information about a specific problems or events. For example, a diagnostic comparative assessment would have the aim of comparing the results with existing data such as found in the DSM-IV-TR (APA, 2000) or the ICD-10 (WHO, 2007) to confirm whether the client matched the criteria for specific conditions such as anxiety or depression. Another example would be mood scores, where results are matched with validated pre-set data to assess the level and risk to the client. In this book there are examples demonstrating comparative assessments for specific clinical diagnosis, for example using the DSM-IV-TR or ICD-10.

The exploratory assessment is used to find new information in relation to the client's symptoms and as such is individualised and aimed specifically at developing a picture of the client's day-to-day lived experience. The clinical interview is the most common form of exploratory assessment, which starts with asking the client to outline their reason(s) for attending and how they see their presenting problems. The interview aims to elicit the duration of the problem for the client, any known precipitating factors, onset, impact and level of intensity. It can also cover significant life experiences, relationships, employment status, current living situation, hobbies, interests, medication, physical condition and past and present healthcare input.

A further aspect of the assessment is an examination of the client's mental state. This takes into account, amongst many things, the potential for self-harming, suicidal intent, mood state, symptoms of psychosis or physically based disorders such as early onset of dementia, alcohol misuse or disordered eating.

To complement the clinical interview, CBT assessment tends to draw on a variety of measures, often taking the form of global symptom questionnaires (e.g. PHQ-9; Kroenke et al., 2001) or more specific records and diaries such as a panic diary. The latter tend to be developed by the therapist and individualised to the client's presenting problems, and a range of such measures can be found in the Appendices of this book.

Case formulation are the next stages in therapy but it seems from reviewing the literature that there is some confusion about these as there are frequent references to case conceptualisation or case formulation as the same thing. Indeed, Westbrook et al. (2011) state that formulation is sometimes referred to as case conceptualisation and Grant et al. (2010) use the terms interchangeably. However, we would argue that they are different and that case conceptualisation is the *initial* stage before formulation itself.

Conceptualisation involves identifying, through a variety of assessment means, the origins, development and maintenance of the problem, whilst formulation is usually the *presentation* or demonstration of the conceptualisation using pictorial or diagrammatic form. The form is most often a model which may be generic or specific to the difficulties experienced by the client. Models tend to represent the theoretical stance of the originator(s) and provide a valuable method of demonstrating connections or patterns that describe or illustrate dysfunctionality. They may examine domains such as thinking, feeling, behaviour, physical/bodily effects and the environment, or may highlight the connections between immediate perceptions, underlying dysfunctional assumptions and belief frameworks.

The other area of potential confusion is with the types of formulations which are commonly grouped into one of three different types: protocol-based – tested in practice and problem-specific; generic – as in Padesky and Mooney's (1990) five aspects model; or idiosyncratic – a combination of generic or problem-specific-based models in conjunction with the client's particular or complex presentation. Protocol-based formulations are also referred to as problem-specific formulations, whilst some authors use the term case formulation to indicate generic or idiosyncratic formulations.

There is much discussion in the literature about which type of formulation should be used, and over recent years there has been a drive for the adoption of those that are protocol-based. This is because such formulations come with a treatment package attached which directs the therapist through a standardised set of interventions, often having been proven effective and efficient in research trials. Due to this evidence base some practitioners argue that therapists have an ethical and professional duty to utilise protocol formulations (Grant et al., 2010), whilst others have been noted to view such formulations as inferior to generic and idiosyncratic ones, stating that in the reality of the clinical situation the latter better support clients who present with complex, co-morbid, chronic, severe or enduring conditions (Kinsella and Garland, 2008). We share the view of Kinsella and Garland (2008) that protocol-driven formulations are a good method of learning CBT skills (being based on good CBT principles), and that they can also be useful for short-term CBT interventions, but we also believe that the generic or idiosyncratic formulations are more bespoke and better able to accommodate additional aspects of the clients' problems that often co-exist in practice. We also value the flexibility of general and idiosyncratic formulations as they give more freedom for clinical decision-making which can not only be based on the individual experience of the therapist but can also assimilate the individual experience of the client.

It may therefore be that the less experienced therapist learns the trade, so to speak, through the use of protocol-driven formulations and that with more experience they gain the skills and knowledge to utilise more generic models. Thereafter, with even more clinical experience, they might go on to develop idiosyncratic models, allowing them to draw on their own clinical decision-making abilities and to individualise the treatment to the specific needs of their client.

Finally, there are also terms such as maintenance formulations and longitudinal formulations which one could argue strictly on definitional terms are not formulations but *principles for* formulation models. The former focus on the problems that are immediate and present and on what is maintaining them in the here and now. It introduces the client to the vicious cycle, a commonly used term in CBT to describe the interrelated nature of the different modalities (thoughts, feelings, behaviours, physical sensations and environment). Maintenance formulations tend to be utilised where therapeutic intervention is short to medium term, with the focus therefore normally being on NATs and assumptions. This approach is most commonly reflected in protocol-driven and generic formulations. Longitudinal formulations, on the other hand, focus on core beliefs that have been formed by environmental and early life experiences, and, as a result, therapeutic intervention tends to be longer. Longitudinal formulations are most commonly idiosyncratic in nature. This view accords with that taken by Kuyken, Padesky and Dudley (2008), who suggest that longitudinal factors should be considered when developing a formulation that may involve predisposing factors, whilst a presentation of the maintenance cycle should be considered where the focus is on more immediate triggers and impact.

In summary, a case formulation is therefore the process by which the identified, presented client problems (conceptualisation) are linked with existing CBT principles so that both the client and the therapist have enough information to devise an agreed treatment plan. There is a variety of forms and models of formulation, a selection of which are demonstrated within the chapters of this book.

Treatment interventions are implemented following the outcome of discussions from the formulation presentation. For problem-specific or protocol-driven formulation there is usually a pre-designated plan of intervention which can be discussed with the client, whilst for generic or idiosyncratic formulations the therapist outlines the most appropriate type of interventions. For this general text covering CBT interventions the treatment interventions tend to follow the generic and idiosyncratic approach, rather than being protocol driven, and these are subsequently differentiated as follows: the level at which intervention takes place within the Stepped Care model and the focus of cognitive intervention as being either NATs, dysfunctional underlying assumptions or core beliefs. In turn these are designated as follows: NATs as immediate interventions, dysfunctional underlying assumptions as intermediate interventions and core belief as core or schematic interventions. For example, a client with mild depression who is referred to a practitioner working in the community is offered intervention based at step 2 of the Care Pathway with CBT treatment following a generic, guided self-help approach where cognitive interventions are aimed at the immediate (NATs) level. Another client presenting with a severe and enduring eating disorder is seen by a practitioner working within a specialist inpatient unit, therefore the intervention is at step 5 of the Care Pathway, formulation is idiosyncratic and interventions are based on cognitive reframing at the schematic (core beliefs) level.

The goal of treatment is to teach the client new ways of coping, thinking or approaching their perceived problems in such a way that they have an increased ability to cope. If the situation cannot be changed or a condition is chronic and enduring then techniques such as mindfulness support more of an acceptance approach to the issues. What is important for intervention strategies to be effective is to have pre-set objectives or outcomes which are realistic and achievable, and not too generalised. Sometimes the objectives may be set at certain points throughout the therapy and sometimes they are set as end goals. Therefore the formulation should provide signposts towards prioritising the problems to be addressed first, and logically these should be the ones causing the most immediate concern for the client.

To progress towards the identified goal the therapist has a myriad of strategies available to them, and rather than discuss these as theoretical premises we have chosen in this text to demonstrate the strategies through their application to the cases presented.

Evaluation of the treatment intervention tends to happen within the last two sessions of therapy and normally takes the form of revisiting the original objectives or goals and evaluating whether these have been met. Evaluation can sometimes be quite quick and relatively simple but in other situations it can be quite complicated and involve referring onwards, planning maintenance strategies, contacting local voluntary groups or managing a situation where the client does not want to leave therapy.

The use of standardised measuring tools is very useful in the evaluation phase of therapy as the client can see the difference in scores or performance and the results also act as reinforcers for further commitment to continue new ways of thinking or to support maintenance of new coping strategies. This approach is sometimes referred to as the case experiment design because it gathers data for wider research regarding the validity and reliability of standardised measuring tools, provides a more scientific basis of knowing whether therapy has been useful to the client and can provide some useful evaluation of the service itself.

Evaluation sessions are also an opportunity to discuss relapse prevention. Whilst this would normally be a consideration throughout therapy, the evaluation stage can present the chance to plan for this more formally by discussing potential areas of vulnerability and identifying strategies to deal with these. Discussion of maintenance strategies should also be part of the evaluation stage and sometimes the therapist and client will together devise a blueprint of all that has been learnt in the therapy to use as a resource to support positive maintenance.

In longer-term work the **end of therapy** phase may be carried out as part of the evaluation and is another area, like socialisation that is not fully studied or researched. The therapy requires high levels of interpersonal skills to retain the therapeutic boundaries as the client is guided towards independence. A decision has to be made as to whether the client can manage without further therapeutic input, which in many cases is the preferred choice of the client. But for others there may have to be referrals to local self-help groups or charities, or referral on to another service. In other situations, maintenance support may involve e-CBT sessions, telephone links or drop-in sessions during periods of perceived stress. This is important as deciding the treatment interventions requires planning *before* the final session(s) as the client has a right to be involved in post-discharge planning and potential long-term support strategies. We have tried to show how this phase of therapy can be difficult in some cases and in others demonstrated the importance of onward referral to other agencies.

In summary this is a generalised textbook providing a case-study approach to CBT interventions and not a specialised CBT manual. It is aimed at the student of CBT and those who are interested in using case studies for learning purposes and its objective is to demonstrate the application of CBT principles in various clinical situations. The case studies have therefore been drawn from experiences in specialist and general services, the intention being to present therapeutic approaches which can be applied in the reality of the readers' day-to-day practice.

1. Which of the principles above do you currently apply in your practice?
2. Which formulation approach do you use most widely and why?

Think about …

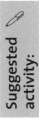

- Discuss with a colleague the advantages and disadvantages of the Stepped Care model.
- If you were entering therapy, what would you like to know about the approach? Think about what would encourage you to engage with the therapy and make a note of these thoughts. Now compare these notes to how you currently socialise clients to your own practice. Do they match?

Suggested activity:

2
Client Presenting with Panic Disorder (without Agoraphobia)

Mandy Drake

Learning objectives

By the end of this chapter you should be able to:

Identify the symptoms and nature of panic disorder
Explain the development of panic disorder from a cognitive perspective
Describe the way in which panic is maintained by the vicious cycle
Discuss the main components of a guided self-help approach
Outline the main cognitive and behavioural strategies used in the treatment of panic disorder
Recognise the central role of safety behaviours and avoidance

---

Diagnostic criteria

DSM-IV-TR (APA, 2000) identifies the central features of panic disorder as recurrent, uncued panic attacks followed by at least one month of persistent concern about having other attacks, worry about the consequences of such attacks and behavioural change as a result. The ICD-10 (WHO, 2007) takes a more flexible approach to the diagnosis but provides consensus of the essential characteristics.

A key consideration is whether criteria are also met for agoraphobia, as panic disorder can be diagnosed with or without this. The essential feature of agoraphobia is feeling anxious in, or about, places or situations from which escape may be embarrassing or difficult or where help in the event of a panic attack may not be available. This anxiety leads to pervasive avoidance of numerous situations, the more common of which include being alone outside or inside the house, being in crowds and travelling on public transport.

Panic attacks can be defined as a sudden and intense experience of overwhelming fear accompanied by strong physical sensations and powerful negative thoughts. They tend to build to a peak within 10–15 minutes and rarely exceed 30 minutes in length. As they are common to a number of anxiety disorders, panic attacks have been differentiated into three types – cued, predisposed and uncued (APA, 2000) – the out-of-the blue nature of uncued attacks being most common to panic disorder.

Many individuals with panic disorder believe that the panic attacks are indicative of a potentially life-threatening undiagnosed illness and may remain convinced of this despite evidence to the contrary. Others fear that the attacks show them to be emotionally weak or to be losing control of their minds or behaviour and they adjust their lives accordingly. It is not uncommon therefore for people to stop doing the things they used to, such as seeing friends, engaging in hobbies and even going to work, but they do not always associate this with the disorder.

Significant comorbidity exists between panic disorder and a number of general medical conditions including dizziness, cardiac arrhythmias, hyperthyroidism, asthma, chronic obstructive pulmonary disease and irritable bowel syndrome. There is also comorbidity with the full range of anxiety disorders as well as with depression, and it is proposed that two-thirds of people with panic disorder will go on to develop depression (APA, 2000).

Predisposing and precipitating factors

There are a number of theories that attempt to explain why panic disorder occurs, but arguably it is the psychological field, in particular cognitive behavioural theory (CBT) that has claimed dominance.

In the CBT model of panic disorder the central maintaining factor is seen to be the fear of bodily sensations, where individuals detect changes in their body and interpret these as a threat. Early work proposed that individuals who had experienced a panic attack found it so distressing that their fear was simply of a repeat attack (Goldstein and Chambless, 1978), but the theory has since moved on. Clark (1986) proposes that the real fear is what the panic symptoms may represent, stating that many sufferers believe them to be indicative of undetected illness, both of body and mind. He further suggests that it is not just symptoms of panic that are open to misinterpretation but any physiological symptoms, with shakiness from not eating and headaches from not drinking being common targets for misconception.

It is such misconceptions that Clark (1986) believes triggers the panic response, which consequently presents as a host of physical and cognitive symptoms that then become the subject of yet further misunderstanding. This is what is known in CBT as the vicious cycle, an elaboration of which will be found later in the chapter.

The success of CBT for panic disorder means that the cognitive model is a widely accepted and adopted understanding of panic disorder, but the sudden, unanticipated nature of the panic attacks has led to the suggestion that a biological explanation may be more fitting. The majority of studies suggest there may be a dysfunction in multiple systems in the brain, rather than any one area but the disregulation of both the benzodiazepine and serotonin neurotransmitters are considered to play a key role, certainly in the aetiology of anxiety (Antai-Otong, 2008). As a result benzodiazepine and antidepressant medication have been used rather successfully in the range of anxiety disorders over the years, but more recently the use of the former has been discouraged in the treatment of panic due to poor outcomes in the long term (National Institute for Clinical Excellence (NICE), 2011). The latter, however, has been shown to be particularly effective with panic (NICE, 2011), thus giving some credence to the biological argument proposed.

Further support for the biological theory includes genetic studies which have found a high incidence rate of panic in identical twins (Stein et al., 1999; Torgerson, 1983) and in first degree relatives of sufferers (APA, 2000). Additionally, some researchers suggest that individuals who experience panic have a heightened sensitivity to physical symptoms and that it is this pre-existing autonomic arousal that triggers panic (Schmidt et al., 2006).

It is unclear what makes an individual particularly vulnerable to panic disorder but it is known that the onset tends to be in late adolescence to the mid thirties, and that developing the disorder after 45 is unusual (APA, 2000). It has been suggested that life events are common around the time of onset, many of which involve the threat of an impending crisis (Clark, 1989). There is also growing speculation that the way in which an initial panic attack is managed may have a bearing, particularly as the physical presentation of attacks means that medical services are usually the first involved. Recognition of panic attacks in such services has been found to be low (Huffman and Pollack, 2003), indicating a delay in appropriate treatment.

Demographic incidence

The exact prevalence of panic disorder is not known, with epidemiological data from around the world suggesting that up to 3.5 per cent of the general public experience panic disorder (APA, 2000) and the Office for National Statistics (ONS) reporting a much lower 1 per cent (ONS, 2010). Similarly, there is a lack of clarity around who is more likely to experience the disorder, with the suggestion of higher rates among women (APA, 2000) being disputed by the findings that the disorder is equally distributed (ONS, 2010).

When applied to clinical samples the prevalence rate soars, with 10 per cent of individuals in mental health services experiencing the disorder. In general settings this is even higher, varying from 10–30 per cent in vestibular, respiratory and neurology settings to as high as 60 per cent in cardiology (APA, 2000). In addition it has been found that up to 25 per cent of patients who presented to accident and emergency met the criteria, all of which may be an underestimation if recognition is as low as reported (Huffman and Pollack, 2003).

Continuum of severity

The severity of panic disorder varies considerably, with some individuals experiencing weekly attacks for a period of months and others having more frequent attacks for only a few weeks. The course tends to be chronic for many, though this may take the form of continuous suffering or of episodic outbreaks followed by years of remission.

Comorbid conditions can complicate the disorder, as can the addition of agoraphobic symptoms, and the lack of early recognition can mean that the condition is much worse by the time psychological services are accessed.

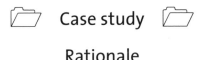

Case study

Rationale

Panic disorder most typically presents as a mild to moderate condition and as such NICE (2011) recommends that treatment should be brief, of lowest intensity and outside of specialist mental health services. The following case study attempts to demonstrate such an approach by following Margaret through step 2 of the Stepped Care model. The treatment Margaret receives is guided self help (GSH) with cognitive interventions being aimed at the immediate level. The setting is Margaret's GP practice where she works alongside a member of the Primary Care Mental Health Team (PCMHT).

Client

Margaret is 64 years old, married and recently retired. Over the last three months she has been presenting to her GP surgery complaining of a number of physical symptoms which the GP thinks are anxiety related. This started after an incident around four months ago where Margaret collapsed while walking her dog in the park. Though she was taken to hospital with a suspected heart attack, subsequent investigations found her to be physically well but Margaret hasn't been able to accept this. Instead she has remained insistent that she has an undetected illness, most probably heart related and her GP has been unable to convince her otherwise. The referral to the PCMHT was an attempt by the GP to alter Margaret's perception of her health and Margaret agreed because she recognised that her concerns were causing her some anxiety.

Assessment session 1

Within CBT there are two common assessment methods; the clinical interview and the use of measures. The clinical interview aims to elicit details of presenting difficulties, and the format utilised with Margaret included current problems, impact, modifiers, onset and history and mental state exam.

Margaret thought that her GP had given an adequate overview of her current problem so the focus initially was on the impact of this, which Margaret identified as anxiety. To break this down further Margaret was asked to recall a recent incident of anxiety, during which she was prompted to identify the thoughts, feelings and physical sensations she had experienced at the time alongside any changes to her behaviour. She was able to recall two incidents very clearly, both of which she stated had come out of the blue. On further discussion, however, it became evident that Margaret was in fact closely monitoring her body and that on identifying palpitations and chest tightness she had misinterpreted these as a sign of a weak heart. It was apparent from the discussion that this had scared Margaret and prompted an escalation in anxiety but what was not clear was how Margaret had responded behaviourally.

It was only when discussing modifiers (strategies that exacerbate or reduce symptoms) that a picture of Margaret's behaviour began to emerge and this is when it became apparent that she was employing both safety behaviours and avoidance.

The aim of safety behaviours is to prevent feared catastrophes and Margaret reported breathing deeply, sitting down, distracting herself and seeking reassurance when she became anxious about her heart. She believed that had she not intervened in these ways her heart would have given way, which was preventing her from seeing the reality of the situation – that her heart would not have failed. Safety behaviours are central to the maintenance of panic due to their role in preventing disconfirmation of the catastrophic belief, and their identification is therefore essential.

Avoidance of situations or experiences that may induce anxiety also serves to maintain panic in that it restricts individuals from experiencing the anxiety and thus discovering that it does not lead to the feared catastrophe. Margaret's only evident situational avoidance was of the park where she collapsed but there was indication that she was avoiding exerting herself in her reports of reduced walks with the dog, reluctance to play with her grandchildren and refusal to push the supermarket trolley.

Margaret agreed that the onset of her anxiety was following her collapse but further revealed that there were also several stressors around this time, some of which remained current. Margaret had retired shortly before her collapse and in the two months leading up to this had been extremely busy and tired. She had initially assumed that over-tiredness had been the cause of the collapse but the consequent investigations into her heart, coupled with a lack of alternative explanation, had left her believing it was more serious. Since retirement she had been isolated and lonely, missing the social contact. She had taken on the role of carer for her grandchildren three days a week and a rescue dog full time, both of which required energy she was afraid to give. In addition Margaret felt distant from her husband, believing him to lack understanding and empathy for her current situation.

Margaret reported two previous episodes of anxiety earlier in her life, both being precipitated by stress and both being characterised by panic. The panic attacks, however, had felt rather different, with thoughts of madness and feelings of detachment, which had prevented Margaret from linking these to her current difficulties. Additional information derived from the mental state exam was that Margaret had lost her appetite and her diet was therefore poor.

It is common practice within CBT to use a range of measures to supplement the information from the interview and these were introduced at the end of the session. Margaret had already completed CORE (Clinical Outcomes in Routine Evaluation), which is a global measure of mental health difficulties commonly utilised in primary care (Evans et al., 2000), and with a score of 19.2 was clearly above the clinical cut-off of 12.9. Due to the high prevalence of comorbid depression in panic disorder Margaret was also asked to complete a PHQ-9 (Kroenke et al., 2001) which, at a score of 10, indicated minor depression of a secondary nature.

Date & Time	Situation (when, where, who with)	Physical (sensations/ symptoms)	Thoughts (what were you thinking/what images came to mind)	Behaviours (what did you do)	Severity of attack (0–10)	Duration (how long did the attack last)
04/05/10 3.00pm	Friend phoned asking to meet at park tomorrow	Heart pounding, difficult to breath, chest tight, dizzy, hot	'Can't go there' 'I will collapse again' Image of lying on floor	Went outside for air Deep breaths Counted apples on tree	9	30 minutes
06/05/10 12.30am	Awoke from sleep	Heart racing, hot, chest hurting, breathing fast, dizzy	'I need to slow heart down' 'I feel dreadful' 'I'm going to pass out'	Woke husband up Took deep breaths Sang a song in my head	8	20 minutes

FIGURE 2.1 Panic diary excerpt

To gather further information specific to Margaret's panic, the panic rating scale (PRS) (Wells, 1997) was administered, which collects details of the frequency of attacks, alongside avoidance, safety behaviours and misinterpretations. A panic diary (PD) aimed at capturing more details of the attacks as they occurred was also given to Margaret who agreed to complete both as homework.

Assessment session 2

A review of Margaret's homework showed that she was experiencing around four panic attacks a week which were severe and of 20–30 minutes in duration. It confirmed the information previously gathered but in addition identified a wider range of physical symptoms and more specific fears of fainting and collapse. An excerpt from her PD can be seen in Figure 2.1

Case formulation

Whilst assessment is continuous throughout treatment, the initial assessment was complete with the addition of the self-report measures. The next stage was to devise a collaborative formulation with Margaret, the aims of which were multi-faceted. Pulling together the information gathered in a way that makes sense to both therapist and client is a primary aim of formulation, as is demonstrating to the client that their story has been understood. It is also an opportunity to socialise the client to the vicious cycle model of CBT which demonstrates how the interrelationship between environmental events, thoughts, feelings, physical sensations and behaviour conspire to maintain their presenting problems. The formulation devised with Margaret followed Williams's (2010) five areas formulation, a vicious cycle formulation based in the here and now with a specific focus on maintaining factors. Margaret's case formulation can be found in Figure 2.2.

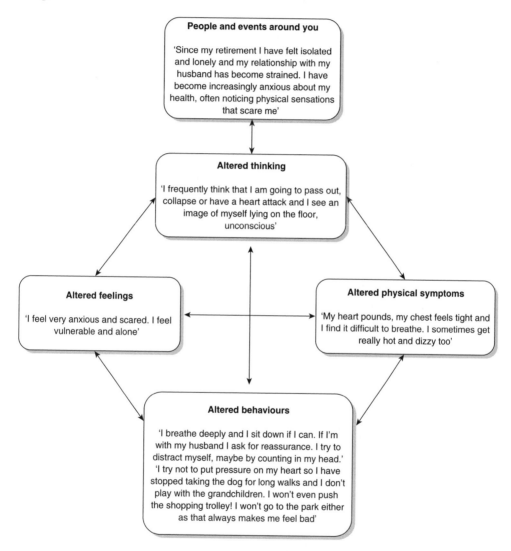

People and events around you

'Since my retirement I have felt isolated and lonely and my relationship with my husband has become strained. I have become increasingly anxious about my health, often noticing physical sensations that scare me'

Altered thinking

'I frequently think that I am going to pass out, collapse or have a heart attack and I see an image of myself lying on the floor, unconscious'

Altered feelings

'I feel very anxious and scared. I feel vulnerable and alone'

Altered physical symptoms

'My heart pounds, my chest feels tight and I find it difficult to breathe. I sometimes get really hot and dizzy too'

Altered behaviours

'I breathe deeply and I sit down if I can. If I'm with my husband I ask for reassurance. I try to distract myself, maybe by counting in my head.' 'I try not to put pressure on my heart so I have stopped taking the dog for long walks and I don't play with the grandchildren. I won't even push the shopping trolley! I won't go to the park either as that always makes me feel bad'

FIGURE 2.2 Adapted from Williams's (2010) five areas formulation. Reproduced by permission of Hodder Education.

A particular aim of the five areas formulation is to assist individuals to recognise how their difficulties are affecting them in order to help them decide what change they want to bring about. Margaret identified the following goals:

1. Understand more about panic
2. Stop worrying about my health
3. Feel positive, not scared and vulnerable
4. Feel better – stop having all those physical symptoms
5. Improve my relationship with my husband
6. Increase my social network
7. Start doing the things I am avoiding.

In order to attain these goals Margaret was asked which of the five areas she would like to focus on initially, the interrelationship of each meaning that change in any one of the areas would result in change in the others. She could see the central role that her thinking was playing and thus decided to work on her altered thinking.

Under the Stepped Care model (NICE, 2011), the least intensive intervention is offered first, which for panic disorder is GSH. Margaret had already shown good motivation and ability to work on her difficulties in the completion of her homework, suggesting she would embrace this type of approach. She also reported enjoying reading and on questioning confirmed that she had no literacy needs. GSH was therefore explained and offered to Margaret and on her acceptance an agreement was made to meet for eight sessions on a fortnightly basis.

Margaret's initial priority was to understand more about panic (goal 1) which was agreed would be her primary focus over the next two weeks. She was given a prescription for a self-help book on panic, available through the local library, and was advised to read the first few educational chapters. She was additionally provided with the details of a panic and anxiety self-help group run by the library and was asked to consider sharing both the reading material and the group experience with her husband in a bid to increase his knowledge too. Whilst NICE (2011) promotes the use of relatives and support groups as standard practice, for Margaret the suggestion was more targeted, working towards goals 5 and 6 being the intention.

Finally, the importance of continuing to monitor her panic was discussed with Margaret who was subsequently directed to a chapter in the prescribed self-help book which would guide her in identifying any emerging patterns or new information arising from the self-report measures.

Treatment session 1

A review of Margaret's report measures identified eight panic attacks over the two weeks but no new data had emerged. A potential pattern to some of the attacks had, however, been recognised in the form of mid-morning panic attacks triggered by shakiness. From her reading Margaret had suspected that this may have been due to low blood sugars from not eating and so had recently introduced breakfast as an experiment, which she intended to monitor. She had also noted a change in the PRS, in that her belief in her weak heart had reduced, and it was clear that her increased knowledge of anxiety had markedly reduced her concerns about her health. Additionally, Margaret reported that her husband had been more understanding after also reading the book, and whilst he chose not to attend the library-based support group he had driven her to the meeting.

Given that her belief in her weak heart had already reduced, Margaret stated that she would like to continue working on this by more directly challenging the thought 'I'm going to have a heart attack.' The verbal reattribution exercises of education and counter-evidence are commonly used for this purpose in panic, the former aiming to correct faulty knowledge and increase understanding, and the latter aiming to gather evidence both for and against the thought. As Margaret's reading had already been successful in correcting knowledge and achieving new understanding, we agreed to focus on evidence, the aim being to generate evidence against her thought and question the quality of evidence for it. My role in the session was to assist Margaret to start this process, whilst modelling the use of the technique, and below is an excerpt from our conversation;

Therapist (T):	What makes you think you will have a heart attack when you are in a panic?
Margaret (M):	Everyone knows that anxiety is bad for your heart.
T:	Is that what you found from the reading you did last week?
M:	Well, no actually, it said that anxiety releases adrenalin and adrenalin is what is given if the heart stops.
T:	So, what do you think now about anxiety being bad for the heart?
M:	It's not really true – just a misunderstanding by the public.
T:	Okay, now let's think about something else. How many panic attacks have you had?
M:	What, ever? A lot … certainly over 100.
T:	So, out of those 100, did any lead to a heart attack?
M:	No, of course not.
T:	Well do you think that there is any evidence against your thought there?
M:	Oh, you mean that I've had panic attacks but not a heart attack?

Within the session Margaret was asked to rate how strongly she believed the thought that she would have a heart attack and on a scale of 0–100 per cent (100 being the strongest possible belief) she stated 45 per cent. An initial evidence

Thought: 'I'm going to have a heart attack'		
Evidence for	**Evidence against**	**Balanced thought**
Anxiety damages the heart – I could have a heart attack	I've been anxious many times but have never had a heart attack	Anxiety and panic will not give me a heart attack
People say you can die of a fright	I've never heard of anybody dying from panic	I will not die from anxiety or from a panic attack
I get symptoms of a heart attack in many situations	These are also symptoms of anxiety – and I do feel anxious	I know that I suffer from anxiety and that this is not harmful
I get tightness in my chest and find it hard to breathe when I do too much	I have over-exerted myself and have not had a heart attack	I get sensations similar to a heart attack when I exercise – they are normal
I often feel my heart beating too fast, like it's under too much strain	I have deliberately put pressure on my heart and I have not died	I am experiencing normal sensations, felt by many. They are not harmful and they will pass

FIGURE 2.3 Evidence chart including balanced thoughts

chart was then constructed before Margaret was directed to chapters on challenging thinking in the self-help guide to both enable her to continue the exercise at home and to prepare for the following session. To assist with evidence gathering, Margaret also agreed to conduct a behavioural experiment, the physical exercise task, which aimed to induce the physical symptoms she misinterprets as a heart attack via exercise, thus demonstrating the benign origin of these. It was agreed that Margaret would skip for five minutes to induce these symptoms, which had the added benefit of directly challenging her fear of exertion, which was at the heart of her avoidance behaviour. Written instructions for the task were provided.

Session 2

Margaret's PD demonstrated a reduction in her panic attacks with none occurring mid-morning since the successful introduction of breakfast. Margaret also reported successfully completing the physical exercise task on three occasions, two with the support of her husband and the other alone. Where she had rated the level of her belief in 'I'm going to have a heart attack' as 45 per cent beforehand, it was only 25 per cent after, and the PRS indicated a further reduction to 20 per cent after review of her evidence chart. The task after reviewing the evidence is to record a variety of more balanced views in relation to the symptoms Margaret experiences and these can be seen in Figure 2.3.

Within the session Margaret was asked to choose one of these balanced views as an alternative to the original thought and she chose 'I am experiencing

Steps:	Goal: To push shopping trolley	Achieved
1	Push small trolley half way around store when going for mid-week shop (accompanied by husband)	
2	Push small trolley all way around store when going for mid-week shop (accompanied by husband)	
3	Push small trolley all way around store when going for mid-week shop (unaccompanied)	
4	Push large trolley half way around store when going for full-week shop (accompanied by husband)	
5	Push large trolley all way around store when going for full-week shop (accompanied by husband)	
6	Push large trolley all way around store when going for full-week shop (unaccompanied)	

FIGURE 2.4   Hierarchy for goal of pushing shopping trolley

normal sensations felt by many which are not harmful and will pass.' She was again asked to rate her how much belief she had in this thought and she gave it a belief rating of 80 per cent.

To test the validity of this alternative thought Margaret agreed to conduct a series of exposure experiments, putting herself in challenging situations currently avoided, hence working directly with her fear of exertion. Margaret's avoidance of pushing the shopping trolley was chosen for the first experiment, for which a hierarchy of steps was drawn up in the session. A hierarchy is a list of activities graded in order of difficulty, the most achievable starting at step 1 (see Figure 2.4). Margaret's aim was to have achieved all of the steps before the next meeting as well as to have developed similar hierarchies for her avoidance of dog walking and playing with the grandchildren. She was provided with materials to assist her with both devising and conducting the experiments, and was asked, as usual, to continue to complete the self-report measures.

Session 3

Margaret had drawn up realistic hierarchies for the avoided behaviours as agreed but despite reporting success with the exposure experiment, the PRS demonstrated that her belief remained at 80 per cent, indicating 20 per cent uncertainty. It was through discussion of the experiment that safety behaviours emerged, with reports of Margaret seeking reassurance or taking deep breaths when she had become a little breathless. Questioning was used to explore why Margaret would need to use these tactics if she believed 'I am experiencing normal sensations felt by many which are not harmful and will pass' and it transpired that there was some residual doubt. Despite this she was adamant that she had been unaware of the safety behaviours at the time and that completing the experiment again without them would be effective at eliminating this doubt.

Session 4

The exposure experiment had been accomplished without any safety behaviours and Margaret had further achieved longer and more intense walks with her dog. Completing the final exercise around playing with her grandchildren was planned for the following week but her increased confidence was already evident. Her belief in the thought 'I am experiencing normal sensations felt by many which are not harmful and will pass' had increased to 100 per cent, demonstrating that the exposure had served to consolidate this new perception. The PRS reinforced this with her original heart attack belief being absent and her PD contained only three panic attacks over the two-week period, none of which related to heart attacks and all of lesser intensity and duration.

The second thought Margaret chose to address was 'I will collapse', which was particularly strong given that Margaret had reported a collapse prior to referral. As with the previous thought, time was taken in the session to define what she meant by this and to explore under what circumstances it had occurred, and with the earlier work on safety behaviours Margaret was able to see that she had in fact placed herself on the ground in an attempt to prevent collapse. She was further guided to the realisation that her fear of collapse was in fact synonymous with her fear of fainting and that the only remaining thought to be challenged was 'I'm going to pass out.' To start the process of challenging this thought Margaret was asked to think back to what she had learnt about anxiety, and my role was again to guide her towards counter-evidence. The physical effects of anxiety in relation to increasing heart beat and blood pressure were discussed before the reasons for fainting were explored. Margaret was able to see that the very low blood pressure required to faint was in fact in direct contrast to the physiological arousal experienced in anxiety and as a result she was able to conclude that fainting in fear would be very unlikely. To continue to challenge this thought, however, Margaret utilised an evidence chart, with counter-evidence being drawn from further education and her increased social contact.

Sessions 5 and 6

Familiarity with the techniques and Margaret's earlier success enabled good progress through the sessions and the alternative thought of 'I'm feeling dizzy because I'm anxious; it will pass' was quickly reached. After a series of exposure experiments challenging her fear of going to the park this was proved valid and the PRS and PD both confirmed a reduction in panic attacks and level of belief. It was therefore agreed that the remaining sessions would focus on evaluation and relapse prevention.

Treatment evaluation – sessions 7 and 8

Several areas were reviewed for the evaluation including the self-report measures, Margaret's goals and a return to the formulation.

The PRS and PD had demonstrated consistent improvement throughout and on review there had been no panic attacks, misinterpretations or avoidance recorded for the past week. All Margaret's goals had been achieved, even those that had not received direct attention, with her relationship with her husband having improved considerably simply as a result of involving him in her treatment. Her social network had similarly increased through attendance at the support group and the library and through meeting people when dog walking and taking the grandchildren to the park. Her physical and mental health had improved significantly, and crucially Margaret reported no concerns about her health. A return to the formulation confirmed the amount of progress Margaret had made alongside the knowledge she had acquired.

Relapse prevention had been incorporated into Margaret's care throughout via discussion of the usability of each strategy, and the potential for future vulnerability and review confirmed that there was no suggestion of vulnerability. In addition Margaret had found the self-help strategies to be highly usable and had developed a resource file from all the materials; therefore it was deemed that she was at low risk of relapse. A final evaluation meeting was made for six weeks later, at which it was confirmed that all gains had been upheld, and it was at this meeting that Margaret repeated the self-report measures from assessment. At a score of 3 from a previous 10 the PHQ-9 indicated a marked reduction that signalled no depression whilst a CORE score of 7.1 from a previous 19.2 demonstrated a significant improvement that brought Margaret far below the cut-off of 12.9.

Discharge strategies

As the referrer, Margaret's GP was informed of her discharge via a letter outlining the treatment she had received. He was informed of the procedure for re-referral and advised that the success of guided self help meant that this would be a consideration in the future. This would depend however on the reason for Margaret's referral, with booster sessions or a different presenting problem being most open to the same approach. Presentation with the same problem would be more likely to require other alternatives, as if Margaret had been unable to retain gains from GSH providing more of the same would be questionable. Referring up to step 3 would therefore be the next option, where CBT sessions could offer increased input and duration and decreased onus on Margaret to self-learn.

Critique of case study

The cognitive model of panic suggests a treatment approach that modifies belief in symptom misinterpretations, reduces safety behaviours and decreases avoidance, and as such GSH has proved a successful treatment approach for Margaret's panic disorder.

Although Margaret's referral indicated that this was her first presentation of panic, it transpired that it was actually her third occurrence, the first experience being 40 years earlier. This posed a risk that Margaret might have formed anxiety-related core beliefs too complex to address in GSH, but fortunately this was not the case. Instead Margaret's thoughts proved to be surface level and only recently altered, making accessing and challenging these much easier.

The five areas formulation worked very well in this case, not least because it brought together in a simple and coherent way the areas of Margaret's life that had felt messy and disjointed. Seeing her life conceptualised in diagrammatic form was the first step towards change for Margaret, as this was when she began to understand that her life had become characterised by panic and that there was a potential alternative explanation for her physical symptoms. The formulation also proved effective in both informing treatment goals and guiding the focus of intervention, and by demonstrating the interrelationship between the five areas it provided good socialisation to the CBT model.

GSH aims to promote self-efficacy in the client by giving them a form of help they will always be able to use, principally through teaching them CBT skills and introducing them to core materials. An additional aim is to help people avoid extensive mental healthcare involvement, and whilst both have been achieved on this occasion it is worth considering when this might not be the case.

A difficulty with GSH is that it has no clear definition and as a result there are wide variations in materials used, therapist input and therapist experience. Individual clinicians will have materials that they personally prefer but this can lead to a lack of quality control. Within this chapter no specific materials have been endorsed but the books-on-prescription scheme, used with Margaret, is advocated as the materials offered have been tried and tested and come recommended by experienced professionals. The amount of self-study required in GSH means that materials are paramount, but unfortunately it is these unregulated materials that can cause treatment to fail.

Therapist input is also central yet disparate, with facilitated sessions ranging from 15 minutes to one hour. The sessions with Margaret were 30 minutes in length which generally allowed for explanation and discussion. With shorter sessions or difficulties arising, however, time would not have been sufficient, and efficacy, it could be argued, would be reduced. In Margaret's case this is supported by session 2 where there was inadequate time to fully discuss exposure experiments. Despite being provided with good materials to guide her through these tasks Margaret's experiments failed, yet following session 3, where experiments were discussed, the outcome was successful.

Finally, therapist experience is a potential key determinant, with some having trained recently and specifically in GSH and others having a longer background in more traditional CBT. Whilst studies consistently demonstrate the benefits of a GSH approach they also build a tentative picture of the greater successes coming from the more experienced practitioner (Drake, 2008); thus when considering the success of this case it needs to be contextualised not only in the materials used and the time available but also in the experience of the author.

Problems arising in therapy

There are some potential challenges in using GSH that, whilst not problematic in Margaret's case, are worthy of consideration. The first is individuals with literacy needs or whose first language is not English, where the mainstream materials cannot be used. There is a growing body of literature that is available in audio CD as well as written form and some of the more utilised self-help guides have been translated into a range of languages. Many therapists will also try to involve translators or relatives in treatment to assist with the communication barriers, but generally the difficulty lies in the amount of time needed to accommodate these added complexities. Offering double appointments is one solution, but the pressure of need in primary care may lead to such individuals being referred on to services that can provide more time and input, usually within the third sector.

The second challenge is homework compliance, which tends to vary among clients. There are many reasons why somebody may not comply and it is essential that these reasons are understood. In GSH many people feel overwhelmed by their own involvement in treatment and ensuring that homework is well planned can help reduce this enormously. Working with the client to determine the time they have available, potential barriers to compliance and plans to overcome such obstacles can increase homework completion significantly, as can ensuring the tasks are logical and relevant. Explaining homework tasks clearly is also important and ensuring adequate time to do this is vital. What is essential, however, is establishing from the start the integral part that homework plays, as, unfortunately, GSH cannot proceed without it. In an approach where therapist contact is minimal, great reliance is placed on the client and if the commitment to the homework is absent the therapy will fail.

Think about ...

1. On which of the criteria did Margaret meet the diagnosis for panic disorder?
2. How was Margaret's panic disorder being maintained?
3. What would happen if avoidance and safety behaviours existed but went unnoticed?
4. Why do we need behavioural experiments when thoughts have been cognitively challenged?

Suggested activity:

- Try to recall a recent time when you felt anxious. Map this against the five areas formulation to see if you can identify the vicious cycle at play.
- Think of something you avoid because it makes you feel anxious (e.g. spiders, crowds, speaking in meetings). Try to draw up a hierarchy that would help you reduce this.
- Ask a friend if they mind sharing a negative automatic thought (e.g. I'm rubbish at DIY). Help them to question their evidence for this and generate evidence against it.

3
Client Presenting with First-onset Depression

Ian Ross

Learning objectives

By the end of this chapter you should be able to:

Identify depression using diagnostic criteria
Understand the development of depression
Discuss the assessment approaches and case formulation
Plan and implement the treatment interventions

Diagnostic criteria

Depression is most commonly identified in clients reporting a change in mood and loss of interest and pleasure in daily activities. Depressive symptoms are varied and often have origins in past events – this chapter and the next discuss first-onset and chronic depression (dysthymia) using the DSM-IV-TR (APA, 2000), code 296.20 to 296.36 and ICD-10 (WHO, 2007), code F32–F33 criteria. Chronic physical disorders or primary psychiatric disorders are excluded as are symptoms that are clearly due to a general medical condition, mood-incongruent delusions or hallucinations.

The DSM-IV-TR criterion states that depression is present if five or more of the following symptoms have been experienced for a period up to two weeks and clearly differs from previous mood, whilst the ICD-10 criterion is virtually the same but states that two or more of the following should be diagnostic criteria for mild depression, four or more for moderate depression and several of the following, with particular emphasis on suicidal ideation, for the diagnosis of severe depression. Clearly depressed mood or decreased interests in daily life are two of the symptoms that have to be presented but there are also symptoms of poor appetite and consequent weight loss (of more than 5 per cent in one month), poor sleeping patterns which differ significantly from prior to onset of the low mood, either physical agitation or retardation (physical processes observably slowing down), general fatigue, loss of libido, awareness of daily poor concentration or recall or indecisiveness and feelings of worthlessness accompanied by excessive or inappropriate guilt. The feelings of guilt can sometimes be presented as delusional and are always more excessive than mere self-reproach, whilst feelings of worthlessness can be so severe that the individual may be plagued by thoughts of death to the point that they may have suicidal intent and act on such, either on impulse or planned.

Depression is therefore a serious condition which causes clinically significant distress and impairment in social, occupational and other areas of daily life and the DSM-IV-TR (APA, 2000) counsels that assessments need to discount the effects of drug abuse, other serious mental health conditions such as psychosis or a history of mania or hypomania, any medication and any physical conditions meeting a medical diagnosis, in order that the correct treatment can be implemented.

Feelings of loss and loneliness are commonly experienced in grief due to bereavement but this differs from depression. However, bereavement can precipitate depression and depression should always be considered if the above symptoms persist for several months after a loss (longer than two months according to the DSM-IV-TR (APA, 2000)).

Depression may also occur as a single episode or be recurrent (with at least two months of remission between episodes) and may therefore develop into a chronic, severe or enduring condition.

Predisposing and precipitating factors

There is no one clear cause for depression; rather it occurs as a result of the interaction of predisposing and precipitating factors. The complex and varied presentation of depression means these factors need to be considered carefully during the assessment of the client.

Predisposing factors are the long-term background factors that, if present, make it more likely that the client may develop depression and may include:

- Family history of depression
- Previous psychiatric disorder, including previous episodes of depression
- Personality – for example, sustained depressive response to life events
- Personality disorder; pronounced traits that limit a client's ability to function effectively, particularly in interpersonal relationships
- Past events or traumas; impact of experiences such as war, migration, suicide in the family, or early childhood experiences
- Poor physical health; especially chronic pain and ill health.

Precipitating factors are recent events and incidents that may lead to the development of depression in individuals who already have a predisposition and include:

- Potentially life-threatening or chronic illness
- Major life events, especially losses and substantial role changes (e.g. relationships, income, worker role, home), family conflict
- Substance dependence and abuse, for example, alcohol.

Demographic incidence

Prevalence is distinct from incidence. Prevalence is a measurement of *all* individuals affected by the disorder within a particular period of time, whereas incidence is a measurement of the number of new individuals who develop a disorder during a particular period of time

It is estimated that 5 per cent of adults will experience an episode of major depression annually, whilst as many as 15 per cent will experience depression during their lifetime. In the UK alone approximately 3–4 per cent of men and 7–8 per cent of women will experience moderate to severe depression annually. The lower prevalence in men is probably due to the lower number of sufferers seeking help from their GPs (NICE, 2009).

Continuum of severity

Distinguishing mood changes between mild and severe and those episodes which occur during the course of normal life activities, remains problematic. It is best to consider the symptoms of depression as occurring over a continuum of severity, with persistence of symptoms being noted. This means that there is often no clear 'cut-off' between 'clinically significant' and 'normal' depression or low mood.

📁 **Case study** 📁

Rationale

This case study outlines the care of Lynda who presented with first-onset depression of a mild to moderate nature. NICE (2009) recommends that such presentations be treated briefly, with low-intensity interventions and outside of specialist mental health services, and as such Lynda's care took place in her local health centre with a member of the Primary Care Mental Health Team (PCMHT). Her treatment consisted of CBT assisted by guided self help, with cognitive and behavioural interventions being aimed at the immediate level. The case demonstrates care at step 2 of the Stepped Care model.

Client

Lynda is a 43-year-old single mother with two teenage daughters, who has been unemployed for five months. She worked as a book keeper for a large building and construction company, which went into liquidation as a result of the major downturn in the market for new-build homes. Lynda was not offered any financial compensation for her loss of employment and is now waiting to hear if there will be any redundancy pay-outs. She receives unemployment benefit and a small child allowance paid by her ex-husband, from whom she has been divorced for six years. The divorce was 'amicable'. Her daughters, aged 11 and 13, live with her during the week and attend the local school. They see their father each weekend.

Lynda has felt increasingly 'down' and helpless and has decided to visit her GP to seek help. She describes low moods, often resulting in tears, tiredness, lack of motivation and a waning interest in food. Her daughters have become aware of the changes in their mother and Lynda feels guilty that she is 'failing as a mother'. She frequently loses her temper when her daughters squabble about what she considers to be insignificant issues. She is alone much of the day and finds it difficult to motivate herself to look for employment. She prefers to lie on the lounge sofa and sleep, often only awaking when her daughters come back from school. She is not aware of any previous history of depression.

At her first appointment with her GP she was prescribed anti-depressant medication and referred to the PCMHT for level 2 Stepped Care model interventions.

TABLE 3.1 Self-report questionnaire data

Questionnaire	Assessment score	Normal range
PHQ-9	14	0–27
HADS	12	0–21

Assessment session

Having confirmed the overview of Lynda's current situation as provided by her GP, the assessment focused on the potential for risk that is inherent in any depressive disorder. The risk is particularly raised in those who experience major depressive episodes, with as many as 6 per cent of hospitalised clients and 4 per cent of outpatients experiencing suicidality (Inskip et al., 1998). Whilst most mental health services will use their own specific procedure, Cooper-Patrick, Crum and Ford (1994) have developed a simple four-question screening tool which, when used with Lynda, did not indicate any suicidal ideation or intent.

There are a large number of psychometric questionnaires that may be used in the initial assessment of depression, and to complement the clinical interview Lynda was asked to complete the Patient Health Questionnaire (PHQ-9; Kroenke, 2002) and the Hospital Anxiety Depression Scale (HADS; Zigmond, 1963) which measures the comorbidity of anxiety and depression. Both have been shown to be adequate measures of depression (Cameron et al., 2008). Scores, as shown in Table 3.1 indicate mild to moderate depression.

Once the formalities of the assessment had been completed, Lynda was asked to devise a problem list and set of patient goals. As a collaborative process this allowed Lynda an early experience of the therapeutic alliance and developed a sense of purpose alongside a confidence that the resolution of problems was underway. Lynda quickly identified her main problems. She described how the loss of her job seemed to be the last straw in an ongoing pattern of 'bad luck'. She said that this had started with the divorce from her husband, and whilst the relationship was amiable and he was approachable, she had found the adjustment to being the sole parent to her two daughters very challenging. Lynda was having some difficulty in obtaining employment and was concerned about money and the needs of her young daughters. She was aware of her lack of motivation and energy. Lynda listed her problems as:

1. Feeling worthless as both a person and as a mother
2. No work, having to scrimp on spending; concerned about future and frustration at lack of progress on compensation by employer
3. Not giving daughters as much attention as she feels that they should have

moods leading to low motivation and constant tiredness
able to concentrate, poor diet, can't be bothered to make meals; relying on
ldy meals for herself and daughters
uck at home, isolated – seldom goes out except if she has to shop; doesn't
ant to meet people from school or work as she will have to explain how she is.

As a prelude to setting goals Lynda was asked how she would like things to be different, following which she summarised her goals as shown in Table 3.2.

As homework between sessions Lynda was introduced to, and asked to complete, a thought diary. For each significant situation that she encountered over the next week, Lynda was asked to record her thoughts, emotions, behaviour and physical feelings, which would subsequently provide the direction for conceptualisation and formulation of cognitive and behavioural interventions in future sessions. Confirmation of what the homework entailed was sought from Lynda before the session ended.

Case formulation

Conceptualisation essentially allows the client to construct a meaningful account of the events that are connected to their depression, whilst the formulation considers possible interventions in the form of a hypothesis: '*If I do this, this will be the result.*'

At the start of session two, Lynda produced her thought diary and decided that she preferred to summarise what she had written down. Thought diaries need to be considered with sensitivity as clients will often write down their most personal insights and feel threatened or embarrassed if asked to show these. Lynda noted that on one morning when she had had been sleeping very heavily she had been awakened by her older daughter requesting breakfast as it was close to school time. Lynda had felt deep guilt during the day, chastising

TABLE 3.2   Lynda's goals

Problem	Goal
Worthless feelings	Find some part-time work as this would be more suitable for the family; salary would ease money worries
Low moods/physical feelings	Restore daily routine and a sense of purpose. Make the girls' life more interesting
Isolation	Get out and make contact with her friends and hear how they are coping. Spend more time with daughters

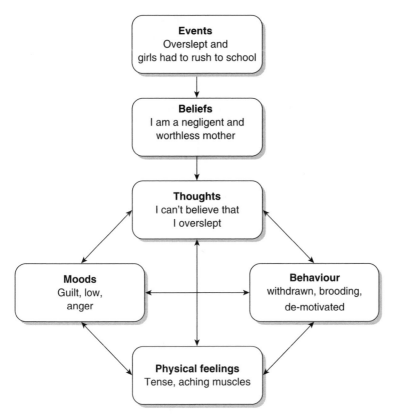

FIGURE 3.1 Adapted from Williams's five areas formulation. Reproduced by permission of Hodder Education.

herself for her negligence and worthlessness. Williams's (2010) five areas formulation was used to conceptualise this incidence as shown in Figure 3.1.

Theoretical perspectives for conceptualisation

Beck's (1976) cognitive model of depression has withstood the test of time and is still considered the most relevant model for the cognitive conceptualisation of depression. It proposes that clients' perception of events leads them to develop assumptions about themselves and the world around them which consequently affect their thoughts, moods and behaviour. In depression, assumptions, which normally guide the assessment of everyday situations, become distorted and result in dysfunctional thinking or negative automatic thoughts. The longitudinal conceptualisation and resulting formulation of the cognitive model is shown in Figure 3.2.

Padesky and Mooney (1990) elaborated on this with the introduction of the five aspects model showing the interaction of the environment with thoughts,

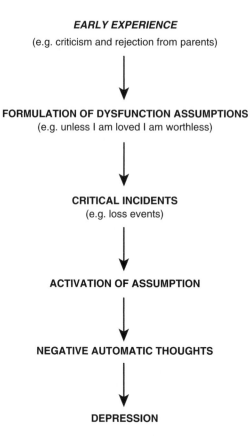

FIGURE 3.2   Conceptualisation of depression (after Beck et al., 1979)

physical sensations, behaviour and moods (Figure 3.3). This picks up from the negative thoughts of the longitudinal model (Beck et al., 1979) and extends the conceptualisation, whilst the combination of Beck's cognitive model and Padesky and Mooney's five aspects model provides a useful visual aid when conceptualising client problems.

Beck et al. (1979) also introduced the concept of the cognitive triad in which he argued that the dysfunctional assumptions that depressed people hold are a result of deep-seated schema and beliefs which typically express themselves in the way in which people hold negative views of themselves, their future and the world. Such views become biased by 'thinking errors' which may seem logical to the client but which are not rational responses. Identifying such errors is therefore important for both assessment and treatment and psycho-education can be a good starting point. The most frequent biases identified by Beck et al. can be found in Figure 3.4.

The strength of the cognitive model and its simplicity make psycho-education a worthwhile intervention. Lynda was a normal mother and professional until

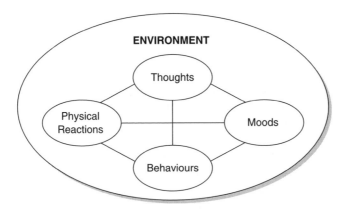

FIGURE 3.3 Five aspects of your life experience © 1986, Center for Cognitive Therapy

1. ALL-OR-NOTHING THINKING: 'black-and-white' categories
2. OVERGENERALISATION: a single negative event is seen as a never-ending pattern of defeat
3. SELECTIVE ABSTRACTION: focus on single negative details to the exclusion of all else
4. DISQUALIFYING THE POSITIVE: reject positive experiences thus maintaining a negative belief that contradicts the positive
5. ARBITRARY INFERENCE: negative interpretation without facts in support; also called mind reading
6. MAGNIFICATION (CATASTROPHISING) OR MINIMISATION: exaggeration or diminishing the importance of events, information, etc.
7. EMOTIONAL REASONING: negative emotions and thoughts reflect reality
8. SHOULD STATEMENTS: 'should' and 'shouldn't', 'must' and 'ought to' lead to feelings of guilt, anger, frustration and resentment
9. LABELLING AND MISLABELLING: an extreme form of over-generalisation and involves highly coloured and emotionally loaded descriptions
10. PERSONALISATION: clients see themselves as the cause of negative external events, but actually have no responsibility for these events.

FIGURE 3.4 Negative processing biases (after Beck et al.,1979)

a decision was taken, without her input or knowledge, to close her job and make her redundant, without compensation. Her reaction to this situation was as would be expected of any normal person experiencing what was an abnormal situation and psycho-education enabled her to normalise this, thus reducing the feelings of confusion and the belief that she was somehow guilty of causing the changes. It also became evident that Lynda was displaying negative cognitive biases typical of depression, and with questioning and prompting she was able to identify these. They are summarised in Table 3.3.

The Hopelessness theory, originally developed by Seligman (Maier and Seligman, 1976) with modifications by Abramson, Seligman and Teasdale (1978), in essence states that with depression there is an expectation that positive outcomes will not occur; moreover, that negative outcomes will instead,

TABLE 3.3 Cognitive biases

Problem	Thoughts	Category
Worthless feelings	'I am a useless mother' 'I am unemployed and have no prospects therefore, I am never going to work again' 'I have failed my daughters by not being with them'	Over-generalisation, Selective abstraction
Low moods/ physical feelings	'I must get my life back together' 'I shouldn't be so de-motivated when I have a family to support'	Should statements
Isolation	'It is my own fault that people don't talk to me – I am so miserable'	Selective abstraction

and that the client has no way of changing this. Embodied within this theory is an element of behaviourism where the client's beliefs prevent them from accepting any reward for positive and constructive behaviours, leading to the lethargy and de-motivation characteristic of depression.

Not only will this lead to social isolation, but as well as losing reward from their own perspective they will consequently lose it from their immediate social environment too. Lewinsohn (1974) suggested that when a person loses this source of positive reinforcement, therapy could focus on re-establishing positive reinforcing activities (activity scheduling) and that maintaining and developing social skills would allow the person to continue to be in contact with sources of positive reinforcement. After a number of modifications (Martell et al., 2001) this approach has become known as behavioural activation or BA, and has been shown to outperform other treatments in depression (Dimidjian et al., 2006).

Activity monitoring and scheduling are the mainstays of BA, being implemented initially with activation assignments, followed if necessary by more specific functional analysis, using the ABC model of Antecedent, Behaviour and Consequence. Activity monitoring and activity scheduling assignments (sometimes described as pleasure and mastery exercises) identify those areas of the client's lifestyle that offer the most positive reinforcement, and through a series of graded exercises based on an activity hierarchy encourages the client to re-engage with these aspects of their life. This may be supported by the functional analysis which attempts to identify those antecedents that might have resulted in behaviour deficits and their consequences. It is a useful technique when simple activation becomes difficult.

Elements of the Hopelessness model apply directly to Lynda, who, having been made redundant from her employment with no immediate financial compensation, has lost one of the main sources of positive reinforcement for

TABLE 3.4 Summary of Lynda's problems and associated interventions and activities

Problem priority	Interventions	Activity
Worthless feelings	Psycho-education	Information retrieval about depression
	Behavioural activation	Activity monitoring and construction of 'experimental' hierarchy
Low moods/ physical feelings	Behavioural activation	Activity monitoring and activation assignments
Isolation	Cognitive rationalisation	Thought and situation diary

her behaviour and self-esteem. Whilst she and her husband have an amicable divorce settlement, contact with him is minimal and so yet another source of potential reinforcement is lost.

Therapists will need to make a judgement on the level of evidence-based information that is offered to the client in the conceptualisation phase. As Lynda demonstrated both interest and understanding, the full conceptualisation was shared openly and she was able to assimilate the theoretical background to her condition well.

Treatment session 1

In session three, the first of the intervention sessions, the therapist and Lynda agreed an agenda which would firstly consider sources of information that Lynda might be able to find to gain a better understanding of her depression (psycho-education) and secondly introduce activity monitoring and a hierarchy of activities for her activation assignments. This is summarised in Table 3.4.

The aims of psycho-education were explained to Lynda and it was suggested that she go on to the internet to read up on depression. Lynda stated that she did not have access to the web as she could not afford the line rental, and the computer that she possessed was too slow for use on the web. This offered the opportunity for the collaborative construction of a behavioural activation assignment, in which Lynda would visit the library and work on the net whilst the children were away at school. Lynda did not feel that this task was too onerous and was curious to see what information she would uncover.

Also in collaboration, a list of 'mini experiments' for Lynda to attempt over the following weeks was constructed and organised into a hierarchy of difficulty. For her first activity Lynda agreed that she would set her alarm to get up at a reasonable hour the next morning; see the children off to school and then walk

Activity	Anticipated difficulty 1–10	Date commenced	Date completed	Actual difficulty 1–10
Visit library	7	3/6/10	3/6/10	4
Meet old friend at library	7			3
Restore daily weekday schedule by getting out of bed at 7am	8	3/6/10	continuous	5
Plan to offer help to daughters when they return from school with homework	6	5/6/10	continuous	3
Plan menu with daughters for weekly tea and shopping outings to buy groceries	7	6/6/10	continuous	4
During half term plan treat for daughters	7	12/6/10	Visited local theme park for the day	2

FIGURE 3.5   Activity hierarchy and assignment monitoring

down to the library, where a good friend worked whom she admitted to look-ing forward to meeting again. She agreed that she would rate her anticipated and actual difficulty on the monitoring sheet before and after the event. Lynda also agreed to continue to keep her thought diary, recording her thoughts, feel-ings, behaviour and physical feelings for difficult and pleasing situations that she encountered during the week. Lynda left the session with the activity sheet shown in Figure 3.5 on which she would record the details of her activities.

Session 2

Lynda gave a report on her activity assignment. She had seen the children off to school and then arrived at the library as it had opened at 9am. She admitted to being very nervous and anxious about meeting people who knew her. Her friend was on duty and was extremely pleased to see her. This helped Lynda relax – the computer systems were booted up and Lynda was able to access a number of sites which she found very helpful including a site giving informa-tion specifically to unemployed people experiencing depression. She was able to complete her search by 10.30 and return home. Lynda had recorded her details on the activity sheet (Figure 3.5).

Throughout therapy Lynda continued to expand her activity repertoire, largely as a result of between-session tasks, recording the results on the activity sheet and bringing this for discussion.

Following the activity schedule Lynda was asked to select parts of her thought diary to discuss and use in a cognitive rationalisation exercise. Lynda was able to discuss the events at the library and the impact that it had on her.

Therapist (T):	So tell me how you felt before and after the visit to the library.
Lynda (L):	I was very anxious after I left you last week and found it difficult to sleep the night before. My alarm woke me up and I organised the kids and got dressed myself. It was a strange feeling because it was the first time that I had dressed to go out — except of course to the shops, but then that was usually in a track suit and trainers. I felt very anxious as I walked to the library.
T:	Let me have an idea of your thoughts as you walked along.
L:	I'll read from my diary ... 'I hope that I can do this. I wonder what Jo will say when she sees me – it must have been at least six weeks since I last saw her ... it was when I took the girls to get some information for their projects.' My hands were sweaty and as I walked around the corner and saw the library I thought ... I am going to turn around and run. But I didn't ...
T:	You didn't?
L:	No. I realised that I had come this far and I needed to see it through.
T:	So you were able to complete the activity – how does that feel?
L:	It was a fantastic feeling to get out of the house and talk to Jo – she was so understanding ... made me realise that my negative thoughts were a bit over the top!

This outcome for Lynda is not untypical of people experiencing first-onset depression – their basic coping strategies are intact but they have become overwhelmed by events and whilst they may feel that they will never recover, the ability to carry out a positive activity helps to re-establish their confidence.

In the second part of the session one of the thoughts that Lynda had noted was worked on with the aim of rationalising this. This can be seen below:

Thought:	'I am never going to be able to find employment again.'
T:	Explain this to me so that I fully understand what this means.
L:	Well I have no job and I doubt I will ever be able to work again.
T:	So you have no job – I wonder if that really does mean you won't be able to work again? You worked until recently.
L:	Yes, I did ... but I was made redundant.
T:	Who made you redundant – did you?
L:	No ... no ... it was because the company went into administration – it was nothing to do with me. I just happened to be doing a good job – the market collapsed and there was no more work.
T:	So you are telling me that you did a good job and that it was not because of you that you lost your job – I don't understand how you can conclude that you will never be able to find employment again.

L: Hmmm ... maybe I am. What did I read? Beck calls that type of thinking – catastrophising or magnifying – I suppose what I mean is that it may be difficult to find employment again, but I have a good CV and it should be OK. Won't it?

T: Well what do you think – maybe you have answered your own question.

Having worked on this thought in the session Lynda was then asked to continue to work on the others by using a thought record. This prompted Lynda to question both the evidence for the thought and to identify thinking errors, both of which encouraged her to develop more rational thoughts.

Sessions 3–5

Lynda continued to work her way through both the thought rationalisation exercises and the agreed activity hierarchy, reporting back the results of her homework. Whilst she progressed well in each area, at the fifth session she admitted that she had become stuck on the activity to meet with her husband. The therapist guided Lynda through an ABC functional analysis which highlighted the anticipated antecedent (A) that her husband would blame her for not being more proactive in looking for work and that she was sitting on her 'bum' doing nothing. The behaviour (B) that Lynda said she might adopt would be to avoid raising the issue with him, but she realised that this would only delay initiating his involvement in her plans: the consequence (C). The thoughts that were associated with this activity were then discussed and Lynda rationalised that it was probably better to wait to meet her husband until she could demonstrate confidently that she had made some progress with her ex-employer, had started to apply for new jobs and that she was coping with the girls and their needs. Lynda was also concerned as to how she might raise the subject with her husband, when he visited to collect the children. Reading material was provided on assertiveness after a discussion about the need for Lynda to be able to express her needs rather than be passive or competitive, both of which would make her husband uncooperative. A short assertiveness role play in the session helped Lynda strengthen her confidence.

Treatment evaluation session

During this final session Lynda's activities to date and the thought rationalisation activities were reviewed together. Lynda reported that she felt much

TABLE 3.5 Summary of therapy sessions and scores on HADS and PHQ-9

Sessions	Therapy	PHQ-9	HADS
1, 2	Assessment	14	12
3, 4	Conceptualisation and formulation	–	–
5, 6, 7	Interventions – working through the activity hierarchy and rationalising the associated thoughts	9	9
8	Evaluation of outcomes. Relapse prevention and ending	7	8

happier and motivated and that she was getting on much better with her daughters. The interventions that Lynda had learnt were summarised and discussed in the context of preventing a relapse and it was agreed that Lynda had demonstrated her ability to work with the CBT model and benefit from the changes that occurred in her daily activities. In addition Lynda's measurement scores had dropped to subclinical levels, which pleased her and by her own admission gave her the motivation to strengthen her newly found coping mechanisms. A figure summarising the therapy session, content and scores on HADS and PHQ-9 is shown in Table 3.5.

Discharge strategies

As Lynda was referred by her GP she was discharged back into his care. Lynda had been informed that she could re-refer herself to the PCMHT if she felt this was necessary and the GP was also made aware of this in a discharge letter. Given the success of the current approach the GP was advised that further low-intensity input would be considered as a future intervention but that should more intensive input be required she could also be referred up to step 3 within the PCMHT.

Critique of the case study

First-onset depression is commonly encountered in therapeutic practice and Lynda was no exception. A good assessment using a variety of rating scales alongside interview and history-taking is important to identify any risk to oneself or others and, had Lynda demonstrated such risk, safety interventions would need to have been considered within the case formulation.

Depression decreases cognitive functioning and increases tiredness and can negatively impact on the motivation of the client to engage in the treatment process. Therapists therefore need to identify positive core beliefs and assumptions in other areas of the client's life to provide examples which can challenge the feelings of helplessness, as such helplessness is often perceived by the client to be their normal reaction rather than a symptom of depression itself.

Problems arising in therapy

CBT for the treatment of first-onset depression relies on the client being able to work with both behavioural and cognitive interventions and so if there are any factors that may prevent this happening, then the success of the CBT in the short term may be compromised. Typically, the lack of concentration, plus any intellectual difficulties or literacy and learning disability will all contribute to problems with the cognitive interventions.

Behavioural activation requires commitment on the part of the client to engage in the homework activities. They may not wish to or be able to for a number of different reasons. De-motivation is perhaps the most common cause – the client will have been reduced to such a low level of behavioural activation that they find it impossible to engage in the intervention. Homework compliance is usually positively associated both with the client's motivation for therapy and the recognition of a positive outcome at a later stage of therapy; the provision of clearly written notes or homework sheets on the activation assignment is a useful client support.

Perhaps the most significant problem in therapy is the existence of external factors that are influencing the client's emotions, but are difficult to manage in the sessions, for example, marital difficulties or bereavement. The nature of CBT is parsimonious and structured, focusing on the 'here and now'. Issues in the client's life may require additional support, not always available in a time-limited therapy such as CBT.

Think about ...

1. Homework compliance can sometimes be a problem with clients – think of other ways in which clients might record their thoughts, feelings, behaviour and physical feelings for use in therapy sessions.
2. Behavioural activation is considered a powerful intervention in depression; how does it integrate with cognitive interventions and does this integration weaken or strengthen its role in therapy?

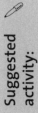

Suggested activity:

- A useful exercise for CBT therapists is to keep your own thought diary and take time to reflect on the entries that you make. This will help you understand the ways in which a client may use the diary and also begin to appreciate how important a diary often becomes to the client – a journal of their experiences.

4

Client Presenting with Dysthymia (Chronic Depression)

Ian Ross

Learning objectives

By the end of this chapter you should be able to:

Identify the symptoms of dysthymia using diagnostic criteria
Explain the development and chronicity of dysthymia
Outline a case formulation and decide on cognitive and behavioural
   interventions
Discuss the implementation and evaluation of the treatment interventions

---

Diagnostic criteria

Dysthymia is a chronic type of depression in which low moods continue or persist over a long period of time. Dysthymia can occur alone, or the client may have episodes of more severe depression. It is long lasting and often resistant to treatment.

Dysthymia should be differentiated from major depressive episodes, the diagnostic criteria for which were presented in Chapter 3. In both the DSM-IV-TR (APA, 2000) and ICD-10 (WHO, 2007) dysthymia, or chronic depression, is

TABLE 4.1   Comparison of criteria for dysthymia and depression

Dysthymia	Major depression
Duration: at least 2 years during which the client will report depressed mood for most of the day, occurring more days than not	Duration: for at least 2 consecutive weeks
At least 2 of the following symptoms: Poor appetite or overeating Insomnia or hypersomnia Low energy or fatigue Low self-esteem Poor concentration Difficulty making decisions Feelings of hopelessness	At least 5 or more of the following symptoms have been present most of the day, every day: Depressed mood Loss of interest or pleasure in usual activities Significant weight loss or gain Insomnia or hypersomnia Psychomotor agitation or retardation Fatigue or loss of energy Feelings of worthlessness or excessive or inappropriate guilt Diminished ability to think or concentrate Recurrent thoughts of death or suicide

diagnosed by the number of criteria the client symptoms match as well as the time scale of the symptoms, the significant difference between dysthymia and major depressive episodes being the time scale of the illness. Table 4.1 compares the two diagnoses.

There is broad agreement between the DSM–IV–TR and the ICD–10. The ICD–10 is less specific than the DSM–IV–TR but recognises the essential feature of dysthymia as a very long-standing depression of mood, which, when onset is later in life, may have resulted from a discrete depressive episode frequently associated with bereavement or other stressful life events.

On the basis of both the DSM–IV–TR and the ICD–10, dysthymia may be considered less severe than major depression, yet the consequences of dysthymia are increasingly being recognized as serious, with severe functional impairment, increased morbidity from physical disease, and increased risk of suicide all being factors. Differentiating dysthymia from major depression is therefore challenging, especially in cases of major depression when there may be only a partial response to treatment.

Predisposing and precipitating factors

Factors predisposing and precipitating dysthymia are not unlike depression and include having biological relatives with depression or dysthymia, being female, stressful life events or the client having a chronic medical condition.

Demographic incidence

Statistics on the prevalence and incidence of dysthymia are difficult to assess, given that it tends to be long-standing. The exact cause of dysthymia is unknown and, as with major depressive disorder, dysthymia occurs more in women than in men and may affect up to 5 per cent of the general population at any time. Both the Cognitive and Hopelessness models (see below) identify a vulnerability to depression; the origins of these can be deep and complex and may be biological, for example chronic illness, social relationship problems or life events which have created dysfunctional behaviour patterns (Barbui et al., 2006).

Dysthymia tends to start earlier in life, often in childhood or during the teenage years, and lasts longer in duration of symptoms than depression. Typically early-onset dysthymia starts before 21 years of age, whilst diagnosis after this age is labelled late-onset dysthymia.

Continuum of severity

Dysthymia is by definition a chronic condition and the long-term outlook for dysthymia is therefore uncertain. Stress and comorbidity, commonly with anxiety and health status factors, will result in lower recovery rates. There is a greater likelihood of a major depressive episode and risk of self-harm and suicide in clients with dysthymia (Hayden and Klein, 2001; Shankman and Klein, 2002).

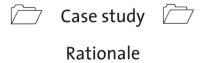

Case study

Rationale

It is not unusual for a number of clients treated for first-onset depression to present some years later with dysthymia. The case for this chapter therefore, will continue with Lynda, who was discussed in Chapter 3. Whilst there is no specific NICE guidance for dysthymia it is arguably best placed under either the moderate to severe category, or that of individuals for who earlier interventions have had an inadequate effect, and it is the latter that this case will address. As Lynda has not retained her progress with the earlier step 2 interventions she has been stepped up to step 3, where her care will incorporate intermediate interventions as well as re-visiting some of the more immediate techniques from step 2. The care will take place within the PCMHT, this time with a mental health practitioner delivering the higher-intensity interventions.

Client

Lynda, now 48 years old, presents to her GP complaining of continual tiredness, fatigue, poor appetite and difficulty with sleeping. The GP's notes show that Lynda was referred for CBT five years previously having been discharged with a satisfactory outcome. Since then Lynda has not requested any repeat prescriptions for the anti-depressants she was originally given.

Lynda confirms that she is still single, that the eldest of her two daughters has left home to take up a job in the South and that the other daughter is commencing college in the coming year. Lynda has had three jobs since the end of therapy, all temporary, with her current one involving working late shifts in a shop selling beers, wines and spirits. Her ex-husband has remarried and sees little of his daughters and has ceased paying maintenance. Lynda is now dependent upon her own earning capacity to provide for herself and her daughters.

Lynda describes her life as 'a long dark existence'; the sense of hopelessness that she had soon after her divorce has returned; she feels de-motivated and despite encouragement by her regional manager to take up training offers in the company she works for, she has done nothing. Lynda admits to wondering what she will do with herself once her younger daughter leaves home as she has few friends and finds it difficult to keep in touch due to her unsocial hours at work.

The GP prescribes anti-depressant medication and refers Lynda on to the PCMHT, Lynda's previous case notes are reviewed in triage and it is decided Lynda be placed on the waiting list for CBT therapy at level 3 intervention of the Stepped Care model (NICE, 2009).

Assessment session

A risk assessment was completed initially, with no significant risk of suicide or self-harm being noted, although Lynda did admit to often wondering 'if it is all worth it', but she acknowledged that she 'doesn't have the courage to leave her daughters alone'.

Lynda reported that the symptoms that she has had of low mood, poor sleep and appetite had been with her almost continuously for three years. Though she had been able to function, go to work and see to her daughters' needs, there had been no respite from the feelings of hopelessness and low self-esteem. When her oldest daughter left home seven months ago, Lynda admitted to being very low. She said that she wakes in the morning feeling tired and fatigued, estimating that she was having about 4–5 hours restless sleep a night, the rest of the time just lying awake worrying. She admitted to drinking wine

TABLE 4.2   Lynda's problems and goals

Problem	Goal
Worthless feelings	Find some permanent work as this would be more suitable for the family; salary would ease money worries
Low moods/physical feelings	Improve daily routine and a sense of purpose, by seeking employment with more regular hours
Isolation	Arrange to visit daughter in new home; increase contact with friends Spend more time with youngest daughter

TABLE 4.3   Self-report scores comparison

	Present assessment	Past assessment
PHQ-9	15	14
HADS	9	12
DAS	112	n/a
ATQ	32	n/a

on occasion to help her sleep but not on a regular basis due to a concern that she might lose her job, if found to be drinking.

Lynda's case notes from the previous sessions were available and she was able to re-evaluate the previous problems she had reported, confirming that these were still much the same. With the departure of her daughter and the final break with her ex-husband, however, she reported feeling even more isolated, and having revised her problems and goals she drew up the list shown in Table 4.2. Lynda admitted, however, to feeling very negative about the process as she was convinced that whatever action she might take, it would fail. She had revisited some of the interventions that she had learnt previously and '... these just did not work'.

Lynda also recompleted the PHQ-9 (Kroenke, 2002) and the Hospital Anxiety Depression Scale (HADS; Zigmond, 1963) self-report questionnaires as she had done in previous sessions. A comparison of her scores with previous scores indicate moderate to severe depression. This is shown in Table 4.3. In addition she was asked to complete both the Dysfunctional Attitudes Scale (DAS) and the Automatic Thoughts Questionnaire (ATQ).

The DAS (Beck et al., 1991) is a self-report that measures the dysfunctional cognitions (assumptions, thoughts) that will contribute to depression and is useful in dysthymia, where the depressive state is likely to have been maintained for some considerable time. DAS was originally developed to test the predictions of Beck's cognitive theory of depression and offers a measure of cognitive vulnerability to depression. Beck (1987) hypothesised that the negative triad of the clients' view of themselves, their environment and the future is maintained as a result of the negative assumptions and beliefs that people hold – the so-called 'silent assumptions' that increase cognitive vulnerability to depression.

The ATQ was originally utilised to measure the frequency of positive and negative self-statements (Hollon and Kendall, 1980). Participants answer each question by choosing a response corresponding to their answer from a Likert scale of 0–4. The range of total scores is 0–60. Lynda's score on both the DAS and the ATQ are also shown in Table 4.3.

Lynda was asked to reinstate her thought diary in preparation for the conceptualisation and formulation session.

Case formulation sessions 1 and 2

Lynda's presentation and symptoms strongly suggest a diagnosis of chronic depression or dysthymia. The time period and the occurrence of the low mood and negative thoughts, poor sleep and eating supports this conclusion. The difficulty with clients with dysthymia such as Lynda is that there is strong evidence that the interventions that were implemented during the first episode of major depression are now failing to relieve symptoms.

Conceptualisation needs, therefore, to focus on earlier events in Lynda's life that have made her increasingly vulnerable to dysthymia. Lynda revealed that some of the thoughts she had recorded during the previous week in her thought diary confirmed that her marriage had been difficult and she consented to elaborating on some of her earlier life events. CBT is thought of as a 'here-and-now' therapy; however, with dysthymia the past offers important clues in the conceptualisation of the client's difficulties. After the birth of her first daughter Lynda was deeply depressed. She was told that this was post-natal depression, prescribed medication and 'told to get on with it'. Her husband had found her mood changes hard to cope with and he became more and more withdrawn. The same problems arose with the birth of their second child. Lynda did not think that she had been depressed as a teenager, nor was there any history in her family; however, she remembers her mother frequently calling her a 'moody cow', and that she tended to keep to herself or with a close clique of friends. She met her husband at college and they married soon after. It was apparent during the conceptualisation process that Lynda had had a number of stressful life events – mostly of loss – and that there was the possibility of previous episodes of depression. A longitudinal conceptualisation based on the cognitive model (Beck, 1976) was collaboratively constructed incorporating these events, which is shown in Figure 4.1.

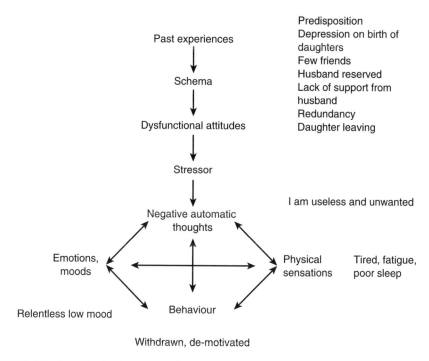

FIGURE 4.1   Longitudinal conceptualisation of Lynda's dysthymia (after Beck, 1976)

Theoretical perspectives for conceptualisation

Beck's cognitive theory argues that the 'silent or negative assumptions' are linked to vulnerability to depression. A study in 2003 (Kwon and Oei) evaluated the causal relationships between automatic thoughts, dysfunctional attitudes and depressive symptoms, following CBT treatment. The results of this study indicated that changes in dysfunctional attitudes, brought about by CBT interventions, effect changes in depressive symptoms through changes in automatic thoughts. These results strongly support the notion that automatic thoughts and dysfunctional attitudes are different in cognitive content, level and the relationship to depressive symptoms. On the basis of these results the Causal Cognition model was developed.

This model proposes that dysfunctional attitudes are more deeply seated and closer to core beliefs than negative automatic thoughts and therefore dysfunctional attitudes have a less direct effect on depressive symptoms, their impact being mediated through automatic thoughts. The implication for therapy is that whilst automatic thoughts will be affected by CBT therapy, for treatment to be effective, interventions should be directed at both negative thoughts and dysfunctional attitudes.

Dysthymia may also be conceptualised using the Hopelessness theory of depression (Abramson et al., 1989) in which a client may have a cognitive vulnerability to depression. This would present as a tendency to make particular kinds of inferences about the cause, consequences, and self-worth implications of the negative life events they experience which, in Lynda's case, is a tendency to view negative events as leading to further negative consequences, and to then construe these events as implying that she is unworthy or deficient.

Formulation of interventions for Lynda recognises the fact that the original cognitive and behavioural interventions implemented during Lynda's first onset of depression have proved ineffective in preventing a relapse into dysthymia. Furthermore, the fundamental assumptions and inferences that Lynda makes about herself and her life experiences have increased her vulnerability to depression. Therefore, formulation of interventions focused on the identification, challenging and restructuring of her dysfunctional assumptions.

Treatment sessions 1–3

The dysfunctional assumptions of the Cognitive model and the negative inferences of the Hopelessness model of depression, should both respond to cognitive rationalisation and restructuring. However, Lynda, like many clients, found the process of identifying negative inferences of dysfunctional assumptions difficult. During session 1, she admitted to being unaware of these deep-seated assumptions and beliefs. This is because they are usually generalised rules which are not easily articulated in words. However, a simple clue to assumptions or beliefs is the use of words by the client such as 'should', 'must' or 'ought'. Fennell (1989) offers a more detailed list of the characteristics of dysfunctional assumptions and this structure was utilized to encourage Lynda to identify her own dysfunctional assumptions and beliefs, which are shown in Table 4.4.

TABLE 4.4 Dysfunctional assumptions (after CBT for Psychiatric Problems by Melanie Fennell (1989) 30w from pp. 202–203. By permission of Oxford University Press.

Dysfunctional assumption characteristics	Lynda's examples
Does not reflect reality	*I am a bad mother*
Rigid, over-generalised and extreme	*Nothing is going right in my life*
Prevent client reaching goals – creates anxiety	*I have had bad experiences in the past, I must avoid doing it again*
Extreme and excessive emotion associated with failure	*Life is described 'as a long dark existence'*
Detached from ordinary experience	*It will never work*

In addition, Burns (1999) recommends the downward arrow technique to assist the client in identifying dysfunctional assumptions. An example of a dialogue with Lynda using this method is demonstrated as follows:

L: I feel very lonely now that my eldest has left home – I sometimes wonder why?

T: I sense that you feel that there may be reasons why she left that you haven't openly discussed with anyone.

L: Yes … I sometimes think that I should be a better mother and talk to them more so that they can let me know what is going on in their minds.

T: It sounds to me like you think that you don't talk enough and therefore, you feel bad about yourself.

L: My problem is that I sometimes get angry with what they say – I ought not to.

T: You avoid talking to them then in case …

L: Well, I am sure that the girls will leave me if I get angry with them. I am a bad mother.

T: So it seems that you have a basic assumption that you are a bad mother.

Once the client has been successful in identifying their dysfunctional assumptions, the next step is for the client to challenge their assumptions and seek an alternative.

Typically, there are a number of questions that a therapist might ask, for example: What is the evidence? What are the advantages and disadvantages of that assumption? How could you modify that belief to make it more appropriate to your present circumstances? Where did this belief come from? Padesky (1993) calls this process of questioning Guided Discovery.

Using this method, the discussion with Lynda continued as follows:

T: So it seems that you have a basic assumption that you are a bad mother. I wonder what evidence you have for this?

L: I don't understand what you mean.

T: I wonder how you would describe a bad mother?

L: Well … she would ignore her children, perhaps not feed them very well, not look after the house.

T: So you have some general thoughts – how many of these would apply directly to you? For example – do you feed your daughters a reasonable diet?

L: Whenever I can – sometimes we will rely on takeaways – but that is because I am busy or they have come in late. They have never been seriously ill and always recover from minor ailments quickly – so they must be healthy; certainly up until the time my eldest left home. I suppose she is still looking after herself.

TABLE 4.5   Summary of therapy sessions and scores on PHQ-9, HADS, DAS and ATQ

Sessions	Therapy	PHQ-9	HADS	DAS	ATQ
1	Assessment	15	9	112	32
2, 3	Conceptualisation and formulation	–	–	–	–
4, 5, 6	Interventions – identifying, challenging and restructuring dysfunctional attitudes	12	7	98	28
7, 8	Evaluation of outcomes Relapse prevention and ending	10	5	86	25

> T: It seems from what you are saying, the evidence that you offer indicates that you are a caring mother, doesn't quite square with your description of being a bad mother.
>
> L: Yes … I wouldn't disagree with your conclusion – but I just feel like I am a bad mother.
>
> T: Perhaps there is room to rephrase that and say something like … I try to be a caring mother, most of the time; sometimes circumstances make it difficult.

Working with dysfunctional beliefs can be slow and difficult for the client and homework can provide an effective way to engage the client in the process. Linda was provided with materials to assist her to continue to challenge and restructure her assumptions between sessions, and as she became more effective at this she was also encouraged to revisit some of the behavioural and cognitive interventions that she had used in the previous sessions, for example behavioural activation. This helped to increase her mood as well as to reinforce the progress she had made with changing her assumptions about herself.

Treatment evaluation session

Table 4.5 summarises the therapy session content and scores on HADS, PHQ-9, ATQ and DAS. The scores indicate that Lynda has improved in terms of her depression and anxiety; however, the higher scores of the DAS and ATQ are in line with the suggestion that she has a cognitive vulnerability to depression, which is fairly typical for dysthymia. Relapse prevention depends on maintenance of a stable routine, avoiding as far as possible any upheavals. In Lynda's case this was proving difficult and so it was agreed that she would have quarterly review sessions.

Discharge strategies

Lynda was not discharged following review but was instead encouraged to maintain her thought diary and to use the downward arrow technique to identify and alter dysfunctional assumptions that she might have developed. These would then be presented for review at the quarterly sessions.

Critique of case study

Dysthymia is an insidious and chronic condition causing relapse in mood and regular bouts of depressive symptoms. Motivation and willingness to engage in therapy is therefore an uphill task and individuals require support outside of therapeutic sessions to make the initial contact and continued attendance. Non-attendance rates can be high initially which can negatively reinforce the individual's underlying dysfunctional assumptions about their ability towards self-help and management.

Dysthymia is a long-term condition that requires long-term management and well maintained strategies. Lynda will be reviewed every three months but there is a potential for review meetings to drift further apart over time, particularly in the case of non-attendance or service changes. For some clients such an outcome can be devastating and even life threatening so ensuring adequate maintenance arrangements is paramount.

Problems arising in therapy

Challenging and changing client dysfunctional assumptions often leads to endless questioning and testing of the alternatives. The assumptions are long-standing and have become a set of unique rules that the client unwittingly uses to manage their life, therefore normalisation is encouraged (how do others think about these issues; do they have the same rules and assumptions?). New ways of doing things can be particularly difficult as the client will feel anxious and exposed. Regular sessions are necessary so that the client is able to discuss their activities and raise any issues they find problematic.

Re-socialisation is also necessary for individuals with dysthymia as they have become isolated and their social skills have become compromised. Lynda was aware of this. Her work during anti-social hours meant that not only was she not able to see her friends during normal social time, but the customers at the store she described as 'either drunk or in a hurry'. The quarterly sessions would aim to progress normalisation and implement re-socialisation activities, such as membership of a sports club or attending local social events. Lynda was also referred to a local mindfulness group.

Mindfulness-based cognitive therapy (MBCT) was developed in response to clients with cognitive vulnerability to depression and who are prone to relapse, as in dysthymia, (Teasdale et al., 2000) and assumes that clients, such as Lynda, who have experienced previous depressive episodes will have dysfunctional assumptions that will re-activate depression when they experience difficult life events. It is an acceptance therapy, as opposed to CBT which is a change therapy, and is most suitable for clients who have chronic depression prone to relapse. MBCT is a manualised group skills-training programme (Segal et al., 2002) that encourages clients to take an open, accepting and decentred perspective on their thoughts, bodily sensations and moods and recognise that where change is not possible, acceptance can be therapeutic.

Think about …

1. On what criteria did Lynda meet the diagnosis of dysthymia?
2. What issues in Lynda's life maintained the dysthymic symptoms?
3. How would you describe the downward arrow technique to a client with chronic depression?
4. How would you, as a therapist, provide guidance and support to Lynda so that she can continue to develop her socialisation skills?

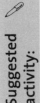

Suggested activity:

- Re-read this chapter and summarise the way in which it is possible to begin to differentiate depressive episodes from dysthymia. What therapeutic interventions are most likely to maintain a reasonable degree of symptomatic management of dysthymia?
- Try to recall when you felt sad; write down as many signs as you can recall in the areas of thinking, feeling, behaviour and bodily (physical) sensation. Make a list of how long these signs dominated your life, which areas began to decrease first and what incidences or strategies helped you? How was sadness different to dysthymia?

5
Client Presenting with Social Phobia

Mandy Drake

Learning objectives

By the end of this chapter you should be able to:

Identify the symptoms and nature of social phobia

Explain the processes involved in the maintenance of the disorder

Recognise the unique contribution of self-consciousness and safety behaviours in relation to the disorder

Outline the key cognitive and behavioural strategies utilised in the treatment of social phobia

Discuss some of the potential difficulties in the treatment of the disorder

---

Diagnostic criteria

The central characteristic of social phobia is a fear of social or performance situations in which the individual is open to scrutiny by others. In such situations it is the negative judgement of others that the individual fears and they anticipate that this will result from them behaving in a manner that is embarrassing, humiliating or in some way unacceptable. Not only do they fear the judgements themselves but in attracting such negative appraisal they believe that the ultimate outcome will be rejection.

The fear experienced is pervasive and evident in everyday life, manifesting in a variety of forms, from an inability to talk to new people or a reluctance to eat in public, through to excessive blushing, stuttering or trembling. Anxiety on exposure to feared situations can be very extreme with panic attacks being a feature of more severe cases. It is not surprising then that feared situations are avoided where feasible or endured with great distress where not.

Where some people will have a fear of only a few performance or social situations (non-generalised), others will fear the majority of both (generalised) and it is the latter that is most disabling (DSM-IV-TR, APA, 2000).

A key feature of social phobia is that the person recognises that their fear is excessive but this may not be the case if the individual is not an adult, in which case it may be assumed that the symptoms are part of the 'normal' adolescent personality (APA, 2000).

Social phobia is often complicated by other disorders, and in adolescent/young adulthood it has been found that up to 72 per cent of sufferers experience at least one other comorbid disorder (Wittchen et al., 1999). The risk of developing depression as a result of social phobia is considered to be high (Kendall et al., 2004; Stein et al., 2001) with about one third of people with social phobia also having depression (Essau et al., 1999; Wittchen et al., 1999). Substance misuse is also common, with estimates of between 24 per cent (Essau et al., 1999) and 41 per cent (Wittchen et al., 1999) of individuals experiencing both.

The most common comorbid condition, however, seems to be other anxiety disorders with 50 per cent of those with social phobia also being found to have another anxiety disorder present (Wittchen et al., 1999). There are certainly similarities between social phobia and panic disorder, and before a diagnosis of the former can be made it must therefore be clear that any avoidance or panic attacks are specific to social or performance situations, as a wider occurrence may be better attributed to the latter.

Finally some medical conditions will result in similar behaviours to those seen in social phobia, for example avoidance of eating in public in eating disorders, or fear of shaking in public in Parkinson's disease. These should be ruled out before a diagnosis of social phobia can be made.

Predisposing and precipitating factors

Unlike some conditions, social phobia does not have a number of theories competing for dominance when it comes to potential causes; in fact the general agreement is that there is a paucity of research into the area (Hodson et al., 2008).

Though there is some suggestion that there may be a physiological or hormonal basis for increased sensitivity to disapproval, or that the brain structures that control fear may be faulty (Antai-Ontong, 2008), on the whole there is a lack of compelling evidence as to a biological cause.

The APA (2000) reports that there is, however, some familial basis, indicated by a preponderance of the condition among first-degree relatives but they also propose a potential sociological cause in their statement that withdrawal and shyness in children is a predisposing factor. Indeed, Antai-Ontong (2008) purports that it is the modelling of such behaviour by adults, particularly the primary care giver, that leads to such behaviours in children, agreeing that this in turn produces a susceptibility to the disorder.

Marks (2001) states that whilst there is no obvious cause, there is a relatively clear age of onset, which he places at between 15 and 25, an age range supported by the APA (2000). He reports that the condition develops slowly over months or even years with no evident precipitator, but whilst the APA (2000) agrees that this is one potential pattern it also states that onset can be abrupt, tending to follow a stressful or humiliating experience.

A cognitive view proposes that socially anxious individuals are pre-occupied with how others perceive them in social situations, resulting in a preoccupation with their own thoughts, physiological symptoms of arousal and ongoing presentation (Hartman, 1986). Rather than identify the factors that may predispose the individual to such beliefs, the cognitive view attempts to explain the maintenance of the disorder and in the cognitive model this is seen to be the focus on the self. The work of Wells and Clark (1997) is arguably the most influential in the area of social phobia currently and their cognitive model will be utilised during the formulation stage of the later case study.

Demographic incidence

Social phobia is a prevalent disorder with studies suggesting that up to 13 per cent of the general population will experience it at some point in their lives (APA, 2000). There is a lack of consensus as to who is at more risk of developing this between men and women, with some studies suggesting it is women (APA, 2000; Wittchen et al., 1999) and others reporting equal distribution (Marks, 2001). One study found it to be less prevalent in children than in adolescents, the prevalence in the latter reportedly being up to 9 per cent (Crawley et al., 2008).

The difficulty in accurately predicting prevalence is that the threshold used to determine both the level of distress associated with the fear and the level of overall impairment is likely to vary widely. Where many members of the general population have a fear of speaking in public, only a small proportion of these are likely to experience enough distress to warrant a diagnosis, and fewer still will have a fear of meeting new people or eating and drinking in public. It is also difficult as the behaviour is dependent on social norms.

Continuum of severity

The onset of social phobia can determine the course of the disorder. If onset is early then impairment in children tends to take the form of failure to achieve expected levels of functioning whereas onset in adolescence may lead to a reduction in functioning, primarily in social and academic performance (Albano and Detweiler, 2001). Timely access to support is also a key determinant, as untreated social phobia in younger people has been associated with such debilitating consequences as failing to complete education, avoidance of age-specific social situations such as dating, and loneliness and isolation (Albano and Detweiler, 2001).

Where social phobia is generalised the impairment tends to be more severe with a noticeable deficit in social skills. Comorbid disorders can also negatively influence treatment and in particular the coexistence of depression has been associated with poorer outcomes (Crawley et al., 2008: Stein et al., 2001).

Finally, the duration of the disorder is frequently lifelong, though it may abate during adulthood. It is more likely that the course of the disorder will fluctuate with life stressors and demands, as will the severity of the impairment.

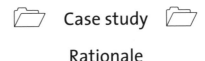

Case study

Rationale

The severity of social phobia is dependent on many factors and thus where a client sits on the care continuum is a matter of professional judgement. Whilst there is no specific NICE guidance to assist this judgement the general principles of the Stepped Care model can still be applied, starting with whether the condition is mild, moderate or severe and moving on to consideration of how intensive the interventions may need to be.

The following case study introduces Janine, a young lady who presents with moderate social phobia which has previously failed to respond to a guided self-help approach. The care provided is consequently at step 3 of the pathway with interventions being aimed at both the immediate and intermediate levels. The care takes place within Janine's own GP practice with a mental health practitioner from the Primary Care Mental Health Team.

Client

Janine, aged 16, is in the first year of college and is finding it difficult to attend. Her GP reports that she has always been a shy, quiet girl and his referral to the

Primary Care Mental Health Team (PCMHT) asks for help with self-esteem and confidence building. Two years previously the GP had referred Janine to the Child and Adolescent Mental Health Service (CAMHS) for the same reason, this time due to her difficulties attending school. The accompanying discharge letter from CAMHS indicated that Janine had lived in a small community where her family had owned one of the village shops. Due to financial difficulties the family had been declared bankrupt and had consequently had to sell their business and home – a very humiliating experience for the whole family. Though the family left the village, Janine continued to attend the school, albeit somewhat erratically. It eventually emerged that Janine feared her peer's rejection, believing that they saw her as a failure and she consequently withdrew from school in favour of home tutoring. During this period Janine was provided with counselling and guided self help but given the recurrence of the same problem her GP wanted to try another approach.

Assessment session 1

The assessment started with the clinical interview which followed a semi-structured format including presenting problems, impact, modifiers, onset and history and mental state exam.

Janine confirmed the information provided at referral, adding that she was afraid that her earlier problems had resurfaced due to having re-entered education. She reported feeling very anxious when at college, saying she found it difficult to join in conversations with her peers and that she was consequently avoiding any social contact with them, preferring instead to stick with her two close friends. She also reported feeling anxious on being asked questions in class and said that on a couple of occasions she had actually left the room to avoid participation. In order to gain a more comprehensive picture of the impact of Janine's anxiety she was asked to recall any recent examples, and on choosing two from earlier that week she was prompted to identify her thoughts, feelings, physical sensations and behaviour within these situations.

Janine was able to identify two very clear negative automatic thoughts (NATs), these being 'I'm going to say something stupid' and 'I'm going to go red', which made her feel anxious. She also reported a variety of physical symptoms and behavioural responses, the latter most commonly taking the form of avoiding eye contact, covering her face with her hands, and smiling and nodding to avoid having to talk. Janine reported using these behaviours to prevent her thoughts from being realised, thus these were identified as safety behaviours.

Safety behaviours maintain anxiety disorders due to the client's belief they are responsible for the non-occurrence of their fears, which prevents them from seeing that their fears are in fact unfounded. In social phobia they can also exacerbate symptoms and interfere with performance and so their identification is essential. Further safety behaviours were identified when discussing modifiers, including taking deep breaths, drinking water and sitting at the back of the class.

A key area for exploration in social phobia is how the individual thinks they appear to others and during the recall of the incidents Janine was asked if she had any particular impression of how she had looked at the time but she said no.

Janine reported that her difficulties were particular to college and that whilst she shared her father's shy personality she functioned well in day-to-day life. The mental state exam, however, identified poor sleep, diet and motivation that could indicate comorbid depression but there was no evidence of further comorbidity.

Prior to the interview Janine had completed the Clinical Outcomes in Routine Evaluation (CORE) questionnaire (Evans et al., 2000) which is a global measure of mental health used widely in primary care. At 24.2 her score indicated a significant clinical presentation, placing her considerably above the cut-off of 12.9. Due to the suggestion of comorbid depression she was also asked to complete the Patient Health Questionnaire (PHQ-9) (Kroenke et al., 2001) which is a measure of both presence and severity of depression. A score of 9 confirmed the presence of minor depression.

To further assess Janine's social phobia she was asked to complete the Social Phobia Rating Scale (SPRS) (Wells, 1997) which measures the frequency and intensity of symptoms over a seven-day period. She was also asked to keep a diary of her anxiety, a specific aim being to elicit the content of Janine's self-consciousness. Both were to be completed as homework.

Assessment session 2

The self-monitoring indicated that Janine had experienced five incidents of social anxiety of moderate distress. The majority related to her fear of blushing with only one being associated with her fear of saying something stupid. Many new safety behaviours emerged, as did physical symptoms and, importantly, she had been able to identify two different images of how she thought she looked to others when anxious. This information can be seen in an extract from her diary in Figure 5.1.

Case formulation

Clark and Wells' (1995) model of social phobia was used to formulate Janine's difficulties, and to aid socialisation to the model the theory underlying it was discussed. This can be found in the summary below, whilst the formulation can be seen in Figure 5.2.

Date & time	Situation	Thoughts	Anxiety symptoms	Image (How you think you appeared to others)	Safety behaviours (what did you do)	Level of distress (0–8)
01/11/10	In class. Girl asks me question about last week's session	I'm going to go red	Feel hot Heart pounding Butterflies	Face colour of post box Hot and flustered	Said I was hot Opened a window Drank some water Deep breaths	4
03/11/10	In town with friend. Two boys from college stop us to talk	I'm going to say something stupid	Hot Heart beating loudly Dry mouth Mind blank	A bit simple – all vacant expression and sort of slow in speech – village idiotish	Pretended to be texting Let friend talk Smile and nod, sometimes laugh Speak quietly	5

FIGURE 5.1 Social phobia diary extract

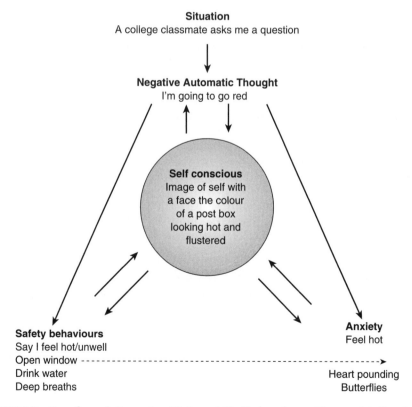

FIGURE 5.2 Case formulation using Wells and Clark's (1995) cognitive model of social phobia

Wells (1997) believes that the central feature of social phobia is a strong desire to portray a favourable impression of the self to others. This is accompanied by a lack of belief in the self's ability to do so; thus on entering social situations the individual appraises them as dangerous, fearing he/she will behave in a manner that is unacceptable or will lead to humiliation or rejection. This fear activates anxiety, the physiological effects of which become a preoccupation for the individual. As a result, the individual then focuses on the self, monitoring their own performance in a manner that prevents them from engaging or observing others. This not only makes performance more difficult but it prevents the individual from acknowledging information that could disconfirm their fears. The focus on the self also generates an often exaggerated internal view which is mistakenly assumed to be shared by others (termed self-consciousness) and a range of safety behaviours are then employed to stop others from seeing them this way. Unfortunately such behaviours are problematic in that not only do they prevent disconfirmation of the feared catastrophe but they can exacerbate the symptoms of the condition and also interfere with performance. Finally, two further mechanisms are considered to contribute to the maintenance of the condition, anticipatory and post-event processing, the former referring to how individuals rehearse and plan for social occasions and the latter to the way they mull these over after the event. Both are felt to overemphasise the negative aspects of the occasion as both are based on the individual's faulty self-focused processing.

Following formulation Janine agreed that she was experiencing non-generalised social phobia and stated that her aim for therapy was to feel comfortable attending college. This was operationalised into the following three goals:

1. To stop feeling anxious
2. To engage with fellow students
3. To participate in class exercises and discussion.

Janine did not think that her depression warranted specific intervention and she chose instead to work on her fear of blushing, which she stated was excessive and debilitating.

In addition to the continued monitoring of her symptoms using the SPRS Janine agreed that between sessions she would keep a negative thought record, the intention being to try to find out the meaning behind her NATs.

Session 1

A good starting point for therapy is assisting the client to see the negative effects of both their safety behaviours and their self-focus, and to begin this process Janine agreed to participate in a role play within the session. This can be seen in Box 5.1.

Box 5.1   Role play exercise

Janine chose a common feared situation which was of the tutor asking her to participate in a group discussion. It was agreed that the question the tutor would ask would be 'can you tell us about a time you've felt happy'. The role play then took place twice under two different conditions:

(1) With Janine practising all of her usual safety behaviours in this type of situation whilst focusing on herself
(2) With Janine dropping all of her safety behaviours and self focus, and instead trying to focus on her role play partner (therapist) and the environment.

Following the role play Janine was asked to compare the two conditions by looking at the three areas of physical symptoms, social performance and self-consciousness. Of these Janine had been surprised to find that under the safety behaviour condition she had felt more anxious and she thought this might be due to her constant worry about whether these were working. She was also aware of being rather fidgety, playing with her hands and fiddling with her water bottle which she thought had interfered with her performance. Certainly under the decreased safety behaviour condition she felt 'stiller' and therefore calmer, though she also felt that her 'redness' was on show. Despite this she still reported feeling more self-conscious when employing the safety behaviours as she was constantly thinking about how red she must look to others. Not thinking about this under the second condition had allowed her to focus more on the conversation, which demonstrated effectively to Janine the negative effects of both self-focus and safety behaviours.

To further demonstrate the negative impact of her current behaviours Janine agreed to repeat the exercise as a homework experiment, but to make it more meaningful it was to be conducted in a real situation. The situation chosen was a small project group meeting and it was agreed that Janine would bring her comparative analysis to the next session for discussion. Also in the next session it was decided that another role play would be conducted but that this would be recorded and played back to Janine so that she could see how she actually presents.

Session 2

Janine had found her homework task difficult and it had taken three attempts before she had successfully dropped her safety behaviours and self focus in the project group. It had, however, reinforced her suspicion that her self focus was increasing her anxiety and her safety behaviours were interfering with her performance, and in the absence of these she felt calmer and less conspicuous. She had also found that when she had focused on the people in her group she had been more able to follow the conversation and she had felt herself wanting to join in.

In preparation for the role play Janine had brought a scenario, which was a boy in her class asking her out; something she had been told was about to happen. Janine was asked to respond as she would normally, with no conditions being placed on her behaviour, and due to the anticipation of the event she reported finding it very realistic.

Before being shown the video Janine was asked to view it as though she was watching a stranger (to increase objectivity) and to visualise how she thought she would appear. Janine imagined that she would present as very red and hot looking with perhaps some signs of perspiration on her face. Earlier experiments had led her to think that she would also be very fidgety and her image developed into somebody who was also unable to sit still. Finally she stated that she would most likely present as boring, uninteresting and tongue-tied.

The reality was very surprising as she came across much better than she had imagined with only a slight colouring to her face and more fluency than she had anticipated. Her behaviour however concerned her, as she thought that she presented as rude and uninterested, but she was able to see that this was due to the safety behaviours which further reinforced their negative impact. Overall the exercise achieved its aim of helping Janine to discover that she presents far better than she thinks and that her self impression is thus misleading, and this in turn increased her confidence to participate in further behavioural experiments as homework, without the aid of safety behaviours or self-focused processing.

Session 3

Janine reported increased integration with her peers, having been on a couple of occasions to the canteen during breaks and having joined in more during group work. When tempted to employ safety behaviours, recalling their negative impact had helped her resist, but she had struggled to divert her focus from her fear of blushing, which had led her to avoid the boy who was going to ask her out.

The thought record confirmed that blushing remained a central fear and suggested that this might be linked to being seen as weak (see Figure 5.3). Janine admitted to thinking that people saw her as weak due to her blushing, reporting that this was preventing her from engaging any further with her peers. To begin to challenge this we agreed to review the evidence for the thought, starting with clarifying the specific observable behaviours Janine

Situation	Thought	Meaning (use prompts)
		• What are the consequences of your thought? • What do you fear will happen if your thought comes true? • What would be the worst others could think? • What are you most aware of thinking?
3 girls from my class say they'll walk to the bus with me	I'm going to go red	• That I'll look silly • They'll think there's something wrong with me • That I'm weak • That people think I'm weak

FIGURE 5.3   An excerpt from Janine's negative thought record

would expect to see in somebody who regarded her as weak. An extract from the conversation is as follows:

Therapist (T):   If a classmate you are talking to thinks you are weak, how would you know?

Janine (J):   I don't know, they're not likely to say so.

T: So, what are they likely to do?

J: They might just ignore me, or they might be quite critical I suppose. Actually, worse than that, they might be all sympathetic and try to molly-coddle me.

T: So is that the sort of behaviour you have been observing from them?

J: No, not at all.

T: Okay, so they are not treating you as you would expect them to if they thought you were weak?

J: No.

T: How are they treating you?

J: Umm ... They are friendly, they invite me places. Some have even started to ask my opinions about things and they know I'm good at assignments so one or two have asked me for help.

T: If you thought somebody was weak would you choose to spend time with them, ask them for their opinions and for their help?

J: I don't suppose I would.

Once operationalised it is easier to gather evidence around the thought, and following the conversation Janine started to compile an evidence chart (Figure 5.4). Though there was little evidence available to support the thought Janine struggled to identify evidence against it; therefore her homework task was to conduct another series of behavioural experiments, this time with a focus on generating-counter evidence.

Thought: People see me as weak			
Internal evidence (own thoughts)	External evidence (outside own thoughts)	Counter-evidence	Balanced thought
I feel like people watch me sometimes	My friends are protective of me – I know they look out for me	Nobody has ever said that I'm weak	
I blush – I must look so weak to them	I have been asked a couple of times if I'm okay by people I don't really know well	People don't behave towards me as I'd expect if they saw me as weak	
I can't even look people in the eye – that's just pathetic			

FIGURE 5.4   Evidence chart

The particular focus of these experiments was to test whether the reactions of others confirmed Janine's belief that people saw her as weak and so she was asked to observe the behaviour of her peers during her interactions with them. She was reminded that she would not be able to gather the evidence needed unless her focus was on her peers, thus self processing was banned.

Janine was then asked whether she had used any particular strategies to prepare for her canteen trips; the specific intention being to identify anticipatory processing. This emerged in the form of rehearsing topics of conversation and ruminating about potential outcomes of these which she was then asked to consider in relation to their advantages and disadvantages. Though she initially stated that they helped her to feel prepared, she then recognised that she usually anticipated the outcomes to be negative and that it was in fact at this stage that her performance anxiety started.

Post-event processing was also evident in Janine's disclosure that she dissected her encounter in detail afterwards, but she stated that she had already recognised the destructive nature of this when she had become aware of her negatively biased self processing. Janine was therefore agreeable to stopping both practices and to utilise behavioural experiments instead as a means of both preparing and evaluating social situations.

Session 4

Janine had engaged in the behavioural experiment on eight occasions, both in the canteen and during the increasingly occurring ad hoc interactions, and the outcome of one of these can be seen in Figure 5.5. The experiments had generated much counter-evidence for her negative thought, which Janine had added to her thought chart, and as a result her belief in the thought had weakened. She was consequently asked as homework, to generate a range of alternative thoughts about how she was perceived by her peers and to decide

Thought	People see me as weak
Prediction	Others will treat me with contempt – they will walk away, be critical or rude or just show no interest
	Or
	They will treat me as if I'm fragile – ask if I'm okay, talk softly to me or be patronising. They'll try to protect me
Experiment	Stay in the situation and focus on the others present. Look them in the eye and take note of their responses. Don't focus on self or I'll miss the evidence I need

Date	Situation	Outcome	Evidence (for and against)
	Went to canteen with some classmates and my 2 friends	Was prepared. Had thought of a topic but was focusing too much on this so abandoned it. Looked at others. I didn't say much but they looked at me and addressed me, just like they did the others. One person in particular asked me questions. Felt like part of the crowd	For: My friend answered for me at first. Against: My friend stopped answering for me when I spoke for myself One person was interested in me Everyone included me
	A girl from my class sat next to me on the bus home	Shocked initially and wasn't able to focus as too aware of blushing. Then focused on her and what she was saying. She asked me questions and we talked about the course. She was friendly and interested and I enjoyed it	

FIGURE 5.5   Outcome of behavioural experiment

on one for our next session. She also agreed to continue with the behavioural experiment, but to just utilise opportunities as they arose, thus incorporating her focus on others into daily college life.

Sessions 5 and 6

It was evident from the experiments that Janine was engaging more frequently with her peers on a daily basis and a review of her evidence chart confirmed that she no longer held a belief that she was seen as weak. Instead

Steps:	Goal: To increase social activity	Achieved
1.	Go into town after school with classmates only	
2.	Join a group of classmates at one of their houses	
3.	Go into town on a Saturday with group of classmates	
4.	Go to a college social evening with group of classmates	
5.	Go out to a social event with group of classmates	

FIGURE 5.6   Avoided activities in order of most achievable first

Janine had identified an alternative thought of 'people would see me as like-able and friendly if I gave them the chance', the latter part having been added as Janine felt that she was still not engaging much in conversations. Whilst her concern about blushing had now disappeared, Janine was still concerned about being seen as stupid, which was the secondary thought identified at assessment.

Treatment therefore proceeded with the development of another for-mulation specific to Janine's fear of being seen as stupid, utilising informa-tion derived from a recent situation. As Janine was already aware of the negative impact of her self processing and safety behaviours, work started immediately with thought challenging. Treatment subsequently followed that outlined for the previous thought of 'people see me as weak' , and due to both familiarity and success with the techniques previously employed Janine quickly reached an alternative thought of 'I'm no more stupid than anyone else.'

Sessions 7 and 8

Despite both of Janine's thoughts having been successfully modified the SPRS identified the continued presence of avoidance, which Janine reported was around social activities with her college peers outside of this setting. She believed that it was just a result of being out of practice and so it was agreed that her social contact would be built up incrementally and a list of avoided activities was drawn up in a hierarchy (Figure 5.6). It was agreed that each step could be achieved first with the support of her two close friends before Janine would complete these alone.

During these activities a new fear emerged coupled with a new safety behaviour, these being that Janine was afraid of revealing her 'true' self for fear of being rejected, resulting in her 'hiding' parts of her personality. She reported having developed a taste for classic literature, poetry and politics during her home tutoring as well as a preference for less mainstream clothing. Her peers seemed not to share such interests and Janine feared that in revealing what she did she would be rejected, which in behavioural terms would mean being ignored, verbally challenged or not being invited to spend time with people. To test this thought it was therefore decided that as Janine continued to work on her hierarchy she would also start to share her interests and preferences and, as with previous experiments, she was asked to observe the reactions of her peers.

Janine progressed quickly and successfully and was pleased to find that others shared some of her interests. Some who did not had expressed this honestly, but interestingly Janine did not see this as a rejection, which showed the progress she had made. This was reflected in the final alternative belief that Janine chose as a culmination of all thoughts that had been modified which was 'I am liked and accepted as an individual.'

Treatment evaluation session

A return to Janine's therapy goals identified that all had been achieved and in relation to her engagement with peers she stated it had been exceeded. Not only had Janine developed a new social network centred on her college peers but she had also started dating the boy whom she had finally allowed to ask her out. Re-completion of the self-report measures reinforced the positive outcome, the CORE (Evans et al., 2000) indicating a significant improvement at a now non-clinical 6.4 and the PHQ-9 (Kroenke et al., 2001) score of 3 signalling an absence of comorbid depression. Finally, the SPRS confirmed the absence of any symptoms of social anxiety, which all together suggested no present vulnerability to relapse.

Given the high prevalence of relapse in social phobia, however, this potential was discussed, with Janine stating that as she had found the exercises used throughout therapy to be beneficial and useful she would feel confident drawing on these. She additionally identified her two close friends as sources of support and she was finally advised of the procedure for re-referral should she want to access the service for booster sessions.

Discharge strategies

As the referrer, Janine's GP was sent a discharge letter outlining the care she had received as well as an invite to re-refer to the PCMHT in the future should this be necessary. It is not unusual for clients to return for a few refresher sessions at a later date, and given the success of the therapy this would be an appropriate course of action in this case.

Critique of case study

The emphasis of treatment in social phobia is on shifting the focus of attention and processing, dropping safety behaviours and evaluating predictions against actual occurrences, and the achievement of this within eight treatment sessions suggests that brief CBT was an appropriate choice in this case.

The failure to identify social phobia during previous intervention demonstrates the difficulties in identifying the condition in young adults, and whilst this could have led to a poorer prognosis there was no indication of this.

There were two significant turning points in therapy: the role play and video feedback. Realising the negative effects of the safety behaviours was instrumental in Janine's progress as it was this that enabled her to engage in the experiments without them. Similarly, directly observing her own presentation was a revelation which acted both to reduce her self consciousness and to further increase her confidence in engaging with the treatment.

A potential criticism, however, lies in the late discovery of a previously unidentified thought and safety behaviour. It was Janine herself who was key to their identification, not the therapist or the strategies employed, and had they not been discovered they would have presented a vulnerability that could have led to relapse. Given the high incidence rate of relapse in this condition it is imperative that vulnerability is as reduced as possible at discharge, and to try to prevent post-discharge deterioration it should be ensured that strategies employed within the sessions are easy and available to use independently should the need arise.

Problems arising in therapy

Janine was motivated to engage and was operating within a social setting, both of which added to the ease with which therapy progressed. Had she not been, however, there could have been many problems, not least in the development of the relationship, which after all is a social encounter itself.

Consideration may need to be given to how to approach somebody who is fearful of interaction with others, particularly as many of the behaviours therapists employ (such as leaning towards the client and maintaining good eye contact) can significantly increase the anxiety of those who are socially phobic. Equally, the aloofness, indifference or rudeness often employed by clients as safety behaviours need to be overcome, and therapy may need to be extended to accommodate this.

Another difficulty arises when people have become so avoidant that they no longer have a social network in which they can carry out the therapy. Not only do the therapist and client have to then actively seek out opportunities for practice but if the situation is perceived to be false it is likely to be less effective. Attempting to identify situations that are meaningful can be challenging but doing so assists therapy to progress more successfully.

Finally, Janine was motivated towards all the tasks but this will not always be the case. To encourage clients to be actively involved in therapy, strategies should be kept simple, explanations clear and activities straightforward, and if they are further encouraged to keep a record of the strategies as they go along they will have a resource file to draw upon post-discharge.

1. Does Janine's presentation fit with what we know about social phobia? Look back over the first section to help you with this.
2. What do you think would have happened to Janine after discharge if the additional thought had not been recognised?
3. Of the strategies employed, are there any you would have difficulty with? Think about this from the perspective of you as a client and then you as a therapist.
4. We can all feel anxious on meeting new people or entering new situations. Think about your own anxiety in such situations and what strategies you employ to 'ease' this.

Think about …

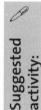

- Using the situation from Question 4 above try mapping this against the cognitive formulation.
- Now ask a friend for a similar example and after mapping this to the formulation practice, explain the maintenance processes to them
- Why not try a behavioural experiment yourself? The next time you are in a meeting or a gathering of friends try focusing your attention on yourself: what you are thinking, how you are behaving and whether there are any physiological reactions you are aware of (e.g. grumbling stomach). Think afterwards how this affected your concentration, interaction and overall performance and maybe you could ask for feedback from those present.
- In a following meeting or gathering focus your attention on the others present, noting their reactions and responses to the conversation. Again, afterwards think about your concentration, interaction and performance in that situation and compare it to the previous one.
- What learning can you take from this?

Suggested activity:

6

Client Presenting with Obsessive Compulsive Disorder (OCD)

Ian Ross

Learning objectives

By the end of this chapter you should be able to:

Identify the symptoms and nature of OCD
Explain the development of OCD from a cognitive perspective
Outline the cognitive and behavioural strategies used in the treatment of OCD
Be aware of factors that may cause a relapse of OCD

Diagnostic criteria

Obsessive compulsive disorder (OCD) is a chronic mental health condition associated with both obsessive thoughts and compulsive behaviour. An obsession (the cognitive component) is defined as an unwanted thought, image or urge that repeatedly enters a person's mind, whereas a compulsion is defined as a repetitive behaviour or mental act that a person feels compelled to perform, often in an effort to reduce the anxiety created by the obsession or as a means of preventing the obsession becoming true. The compulsions may be overt and easily recognised behaviours, for example hand washing and checking, or covert and less obvious, for example counting and word repetition. Both are used to avoid unwanted outcomes and relieve the associated stress. The point at which the client recognises that the obsessions and compulsions

TABLE 6.1 Obsessions and compulsions

Obsession (cognition)	Compulsion (behaviour)
• Fear about contamination with dirt, germs, viruses • Worries about danger or harm from doors being unlocked, electrical items switched on • Need for order, tidiness, conformity, symmetry, precision • Intrusive thoughts or images: blasphemy, swearing, sexual acts, harm to self and others • Need to hoard and store; fear of loss	• Frequent hand washing, disinfecting surfaces, avoidance e.g. public spaces; touching door handles • Constant checking and rechecking • Rearranging, counting, moving and organising objects; grooming and dressing • Suppression or distraction to neutralise cognitions e.g. checking hand brake on car • Hoarding of items; lock up perceived valuables

are becoming problematic is variable and will depend very much on the client's insight into the excessiveness and unrealistic nature of OCD.

Some forms of compulsive behaviour, such as an addiction to drugs or gambling, may offer a certain sense of pleasure or satisfaction. A person with OCD, though, gets no pleasure from their compulsive behaviour; in fact they often find the compulsion very disturbing and can recognise that the behaviour and obsessive thoughts are abnormal. Table 6.1 lists typical obsessions and compulsions.

OCD is classified in the DSM-IV-TR (APA, 2000) as an anxiety disorder whilst the ICD-10 (WHO, 2007) states that symptoms must have been present for a minimum of two weeks. For the DSM-IV-TR up to five symptoms should be present from the following, while the ICD-10 has a similar criterion. For obsessions the individual has recurrent and persistent thoughts, impulses, or images which are experienced as unpleasantly intrusive and inappropriate and cause marked anxiety or distress and are more marked than excessive worrying about real-life issues. The individual is aware that such invasive thoughts, impulses or images are a product of their own perception and makes repeated but failed attempts to suppress or weaken their influences by distraction into other thoughts or actions.

Compulsions are present if the individual has repetitive behaviour or mental acts in response to an obsession that the person cannot control and the compulsions are perceived as preventing a dreaded event or situation. Unfortunately the compulsive acts are not normally realistic behaviours which would be able to prevent the perceived event or situation, but they are not usually recognised as such by the person carrying out compulsive acts. Usually one thought or act becomes the focus of continuous but unsuccessful resistance although there may be a number of obsessive or compulsive behaviours that co-exist. However, to add to the misery of the condition, the individual does become aware that the compulsive behaviour is unreasonable and excessive, sometimes taking more than one hour per day, significantly interfering with daily living activities and providing no pleasure, as the release of tension or anxieties is short-lived.

Assessment should consider whether the intrusive thoughts and compulsive acts are outside another DSM-IV-TR axis 1 condition such as depression, as the level of OCD comorbidity is high whilst some aspects of the criteria can be found in unrelated physical or medical conditions or substance misuse.

Predisposing and precipitating factors

OCD is thought to be familial which is due in part to genetic factors. However, despite a number of candidate genes being identified, no conclusive studies have yet been published. Young adults and women appear to be at most risk of developing OCD and in these high-risk groups there does not seem to be a typical symptom onset pattern, though stressful life events may be precipitating factors.

Salkovskis and colleagues (2000) identified the cognitive component 'inflated responsibility' as a core feature and predictor of OCD. Individuals who experience OCD have heightened beliefs that it is essential that they are responsible for preventing harm or crucial negative consequences to themselves or others. The cognitive model of 'inflated responsibility' is explored in detail in the section on conceptualisation and formulation.

Demographic incidence

OCD is one of the most prolonged anxiety conditions and has a lifetime prevalence of about 1–3 per cent of adults and 2 per cent of children and teenagers (NICE, 2005c). OCD symptoms usually begin in men during adolescence and in women in early adulthood. They can, however, begin at any time, including childhood, though it may take 10–15 years before the individual will seek help. Whilst psychotherapy may assist in the management of the condition, a complete remission is rarely achieved. OCD has comorbidity with depression, anxiety, substance misuse and, less frequently, body dysmorphic disorder (BDD) and eating disorders.

Continuum of severity

One of the difficulties in working with OCD is that clients will often not present for treatment until they recognise that the disorder is having a serious impact on their daily routines. This referral may only occur well into the progression of the condition and exacerbate the disorder. Severity at presentation is complicated by the comorbidity of OCD with a number of other disorders. Bienvenu and colleagues (2000) in a family study, identified high prevalences of comorbid spectrum conditions such as somatoform disorders (especially BDD), anorexia nervosa and bulimia nervosa, hypochondriasis, pathologic nail biting, trichotillomania and kleptomania, which are apparent in families of patients with OCD. Periodic increases in symptom severity have been observed, particularly at times of stress. However, spontaneous remission of symptoms has a very low occurrence.

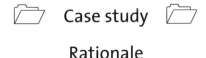

Case study

Rationale

As already mentioned clients rarely present in the earlier stages of OCD and so Stepped Care is frequently at the higher levels to account for the severity of the symptoms. The case of Derek is one such example of a late presentation where symptoms had progressed to the moderate stage. NICE (2005c) recommends that in cases where symptoms are moderate the treatment offered should be CBT, incorporating Exposure and Response Prevention which is aimed at both the immediate and intermediate cognitive levels. Treatment should still be offered outside of specialist mental health services at this stage. Thus the following case study demonstrates a care approach carried out by the Primary Care Mental Health Team at step 3 of the Stepped Care pathway.

Client

Derek is a male client, aged 57 years, married with one adult female daughter, Clare, aged 22. Clare recently finished her training as a secretary and approximately eight months ago decided to move out of her parents' home to take up employment with an organisation located about 40 minutes' drive away. She has rented accommodation locally, which she shares with her partner. Approximately 18 months ago Clare had been ill with a respiratory infection which was later diagnosed as influenza. She was admitted to hospital and placed in a High Dependency Unit for four days to stabilise her condition, particularly her breathing. Both her parents remained at her bedside and Derek admitted to being extremely anxious about her during this time. She made a full recovery and was able to return to work six weeks later.

Since Clare has moved away, Derek reports that he has persistent, intrusive and unwelcome thoughts that his daughter will come to some harm. He initially found that he could counter these thoughts if he repeatedly washed his hands with liquid soap and hot water exactly four times, before meals. This has since increased and he now washes his hands at least eight times before meals and after any visit to the toilet. He also admits to silently reciting in his mind a line from a childhood prayer, before he goes to bed each night. The excessive hand washing has caused the skin on his hands to break down, leaving him with open sores on his palms and fingers which are unsightly, itchy and prone to oozing blood. On closer questioning by the GP Derek reported that he had suffered from compulsive behaviour and obsessional thoughts as far back as he could remember. His daughter's illness has served to exacerbate his symptoms.

Derek experiences high levels of anxiety if he is unable to complete his washing rituals. He works in a large open-plan office which means that he has to walk across the office to access the washrooms. As he now has to spend an increasing amount of time in the washroom – often up to 15 minutes – this makes him feel uncomfortable and embarrassed and as a result he is missing work. This has concerned his employers and in an interview with HR it was suggested that he took sick leave. Derek's GP prescribed anti-depressants and referred him on to the Primary Care Mental Health Team, where he attended two sessions of psycho-education to help him to understand his condition. Following this it was recommended that Derek be moved up to step 3 for CBT, due to both the chronicity and severity of his difficulties, and his scores on the PHQ-9 and Generalised Anxiety Disorder Assessment (GAD-7) supported this decision. Prior to the first session any primary disorders such as schizophrenia had been ruled out.

Assessment session

The aims of the assessment session with Derek were to obtain information about, firstly, the obsessional and compulsive symptoms, secondly, the triggers associated with each, and thirdly, the meaning and significance of the obsessions and compulsions. This was accomplished through a clinical interview and the completion of self-report measures. Salkovskis et al. (2000) offer an extensive checklist to guide the therapist in an investigation of the cognitive, behavioural, emotional and physiological features of the client's problems. It is important to gain a clear picture of the client's obsessional and compulsive symptoms, which may take a number of sessions, during which the client is encouraged to make notes and maintain log sheets. These will be described later.

Derek was asked during the assessment session to identify his goals and expectations for therapy. He stated that his primary goal was to reduce his excessive hand washing. He described how the compulsive behaviour starts when he wakes in the morning. He is immediately aware of thoughts that his hands may have been contaminated during the night and that he may contract a serious illness. He says that he feels his anxiety rising; he feels hot and his hands become sweaty. This anxious reaction causes the skin on his hands to hurt and tingle as the excessive washing has caused a dermatitis which is sensitive to sweat and the washing gel he uses. He is unable to identify the contaminant on his hands, but will get out of bed and immediately commence washing his hands at least eight times.

When asked to describe the routine, Derek described how he would firstly take a disinfectant wipe to clean the taps on the basin and the hand wash gel dispenser before squirting hand wash gel onto his hands and rubbing for at least one minute. He then reaches down and turns on the taps, adjusts the temperature and rinses his hands thoroughly. The routine is repeated at least seven more times until he feels his anxiety reducing. Derek confirmed that he also carried out this routine whenever he thought that he might have touched surfaces or objects that other people could have touched.

Derek went on to describe how, whenever he thought of his daughter, he worried and obsessed that she would come to some harm and that he felt the compulsive need to wash his hands. He recognised he had feelings of anxiety which revolved around contamination by human 'germs' and was sure that his daughter had become infected with influenza through touching surfaces or objects that other people had handled. He felt that he might not have fully educated her as a 'little girl' to thoroughly wash, and therefore he had to shoulder some of the blame for her serious illness. The logic he adopted was that because he had failed to prevent her illness, he caused the harm. He said he felt reassured that if he washed repeatedly he would ensure that he at least would not be contaminated by other people's germs. He said that as he washed he felt mildly relieved, but could never be sure that he had actually washed enough, so he would repeat the procedure.

A crucial element of the assessment process is that the client is encouraged to accurately record the obsessional thoughts and compulsive behaviours, as details are often omitted from their verbal descriptions due to the familiarity of these to them. It can also be useful for the client to demonstrate some compulsive behaviours during the session, for example checking. However, practical difficulties could arise as in Derek's hand washing which required additional facilities. The client may also not wish to discuss their compulsions and obsessions, due to being frightened or embarrassed, or they may perceive that they will be judged or ridiculed, for example in cases of sexual obsessions or compulsions.

A simple monitoring sheet aimed at eliciting details about the obsessive thoughts and compulsive behaviours may be set as homework after the initial

Situation date	Time	Trigger	Thoughts at time of trigger	Intensity 0 = acceptable 5 = extreme discomfort	Activity: Describe what you did	Thought, feeling, mood after completing activity
Before breakfast 21/3/09	7.10am	Hands feel dirty	'I need to wash my hands to stop an infection'	5	Washed hands slowly and repeated procedure 7 times	Some relief, but late for breakfast and work
Lunchtime	12.45pm	daughter	'I should have protected my daughter – I will wash my hands in case I become contaminated'	3–4	Washed hands 5 times	Felt relief that at least I was protecting myself

FIGURE 6.1   Situation sheet for Derek after second session

Thought	Frequency and when	Means to me	Rating of anxiety 1= low; 5=high
1. I was responsible for my daughter's illness	Early am when I wake and hands are sore and itchy	I didn't show her how to keep her hands clean	3
2. My daughter will get ill again	Similar	As a father I have failed to educate her correctly in personal hygiene and I must not let this happen to me	4
3. That desk top is dirty	In the office	Someone may have sneezed on the surface	4
4. The TV remote control may be contaminated	At home	There may be virus contamination	2

FIGURE 6.2   Thought diary

assessment session and such a sheet was given to Derek to complete each time he felt the compulsion to wash his hands. He was asked to fill in the details of his routine, to record associated thoughts and emotions and enter these onto the situation sheet. Derek's completed sheet is shown in Figure 6.1. A thought diary may also be introduced at this stage; this will be ongoing and allow adjustments to conceptualisations and formulations to be made if additional beliefs and intrusive thoughts become obvious. An example of thought diary entries is shown in Figure 6.2.

TABLE 6.2 Assessment session self-report scores for Derek

Questionnaire	Score
OCI	92
PHQ9	18
GAD7	17
RAS	4.7

Self-report questionnaires were completed by Derek in the assessment session. These provide a baseline measurement of obsessive thoughts and compulsive behaviours and when repeated mid-way and at the end of therapy serve as a measure of therapy progress.

One of the most frequently used questionnaires is the Obsessive Compulsive Inventory (OCI; Foa et al., 1998). The subscales of this inventory record washing, checking, doubting, ordering, obsessions, hoarding and neutralising. Anxiety and depression may be measured using the Hospital Anxiety and Depression Scale (HADS) (Zigmond and Snaith, 1983); Patient Health Questionnaire (PHQ-9, Kroenke et al., 2001) and Generalised Anxiety Disorder Assessment (GAD-7) (Spitzer et al., 2006)

Salkovskis et al. (2000) studied responsibility attitudes and interpretations and found these to be characteristic of OCD sufferers. The Responsibility Attitudes Questionnaire (RAS) was developed as a general belief measure linked to responsibility assumptions characteristic of obsessive compulsive disorder.

Derek was asked to complete OCI, PHQ-9, GAD-7 and RAS questionnaires during the assessment session and Table 6.2 shows his scores. These scores confirm the initial diagnosis of OCD. There is a moderate score on the PHQ-9 and GAD-7 indicating comorbid anxiety and depression. OCD is clearly demonstrated in the OCI score with the RAS score supporting the hypothesis that OCD sufferers have strong responsibility assumptions and beliefs. This is true for Derek who feels a strong sense of responsibility for his daughter's illness.

Case formulation

Conceptualisation is about making sense of the origins, maintenance and development of the client's difficulties. A working hypothesis for testing and verification after appropriate interventions is developed along with the goals. A working hypothesis agreed with Derek was that if he undertook the interventions agreed during formulation, then the goal would be achieved, expressed as 'if I carry out the interventions, these will help me manage my hand washing'.

Theoretical basis of conceptualisation

There are a number of theories for the causes and maintenance of OCD which could be used by the therapist in conceptualising Derek's problem. Collaboration between client and therapist at this stage is crucial to ensure successful socialisation of the client to the CBT model and to strengthen the therapeutic alliance.

Behavioural theory was originally proposed by Mowrer as early as 1960, and is an appropriate explanation for the maintenance of anxiety. Essentially Derek maintains hand washing behaviours to reduce the fear of infection and the associated concerns about himself and, particularly, his daughter becoming ill again. In classical behavioural terms, his behaviour becomes negatively reinforced by the reduction in anxiety after his compulsive hand-washing activity. This theory does not, however, consider the initial triggers, which in this case would seem to be his fear of infection, his daughter's illness and his 'inflated responsibility'; the behavioural response has become separate from these events and obsessive cognitions. One explanation for the classical behavioural conditioning is that the normal passive avoidance behaviours or operant conditioning, for example washing hands only once to remove dirt, are insufficient to eliminate the anxious response to the obsessive thoughts, and so a much stronger conditioned compulsive behaviour pattern develops to respond to Derek's concerns about contamination and illness.

Cognitive theories rely on the fact that a faulty appraisal style underlies the intrusive obsessional thoughts. Salkovskis, Richards and Forrester (1995) suggested that the interpretation of obsessional thoughts leads to increased anxiety: greater focus on and accessibility of the thoughts and active and counter-productive attempts to reduce the discomfort and anxiety associated with the thoughts (safety or avoidance behaviours). In the case of Derek, his attempts included compulsive and frequent washing of his hands. His actions actually prevent the extinction of the anxiety caused by intrusive thoughts, as he perceives that by washing his hands he is in fact preventing an illness and therefore, as he apparently does not become ill, there is a compulsive need to continue. This disconfirmation makes therapy for OCD more complicated than for other anxiety disorders.

In a later publication, Salkovskis et al. (2000) investigated the dysfunctional belief systems linked to the intrusive thoughts and the causes of faulty appraisals. For example, it is not the thoughts Derek has about his daughter's illness, but the appraisal he makes of the intrusive thoughts, that lead him to an anxious compulsive response. A feature of beliefs linked to obsessional thoughts is a strong sense of responsibility and blame where Derek believes that the thoughts are potentially harmful to both himself and others. Derek has an associated feeling of responsibility for these thoughts, termed 'inflated responsibility', in which he, the sufferer, believes that it is essential that he prevent any possible negative outcomes. Derek has a dysfunctional belief that he must wash his hands frequently to prevent infection from potential contamination which may have come from dirty surfaces or objects. It was such an infection, he believes, that hospitalised his daughter and he sees himself as at fault for not preventing it.

Initial entries in Derek's thought diary (Figure 6.2) indicate a faulty appraisal style in which he attaches inflated responsibility and blame to the possibility of contamination, to both himself and his daughter. This becomes part of the conceptualisation and formulation process. As part of normalisation of the appraisal of these intrusive thoughts, an activity was introduced in the following session; Derek was asked to do some research into potential infection by the influenza virus. This information would be used to challenge some of his faulty appraisals and beliefs. In addition, for homework Derek continued to record his OCD behaviours and thoughts and use the conceptualisation diagram to assist his understanding of his condition.

Treatment session 1

The agenda for this session focused on the information that Derek had collected on influenza and using this to normalise his experiences.

Derek produced a summary of information about the influenza virus as homework by searching the internet. Derek discovered that indeed the main route of transmission of the influenza virus was either droplets, for example sneezing, or contamination of surfaces or objects after handling by people with unwashed hands. However, he also read that the influenza virus was relatively unstable and could be eliminated by simple washing or application of disinfectant gels. Derek recognised that whilst his compulsive behaviour was correct in principle, that is washing would significantly reduce the risk of infection, his behaviour had become dysfunctional or, as he described it, coincidentally, 'overkill'. As an additional measure the therapist asked Derek to carry out a poll amongst his colleagues and ask them how they thought the virus might be killed on hands and he was mildly surprised to hear that in polls of this type, most people agreed that a single wash was adequate.

Clients with OCD are often reluctant to seek help as they believe that they are abnormal. Whilst they recognise that their obsessions and compulsions are dysfunctional they believe they are powerless to stop them. Normalising the OCD experiences of the client are essential in building the therapeutic alliance. Often the difficulty in the normalisation process is deciding upon the boundaries of normal or safe behaviour which will ensure that the client remains safe. Derek was reassured that it was not uncommon for people to have obsessions and compulsive behaviours and was asked to recall an obsessive thought he may have had that was not connected to his present problem. He acknowledged that both he and his wife were prone to checking at least once that the front door was locked when they left for work in the mornings, but that they did not consider this abnormal, but rather essential to check the security of the house. Derek responded positively to this type of risk normalisation activity concluding that he was not going mad, a phrase he had used early in the assessment session. Whilst there are benefits in this psycho-educational intervention of normalising risk, there also needs to be an awareness of the additional anxiety that the client may develop with detailed knowledge of their condition, particularly with chronic life-threatening diseases.

Finally at the end of the session, Derek summarised the typical triggers and thoughts that accompanied his obsessive behaviour from his weekly diary. As homework Derek agreed to construct a hierarchy of situations which triggered his OCD, which would be used in session 2 exposure activities.

Session 2

At the start of the session the issues around Derek's OCD were reconceptualised; to be precise that Derek washes his hands repeatedly to gain some relief from the anxiety that he constantly associates with thoughts of contamination from dirt and infections and the illness of his daughter.

Derek was then introduced to the next intervention, Exposure and Response Prevention (ERP) (Foa et al., 2005), which needs to be initiated within a cognitive context, simultaneously challenging faulty appraisals and beliefs linked to the compulsive behaviour.

Exposure procedures will habituate Derek to the anxiety he fears and will thus reduce the negative reinforced behaviour he experiences. From his homework Derek provided details of his hand-washing procedures which he had constructed into a hierarchy of situations from most to least threatening, shown in Table 6.3.

A series of prolonged exposure experiments were then collaboratively devised, as shown below.

TABLE 6.3 Hierarchy of situations for Exposure and Response Prevention

Situation hierarchy	Anxiety level (1 lowest–5 highest)
Touching objects and surfaces in his home	2
Touching surfaces, objects in office	3–4
Touching objects in public places	5

T: We have agreed on the effect that exposure will have on your behaviour of frequent hand washing – I need to explain to you how we are going to carry this out.

D: I understand – I have my list of worst situations here.

T: Well we will start with an experiment where you deliberately soil your hands and then refrain from washing your hands for an increasing length of time. Which is the least anxiety provoking situation you have identified?

D: Touching surfaces in my home, I find least difficult. For example the front door handle; the loo-flush handle.

T: Which would you prefer to use first?

D: Hmmm ... I'll try the front door handle.

T: Good – so let's agree that at a specific time of the day you will deliberately touch the front door handle, grasp it as if you were entering the house and then hold back from washing your hands for say five minutes to start with. You can record your SUDS [Subjective Units of Distress Scale] number at the time of touching the handle and then at five minutes after and finally after you have washed your hands. How does that sound?

D: I think that I will be able to manage.

T: Once you find that you are able to touch the handle and your anxiety remains fairly low for say up to 15 minutes, then you can decide to repeat the same experiment on the next item on your list. Is that OK?

D: Yes – one question – do I do all the experiments in one day?

T: Ideally you should repeat each over perhaps a couple of hours until you feel comfortable before moving on. How about we agree that you work on the front door handle in the morning and then if all goes well, you start on the loo handle in the afternoon. Don't forget, it is important that you become comfortable with not washing your hands for a while. The loo handle will present us with an interesting point – would you normally wash your hands after going to the loo?

D: Yes of course, straight after. The problem is that I can't stop washing my hands though.

T: So it is quite normal to wash your hands after using the loo, the challenge is to refrain from doing it again and again. So for the loo handle we can agree that you touch the handle and then wash your hands once and then start experimenting with time intervals as we do with the front door. Do you think you can manage?

D: Yes.

Derek was given a series of sheets on which to write down the conditions of each exposure and he confirmed that he understood the homework exercises and was happy to proceed.

Session 3

At the beginning of the session, Derek reported that within three days over the weekend, he was able to reduce and maintain his anxiety at SUDS 1–2 until he next needed to go to the toilet and touch the loo handle. He was very proud of his achievement and discussed his SUDS results with the therapist. The next set of exposures and the procedures were then agreed for homework.

Clients often fall into avoidance behaviour during these experiments; they resist going about their normal routine to avoid triggers for the impulsive behaviour. Derek was able resist the urge to wash again until he considered it a normal behaviour, for example after going to the toilet. The choice of the loo handle was a useful way of normalising washing behaviour as this is a situation where it is important to wash hands to prevent infection. Derek reported an additional benefit from these activities which was that the less he washed the less irritated his skin was, reducing one of the physical triggers to his OCD.

Cognitive restructuring and generation of alternative thoughts and beliefs are usually initiated along with normalisation and ERP. Derek maintained a thought diary in which he recorded unwanted obsessional thoughts. A section of Derek's thought diary is shown in Figure 6.2.

The thought diary, alongside Clark's (2004) analysis of faulty appraisals helped Derek to identify both his own faulty appraisal styles and more appropriate alternative responses, as can be seen in Figure 6.3.

Sessions 4–6

During these three sessions Derek progressed his ERP experiments to the most feared situations, touching objects in public places and refraining from washing his hands for long periods of time or until it was appropriate, for example meal times. He also worked his way through his thought diary and was pleased with the manner in which he was able to offer more 'realistic' explanations for his thoughts.

Treatment evaluation session

This session focused on evaluation of intervention outcomes linked to Derek's therapy goals. The self-report questionnaire scores are shown in Table 6.4.

Whilst Derek scored noticeably lower on the PHQ-9 and GAD-7 questionnaires, his OCI and RAS scores improved less. This is not unexpected because the cognitive processes involved in OCD are more complex than the

Thought Diary		
Faulty appraisal	Alternative response	SUDS rating before and after alternative
Thought 1: Blame	You may have not fully educated your daughter but at the age of 18 she is her own person and needs to take responsibility for her own safety. There has been a major campaign on the TV and radio about hygiene precautions to prevent spread of the virus.	3 → 1
Thought 2: Inflated responsibility	Sitting by your daughter's bedside when she was in the HDU was a traumatic experience. Your presence and support would have been very important to her. Has she ever blamed you?	4 → 2
Thought 3: Overestimated threat Someone in the office has the active disease and that the virus has survived on the desk	Someone may well have contaminated a surface but based on your information the chances of the virus surviving is remote and if the person had active infection they would be on sick leave and you are not aware of any of your colleagues being ill. In addition an office memo reassured staff that extra cleaning procedures had been introduced as well as antiseptic gel dispensers and personal disinfectant gel hand tubes	4 → 2
Thought 4: Overestimated threat. My wife or I may be harbouring contamination which could make me ill	Is this likely? – neither of you have been ill.	2 → 1

FIGURE 6.3   Faulty appraisals and alternative thoughts

TABLE 6.4   Final self-report scores

Questionnaire	Final score	Assessment score
OCI	31	92
PHQ-9	9	18
GAD-7	6	17
RAS	4.0	4.7

behavioural elements. Salkovskis et al. (2000) note that the cognitive process of inflated responsibility is particularly deep–seated in OCD client beliefs and may prove difficult in the long term to restructure. However, CBT is a parsimonious process dealing with the 'here and now' and in the case of Derek he reported sufficient relief from his compulsive behaviour to return to work at the end of therapy.

Discharge strategies

Derek required no forward referral and was discharged from the PCMHT back to the care of his GP. The GP was informed of the risk of relapse and he agreed to monitor and support Derek and also informed him of a number of local support groups.

Critique of case study

Derek had a sympathetic and understanding GP who supported his therapy within the surgery. The GP had also undertaken a good initial assessment, ruling out other causes for the OCD, enabling a timely and accurate referral.

Derek's obsession was focused on hand washing, which created an additional requirement for relevant resources so that he could demonstrate the behaviour to the therapist. Therapy is more difficult if the OCD focus is on an activity or intrusive thoughts that are socially or personally unacceptable to the client, for example unkind thoughts or a compulsion to cause pain.

Finally, Derek is not alone in not seeking therapeutic support; normal habits can develop into OCD and there is a general reticence to seek help. In this case Derek was initially encouraged to get help by his employer but many individuals can have the condition for a number of years before therapy occurs and many treatment sessions may therefore be required before progress can be observed.

Problems arising in therapy

A number of studies have shown OCD to be a chronic disorder and the client is likely to relapse at any stage following the end of therapy (Clark, 2004). Stressful life events and mood fluctuations may cause a relapse in symptoms. At the outset of therapy the client needs to be made aware of this possibility and to understand that CBT therapy offers a number of coping interventions for future use. These can be enhanced by client attention to potential triggers, continuing psycho-education and provision of continued support via self-help groups. In the case of Derek, he required no further intervention from the PCMHT but he did choose to join OCD-UK, a national charity, independently working with and for people with obsessive compulsive disorder (OCD).

One of the most difficult aspects of OCD is the difficulty the client often feels about engaging in therapy. They frequently recognise the dysfunctional nature of their behaviour and thoughts and this has often become an issue within the family – in the case of Derek his wife admitted to frequently becoming very impatient with her husband and feeling helpless to respond to his dysfunctional behaviour and thoughts. Then there were occasions when she admitted collusion with him by acknowledging the relief he gained from his obsessive washing, which was in fact a relief to her. This unpredictable environment can make it difficult for the client to admit to needing therapy.

1. OCD sufferers often realise that their obsessive thoughts and compulsive behaviour are abnormal – as a therapist how would you initially work with a client who was convinced that he was, as Derek, said 'going insane'?
2. Clients with OCD frequently relapse and their thoughts and behaviours return after therapy. Describe one way in which the client can monitor their thoughts and behaviour and use this record as an early warning to seek help?

Think about ...

• Do you have any obsessive thoughts or compulsive behaviours? Use Table 6.1 as a guide and work through a conceptualisation and formulate appropriate interventions. You might like to try these out and see if they work.

Suggested activity:

7

Client Presenting with Generalised Anxiety Disorder (GAD)

Matt Bowen and Dennis Turner

Learning objectives

By the end of the chapter you should be able to:

Identify the nature and symptoms of Generalised Anxiety Disorder (GAD)
Explain the development and maintenance factors of GAD from a cognitive perspective
Outline a cognitive and behavioural strategy used in the treatment of GAD

Diagnostic criteria

Generalised anxiety disorder (GAD) is characterised by excessive, intrusive and difficult to control worry. It is a 'free-floating' worry that, as noted in the DSM–IV–TR code 300.02 (APA, 2000), is not focused exclusively on having a panic attack (panic disorder), concerns about contamination (OCD), anxiety about social contact (social phobia), physical complaints (somatisation disorder) or illness (hypochondriasis). The anxiety and worry may well revolve around a number of the above issues; however, the 'free-floating' nature of the anxiety often means that the specific nature of the worry seems difficult to identify as it moves from one area to another. This feature is supported by Stober and Borkovec (2002) who noted the limited capacity of individuals experiencing GAD to provide concrete and specific accounts of their worries.

For a clinical diagnosis, using the DSM-IV-TR (APA, 2000) criteria, the excessive and difficult to control worry must have lasted for at least six months and to have been present for more days than not during that time. Additionally the client must demonstrate at least three of the following symptoms: restlessness, fatigue, difficulty concentrating, irritability, muscle tension or sleep disturbance. It is commonly the somatic problems that bring the individual into contact with services rather than their concern about their difficulty in controlling worry (Flint, 2005).

The ICD-10, code F41.1 (WHO, 2007), definition of GAD is less specific regarding the duration of the anxiety, stating that it must be for most days of several weeks or several months. Research by Slade and Andrews (2001) indicated concordance between the DSM-IV-TR and ICD-10 diagnostic criteria; however, one difference is that the DSM-IV-TR indicates that GAD must lead to clinically significant distress or impairment, which suggests the DSM-IV-TR diagnostic group shows a higher level of acuity.

There is evidence of considerable comorbidity with GAD and depression (e.g. Mennin et al., 2008). The DSM-IV-TR criterion acknowledges this and notes that a clinical diagnosis of GAD cannot be made if the symptoms only exist whilst there is a mood disorder. The ICD-10, by contrast, indicates that if the client meets the full criteria for a depressive episode that this excludes GAD as a clinical diagnosis. This difference reflects some debate about whether GAD is actually a diagnostic category in its own right or whether it should be regarded as prodromal or a marker of severity in depressive states (e.g. Kessler, 2000; Mennin et al., 2008).

Predisposing and precipitating factors

Unlike some other anxiety disorders, there is no compelling evidence of a strong genetic factor in the aetiology of GAD (Kendler et al., 1995). A meta-analysis by Hettema, Neale and Kendler (2001) noted that GAD exists with high frequency within families but without a strong genetic influence, suggesting a learned response, whilst Moffit and colleagues (2007) have indicated low socioeconomic status and maltreatment as specific risk factors. McLaughlin, Behar and Borkovec (2008) also suggested that having another family member with a history of an anxiety disorder is a substantial risk factor – more so than having a family member with depression.

Koerner and Dugas (2008) have proposed a high intolerance to uncertainty which has a strong association with trait levels of worry and is increasingly viewed as significant in the aetiology of GAD.

Due to the disproportionate prevalence of GAD from midlife onwards there has been some interest in the precipitating factors of GAD in the older population. At a broad level, both the work of Jordanova and colleagues (2007) and Beekman and colleagues (1998) support a stress-vulnerability model of anxiety disorders with life stressors playing a more significant role in the development of anxiety disorder in the elderly, including GAD, than recent stressors.

Demographic incidence

The incidence of GAD globally is high, though there is considerable variation between nations. Maier and colleagues (2000) using World Health Organization statistics for primary care patients indicated a one month prevalence rate of 7.9 per cent for GAD, which was more significant than any other anxiety disorder and comparable to depression. The data also indicated the high comorbidity of GAD with other psychiatric disorders.

The largest community study was the National Comorbidity Survey (Wittchen et al., 1994) which indicated in the USA that women were twice as likely to have experienced GAD as men (6.6%:3.6%). This has been supported by more recent studies by Carter and colleagues (2001) whose community-based work indicated a prevalence of GAD, using the DSM-IV-TR criteria, of 1 per cent men and 2 per cent women and a sub-threshold level of 3.6 per cent. Flint's (2005) review of research into comorbidity confirmed the high levels, especially with depression, indicating that in the elderly population experiencing GAD, only one third are not comorbid with another mental disorder.

Continuum of severity

GAD should be viewed as being a potentially chronic and severe condition which significantly impairs the individual, particularly within relationships, at work and in social functioning (Henning et al., 2007).

As noted earlier, one of the striking features of GAD is the high prevalence of comorbidity. For example, Carter et al.'s (2001) research into the prevalence of GAD identified that 59 per cent of clients reported a major depression compared to 7.5 per cent of respondents without GAD. And 55.9 per cent of the respondents experiencing GAD reported comorbidity with another anxiety disorder. This high prevalence is a significant aspect of the severity continuum and should be reflected in the assessment process and subsequent treatment package.

Typically clients experiencing GAD have been high users of primary care services rather than specialist mental health services (Wittchen at al., 2002). Indeed, there is evidence that clients have typically experienced symptoms for between five and ten years before accurate diagnosis and treatment (Ballenger et al., 2001). This raises the question about the degree to which the problem is typically chronic and to what degree there has been a lack of appropriate assessment and treatment available for this client group.

Stanley and colleagues (2003) examined the efficacy of CBT for an older population of clients with a diagnosis of GAD and their findings indicated efficacy, but results were less promising than those for a younger population. They found that in post-treatment 55 per cent of the research participants who received CBT no longer continued to meet the GAD criteria; however, only one individual met the criteria for high end-state functioning. This may reflect the severity of the disorder within the older age group and the need for some caution about treatment outcomes.

Wittchen (2002) noted that the relatively poor prognosis of GAD had at times raised questions about whether GAD should be regarded as a character-ological disorder (and as such placed on the Axis II of DSM-IV-TR with the personality disorders); however, there has been little support for this position.

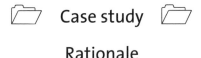 **Case study**

Rationale

The case study introduces Louise, aged 63, who presented with typical GAD symptoms. Louise had initially received a low dose of benzodiazepine from her GP, but on not responding was referred to the Primary Care Mental Health Team. Her referral was for CBT, which was offered at step 3 of the Stepped Care model with interventions being aimed at the immediate level of NATs.

Client

Louise's referral reported that she had been seen frequently over the last six years for a range of somatic complaints, specifically upper back and neck pain, recurrent headaches and flu-like symptoms. One month ago she presented to the surgery with muscular pains, headaches, poor sleep and fatigue during the day and she was prescribed a course of benzodiazepines for a month. She reported, however, that this had not provided her with much relief, as not only was she was lying awake at night ruminating about problems within the family but she was consequently feeling fatigued during the day.

Assessment session 1

As Brown, O'Leary and Barlow (2001) note, the reliability of diagnosing GAD is poor compared to other anxiety disorders, and assessments should be particularly vigilant if someone has been referred with a possible diagnosis of this. The assessment therefore may have to simultaneously attend to a number of important tasks, with the most obvious and overt being to make an accurate diagnosis that can inform an evidence-based treatment package. The assessment process is usually the first opportunity to start to socialize the client to the treatment model and is an important part of establishing a trusting relationship with the client.

The Anxiety Disorder Schedule for DSM-IV (ADIS-IV; Di Nardo et al., 1994) provides a semi-structured schedule to assist the accurate diagnosis of GAD. The schedule draws out information regarding excessiveness and lack of control, scoring these on a 9–point Likert scale matched against the DSM-IV-TR (APA, 2000) criteria. Given the relative complexity of diagnosis it is advisable to utilise this type of tool and when used with Louise it facilitated the identification of a wide range of worries in relation to her health, that of her family, the finances of her family and others' opinions of her socially.

Louise reported having always been worried but stated that she finds it hard to pinpoint when this became problematic. She stated that she had worried a lot when her daughter was pregnant, which she knew had annoyed her daughter at times and it was during this period that Louise had started getting headaches. She now worries whether her daughter can afford to be unemployed and, with her granddaughter also now being at school, whether she is okay. Louise stated that she wished that she and her husband could provide more of a financial safety net for them and that such thoughts keep her awake at night which means that she is then tired for much of the day. At times her back aches the most, at other times it is her head, but generally she feels pent-up and thinks that something awful is about to happen. This has made it hard to go out and she has started to turn down invitations to meet with friends. She insists that this is not because she does not like being with them but because she is so tired during the day that she has no energy. The findings of the assessment against the diagnostic criteria can be found in Table 7.1.

To supplement the diagnostic interview there are a number of self-report questionnaires that are helpful in the assessment of GAD, one of the most common being the Penn State Worry Questionnaire (PSWQ; Meyer et al.,

TABLE 7.1   Identified areas of priority and related scores in areas of excessiveness, lack of control and somatic severity

	Excessiveness (From total 9)	Lack of control (From total 9)
Minor matters – state of the garden	5	6
Family – especially daughter and granddaughter	8	8
Finance – both own and daughter's	6	7
Health (self) – that she's 'falling apart'	6	7
Health (other) – granddaughter will die	7	7
Somatic complaints	**Severity**	**Frequency**
Restlessness: feeling keyed up or on edge	7	Most days
Being easily fatigued	7	Most days
Difficulty concentrating or mind going blank	7	Most days
Irritability	3	Rarely
Muscle tension	6	Most days
Difficulty falling asleep/staying asleep	7	Most days

1990) which has demonstrated good internal consistency and reliability. It has also proven to be reliable with the older person (Molina and Borkovec, 1994; Wetherell and Gatz, 2005). This 16-item questionnaire is focused specifically at trait levels of worry and does not address somatic complaints. The absence of questions related to somatic complaints may be confusing to the client and this is a good opportunity to start to make the links between beliefs (traits), dysfunctional underlying assumptions, negative automatic thoughts (NATs) and somatic complaints, through explaining the vicious circle that is maintaining her generalised anxieties, and using psycho-educational approaches. Discussions can highlight the importance that worry plays in somatic complaints and the evidence that addressing the worry will lead to reducing the somatic symptoms (Dugas et al., 2003; Ladouceur et al., 2000). Louise was asked to complete the PSWQ before returning to the second assessment session and was also asked to keep a worry diary in which she recorded three worries each day (Figure 7.1).

Assessment session 2

Louise scored 70 on the PSWQ which clearly indicated a level of worry indicative of GAD (Fresco et al., 2003). Louise also produced her worry diary which facilitated a discussion of its role in helping her to become more familiar with her worries. It was explained that identifying her thoughts more clearly would help her to begin to make more sense of their connection to the other modalities: namely, her feelings, physical sensations and environmental factors. An extract from her diary can be seen in Figure 7.1. An incident from the diary was then used to inform the case formulation.

Date and Time	Worry	Anxiety (0–8)	Worry type (Current problem or hypothetical situation)
10/9/09 9.00am	Granddaughter contracting swine flu	7	Hypothetical situation
2.00pm	I'm a physical wreck	7	Current situation
10.00pm	No one to look after them – daughter and granddaughter We are too old	7	Hypothetical situation
10.00pm	Garden becoming overgrown	5	Current situation

FIGURE 7.1   Worry diary form

Case formulation

The cognitive model promoted here is that of Dugas and Robichaud (2007) and in order to socialise Louise to this model the case formulation was kept deliberately simple. An aim of this stage is to engage clients with the key concepts of intolerance to uncertainty, worry and the somatic responses, and due to the pre-occupations and poor concentration inherent in the condition this simplicity is paramount. The situation used was of a particularly powerful worry that Louise's granddaughter would get swine flu, which culminated in Louise having an incapacitating headache. Louise was guided to identify the initial trigger for the worry which she named as an article in the local newspaper and she was then asked whether she recalled what she had thought prior to her worry. In GAD a key maintaining factor is the 'what if?' question, where individuals prompt themselves to worry by imagining what if. In Louise's case she remembered thinking 'what if my granddaughter got swine flu?' when she read the article and she confirmed that this had then led on to her worrying about the potential consequences, which in turn precipitated a headache. Discussion of the formulation helped Louise to see the central role that intolerance to uncertainty has in maintaining GAD (the 'what if?' question) and this formulation can be found in Figure 7.2.

Treatment session 1

Dugas and Robichaud (2007) propose four main features in their cognitive-behavioural model of GAD. These are the intolerance of uncertainty; positive beliefs about worry; negative problem orientation; and cognitive avoidance. In proposing a treatment strategy, Dugas et al. (2003) suggest the intervention should be structured in six stages based on a CBT approach, and the interventions should build tolerance and acceptance of uncertainty at each stage of treatment. The stages are: presentation of treatment rationale (learning to live with uncertainty); worry awareness training; re-evaluation of the usefulness of worrying; problem-solving training; cognitive exposure; and relapse prevention.

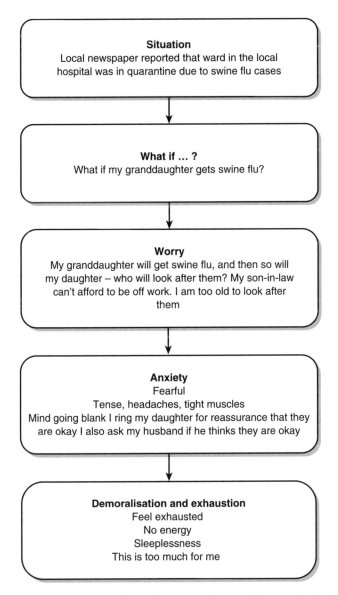

FIGURE 7.2 Presentation of formulation based on the cognitive model of GAD proposed by Dugas and Robichaud (2007)

Stage 1

Session 2

The first session of treatment took a psycho–educational approach with a number of points from earlier therapy being reviewed, including the principles of CBT and information about generalised anxiety disorder. After describing the diagnosis of GAD and its associated symptoms Louise started to understand it better, particularly how it can be characterised by worries about daily events that are excessive and difficult to control.

The basis of treatment within Dugas and Robichaud's (2007) model is that an individual's response to uncertainty is an important source of worry and anxiety and therefore the outcome of treatment is to enable the client to cope with uncertainty.

Stage 2

Sessions 3–6

In the second stage of treatment, Louise became more aware of her worries and their effects through further worry awareness interventions, sometimes known as worry awareness training. This approach allowed Louise to begin to develop a greater tolerance of uncertainty and involved identifying the domains related to worry such as physical symptoms, thoughts, emotions and her immediate environment, and placing her worries into two categories of current problems and hypothetical situations. To get an idea of which domains were dominant Louise was asked to record any worries she was experiencing at three separate times during the day. She was also asked to note her level of anxiety and the type of worry she was experiencing at that moment (Figure 7.1).

Working with Louise's worry record, therapy was able to identify concerns about her family, particularly her granddaughter's health (hypothetical issue), and her own health (current issue). Using a Socratic approach (Padesky, 1993), Louise was able to identify the recurring themes of her worry, the length of the time spent worrying daily, the influence of her worry on her day-to-day living and her worries about the future.

Despite the lack of certainty regarding the outcomes of her diary Louise was able to recognise worry episodes as they occurred and also to distinguish between external and imaginary anxieties through categorising of current and hypothetical situations. The diary entries were discussed with Louise and she volunteered the information that her tolerance levels had gradually increased and she was experiencing fewer anxieties about whether she could control aspects of her daily life. Exploring the relationship between intolerance of uncertainty and excessive worry was important because studies have indicated that when people learn to increase their tolerance regarding uncertainty they tend to worry less (Dugas et al., 2004; Ladouceur et al., 2000).

The next session therefore helped Louise to recognise and develop an even greater tolerance for uncertainty. The central goals for the therapy at this stage were to ensure that Louise understood the primary role of intolerance of uncertainty in the development and maintenance of excessive worry and anxiety, and to encourage her to begin recognising and dealing with uncertainty in her daily life. This initially took the form of psycho-educational information-giving about the relationship between intolerance of uncertainty and excessive worry, and in this context Louise's worry about her health and that of her family was explored.

Louise explored the development of anxious thinking through hypothetical examples. For example, one area she explored was the link between irrational thinking and its reinforcement or maintenance of other domains such as feelings and physical sensations by discovering that most people dislike uncertainty and tend to become anxious. For some people a small amount of uncertainty may cause a deeper response of worrying and anxiety. For example, Louise was asked to consider her thoughts about a person who is intolerant of uncertainty who worried that a partner travelling home in a car might crash, even though there was a small chance of this happening. She began to see that worrying about this type of example regularly may cause a loss of confidence in the fact that the chances of a crash are unlikely and that this in turn would heighten anxiety. Any media items or conversations regarding car accidents would then serve to reinforce this negative thinking, thus activating the vicious cycle which would eventually develop into a negative and intrusive anxiety.

Louise started to understand that when she is intolerant of uncertainty she worries excessively and that her worry can be seen as an attempt to consider all potential eventualities of a future situation; in other words she was attempting to reduce uncertainty by thinking about every possible outcome for a given situation. Louise started to discuss how her own intolerance of uncertainty had increased her worrying and anxiety, and in therapy she considered that if she was no longer intolerant of uncertainty whether there would be any need to engage in her prolonged mental activity of excessive worry. She also began to identify the links between her excessive concerns about her family's health and her own health problems.

Louise recognised that certainty about all aspects of her life was impossible to attain and set the goal of this stage of therapy as further developing her tolerance of uncertainty. One way of achieving this goal was for her to break down the intolerance of uncertainty into its two component parts: intolerance and uncertainty.

Clients seeking to reduce their worry can either chose to address the first component (increasing certainty) or the second component (increasing tolerance) and by the use of Socratic questioning the therapist can help clients discover which of these goals is more realistic, more attainable and more likely to lead to a lasting reduction in their worry and anxiety levels. An excerpt of the Socratic dialogue was as follows;

Therapist (T):	We could start by looking at the two components [intolerance and uncertainty] if you wanted to reduce your level of worry and anxiety. We've discussed them a lot. You could perhaps choose to either increase your tolerance or your certainty. Which of the two have you been using?
Louise (L):	Not sure, but I think I have been trying to increase my certainty.
T:	Has this been helpful to you?
L:	No, I still worry a lot.
T:	Why do you think it's not working even though you keep trying?
L:	I'm not sure, but I seem to make sure that everything has to be right, you know, preparing for all eventualities.
T:	I know that takes up a lot of your time every day. How do you feel after you've prepared for every eventuality?
L:	I feel exhausted. I can see now … how often I feel exhausted.
T:	I know it's exhausting for you, especially as we cannot, with certainty, know or plan for all eventualities. Perhaps, in view of the fact that you have tried every day to increase certainty and it's not been that helpful, we need to think about how we could increase your level of tolerance for uncertainty? What do you think?
L:	I agree. It's worth a try anyway.

Within this stage, therapy was helping Louise to identify the manifestations of intolerance of uncertainty. It is important to help clients to recognise the different ways in which their intolerance of uncertainty manifests itself in their lives and to deal with uncertain situations. Very often clients are not aware of how uncertainty manifests itself or the impact it has on their lives, and attempts to eliminate or circumvent the experience of uncertainty often maintains the intolerance. Two categories of intolerance of uncertainty are identified: approach and avoidance strategies.

Approach strategies are behaviours that involve approaching a given situation in order to eliminate one's feelings of uncertainty, for example seeking reassurance from others or collecting excessive information before making a decision. Louise was already aware that she sought constant reassurance from her husband and her daughter, which had become problematic in her relationship with both.

Avoidance strategies involve attempts to circumvent uncertainty by avoiding uncertainty-inducing situations, for example putting off doing a job, so that the feelings are only there for a short time. Louise suffered from severe headaches and would often spend the day in bed to avoid an episode because she believed that she was intolerant to light. By staying in a darkened room she felt she reduced the likelihood of headaches occurring but this also meant that she avoided uncertainty-inducing triggers.

Increasing Louise's awareness of these two strategies, approach and avoidance, meant she could start to take actions to achieve the potential benefits of increased tolerance to uncertainty.

Stage 3

Session 7

The third stage of treatment was to support Louise in re-evaluating the usefulness of worry by identifying her beliefs about the usefulness of worry and to begin a re-evaluation of these beliefs through behavioural experiments. Research suggests that individuals experiencing GAD hold positive beliefs about worry from any of the following: worry helps them find solutions for their problems; it can serve as a motivating function, thereby aiding them in getting things done; worry can serve as a buffer for negative emotions thus preparing them for negative outcomes should they occur; worry in and of itself can prevent negative outcomes from occurring (sometimes referred to as magical thinking or thought–action fusion); and worrying about people or situations shows that they are compassionate and caring. Worrying in context can therefore be useful; however the usefulness of worrying decreases as worrying becomes excessive, as in the case of individuals experiencing GAD.

Louise was helped to identify her beliefs about the function of specific worries as many of her beliefs fitted the above. Once she was able to identify her beliefs Louise began the process of challenging their actual usefulness. One behavioural experiment involving her excessive worry about the well-being of her daughter and granddaughter had led to her seeking constant reassurance from her daughter, so Louise monitored this pattern as a homework exercise and talked to her daughter about the impact of this on their relationship. The new information was invaluable to her in re-evaluating the usefulness of her excessive worry as a way of preventing negative outcomes from occurring and of demonstrating her caring nature. This process of evaluation can be seen as cognitive restructuring, with the goal being to help Louise acknowledge that her beliefs are thoughts and not facts, and by doing so she can carry out behavioural experiments to develop a more flexible beliefs system.

Defining the problem

My garden is overgrown and untidy

Problem-solving goals

To tidy the garden and to prune the small trees

Generating alternative solutions

- I will attempt to tidy and clear the garden. Unfortunately this causes a lot of pain later on
- Contact and hire a retired local gardener to work on the garden
- Wait until I am feeling better to attempt to tidy the garden

Choosing a solution

Contact the local retired gardener to establish his cost and availability

Implementation

Gardener contacted and discussed his costs and the job. Starting next week

Review

Fortnightly

FIGURE 7.3   Worry plan to address problems with Louise's garden

Stage 4 – problem-solving training (PST)

Session 8

Problem-solving training could be helpful with some clients, as rather than worrying about current problems the client could, with therapeutic support, attempt to solve them.

An identified current problem for Louise was her back pains and headaches. This problem was therefore used as an example of how to use problem-solving skills and Louise explored a range of options to approach her aches and pains. Therapy techniques such as behavioural experiments and psycho-education had already demonstrated to Louise the links between her excessive worry and her somatic problems, and so this more focused stage enabled Louise to see the somatic benefits of ensuring that she also re-started activities that she had previously enjoyed, for example reading. Louise agreed that her homework was to practise her problem-solving skills by constructing a plan to address a relatively minor worry with regards the state of her garden (Figure 7.3), whilst sessions provided the opportunity to reinforce the point that it is almost impossible to have complete control (certainty) over one's social environment, and Louise began to see how events may happen outside her control. For example one diary excerpt review showed that Louise's gardener was once unable to attend, and rather than become more anxious she began to see that she could not change the situation and she became slightly more accepting of it.

Stage 5

Sessions 9–10

Louise had by now identified how she avoided situations if she thought they would be uncontrollable or anxiety-provoking. She therefore began to challenge this area of cognitive avoidance by using hypothetical situations, and therapy supported her as she engaged in imaginal exposure to the fears that underpinned her concerns.

Imaginal exposure usually involves two aspects; gaining a mental image of a threatening situation and understanding the subjective feelings and physiological effects induced by the anxiety. Imaginal exposure is useful when the client is challenging general anxiety disorder symptoms, as in their normal day-to-day living the individual with GAD develops an avoidance of mental images when thinking about threatening material and tends to fear their own anxiety responses. It requires support in therapy but can have positive outcomes relatively quickly which act as counter-conditioning to the usual negative thinking inherent in GAD.

In the initial phase, Louise attempted to avoid thoughts about her fears of her granddaughter dying, but by challenging this position she was able to understand that it was actually counter-productive and paradoxically led to increased preoccupation. She began to discuss her normal approaches to worry which involved avoiding the things she feared, because at least this initially made her feel less anxious. However by continuing to avoid these thoughts the strength of the fears increased and she continued to be afraid of them. Attempting to reduce anxiety by avoiding or neutralising fears was less effective in the long term than gradually exposing herself to the feared situation through imaginal techniques.

Therapy helped Louise to identify such fears and which ones she wished to target by the use of the downward-arrow technique. An example includes Louise stating; 'What if my granddaughter caught swine flu?' and the response being: 'If your worry came true, what do you think might happen next?' This line of question was pursued to challenge the dysfunctional underlying assumptions held by Louise and she was able to write up the exposure scenario and subsequently record it as a future blueprint for her own self-supporting strategies.

The next stage involved Louise visualising the feared scenario, as well as experiencing and tolerating the anxiety. The exercise of imaginal exposure continued until her anxieties returned to a baseline level. Therapy needed to balance helping Louise address her fearful outcomes while still being exposed to uncertainty, but after three exposures Louise was able to demonstrate a reduced excessive worry regarding her granddaughter's health.

Stage 6

Session 11

The final stage of treatment was the prevention of relapse following the completion of the treatment. The objective here was to help Louise maintain her progress following treatment and to prevent any future relapse. The final session discussed the main issues covered during all the stages of treatment and focused on her strategies regarding relapse prevention. Three components for preventing relapse were identified in the programme: daily maintenance; identifying at-risk situations; and preparing for at-risk situations.

Louise was encouraged to develop a positive maintenance plan by first recognising those factors that increased her worry and her anxieties. She was encouraged to think of the strategies that had helped her to improve her coping abilities, especially her tolerance levels, which had been recorded in a personal portfolio in order to improve her future and continued progress. Louise also identified at-risk situations and those stressors she was likely to experience, her interpretations of these situations and what she thought were her realistic expectations of coping following treatment. The final session discussed her plan of action and reviewed her progress before the ending of therapy.

Treatment evaluation session

In the final session Louise complete the PSWQ and her score had reduced to 45, indicating a trait level of worry but below a clinically significant threshold. The Anxiety Disorder Schedule for DSM-IV-TR (APA, 2000) criteria (ADIS-IV; Di Nardo et al., 1994) was also repeated. This indicated a reduction in the level of excessiveness and control of her identified worries about family, health and minor matters, but she remained concerned about issues related to finance and retained an underlying concern that she and her husband could not provide a financial safety-net for her daughter's family.

Significantly, many of the somatic symptoms were markedly reduced and Louise no longer experienced difficulties with sleep, which in itself reduced her daily experience of fatigue. She also reported that she no longer experienced intense or frequent somatic symptoms of anxiety.

Discharge strategies

Following treatment, Louise was discharged from therapy and a discharge letter sent to her GP requesting that he monitor her ongoing progress. The GP was advised that if there were signs of relapse then the team would consider it appropriate to re-refer Louise for booster sessions but it was expected that Louise would be able to instigate her self-help strategies on a day-to-day basis. Louise was also informed that she could self-refer back to the Primary Care Mental Health Team should she feel the need.

Critique of case study

Louise progressed well once she had understood the relationship between her avoidance behaviours, attempts to control uncertainties and improving her tolerance levels, but this was a chronic condition so initial attempts at counter-conditioning were not successful. Louise tried to challenge her control of uncertainties but her attempts actually increased the frequency of anxieties and related somatic complaints and it was through the Socratic dialogue that she began to see that she did have other options – one being to work on her tolerance levels where she gained more success. It is important when working with GAD to achieve early success in order to have reinforcers to support the work done in psycho-educational sessions, and this was difficult for Louise. It is not uncommon for clients to understand their conditions and symptoms but still not know how to decrease their distressing impact or develop more positive maintenance strategies, and attempts to deal with the condition without support may consist of trial and error. Despite the slow start she progressed quickly through therapy and became quite adept at developing counter-conditioning strategies. Nevertheless, it has to be acknowledged that CBT is more useful as a management and positive maintenance strategy for this type of chronic condition rather than a restorative treatment.

However, it may be that mindfulness-based CBT (Crane, 2009) would have enhanced the thought-challenge exercises and behavioural experiments that Louise completed outside of therapy sessions, whilst a referral to a local support or self-help group might have provided more certainty for her at discharge. The new third wave of CBT practices such as the assimilation of family therapy might also have been beneficial to Louise as some psycho-educational sessions with her husband and her daughter could have provided more understanding and support in the immediate family environment.

An alternative approach to the model used could also have been the problem-specific meta-cognition model developed by Wells (1999). This has been an influential approach to a theoretical model and treatment package for GAD. Wells considers meta-cognitions to be central to the understanding of GAD and his treatment model emphasises the importance of addressing the positive attributions to worry which may have provided an alternative approach for Louise to challenge her general anxieties.

Problems arising in therapy

One of the key problems for individuals working with their GAD symptoms is that, whilst there is strong evidence to support CBT as the treatment of choice, there is evidence that a significant number of clients retain clinical features of GAD and the majority retain an underlying pattern of worry (Stanley et al., 2003). It is this relatively poor prognosis that has given rise to the perennial question of whether GAD is a characterological disorder (Wittchen, 2002). Louise provides a good example of an individual who responds positively to CBT treatment yet retains clear cognitive vulnerability to relapse, possibly due to the positive attribution of worry.

The theoretical models may also cause problems for clients and the importance of socialisation to the CBT model cannot be underestimated; an introduction to its terms, definitions and underlying principles may need some time to explain to an individual experiencing poor concentration and overall tiredness. It does not help that the terms are 'jargonistic', and if they occasionally baffle the practitioner then they will most likely confuse the client too. Psycho-educational approaches play a part in deciphering and translating the language used amongst CBT practitioners into one which is understandable and positively accepted by the person undertaking therapy. In situations where a person presents with GAD symptoms the initial socialisation and psycho-educational aspects may take more sessional time and this should be considered when developing the case formulation.

Think about …

1. What is the key characteristic of GAD?
2. What do Dugas et al. (2003) consider to be the central cognitive vulnerability for GAD?
3. What are the differences between approach and avoidance strategies?

Suggested activity:

- Recall an incident when you used a 'what if' question that led to you worrying.
- Identify whether this worry was about a hypothetical or a current problem.
- Identify if you have used avoidance strategies to manage the worry.
- Draw up a problem-solving strategy for how you could or did tackle the problem.

8

Client Presenting with Conduct Disorder

Mandy Drake and Mike Thomas

Learning objectives

By the end of this chapter you should be able to:

Identify the presentations for conduct disorder

Describe the development of conduct disorder from a cognitive
   perspective

Describe how anger is maintained through maladaptive coping
   mechanisms

Outline the main strategies used in the treatment of anger management

Understand the importance of trust and relationship building in the treatment of anger management

---

Diagnostic criteria

Anger as a diagnosis is usually not included as a single mental health disorder as it is within the emotions commonly observed and experienced. Anger
itself is usually a normal response to a situation which causes anxiety, stress
or frustration and therefore remains an emotion within cultural, social and
psychological parameters. The DSM-IV-TR (APA, 2000) and the ICD-10

(WHO, 2007) classify anger management difficulties under conduct disorders, the former within the criteria 312.81, 312.82 and 312.89 and the latter within F91.0, F91.1 and F91.2. Some of the ICD-10 criteria may be found amongst other symptoms of mental health conditions such as depression, development disorders, psychosis and diurnal mood disorders, and these should be discounted as differential diagnoses.

The conduct disorder itself is usually sub-categorised as follows:

- Conduct disorder confined to the family context (ICD-10 F91.0) wherein the behaviour is almost exclusively with close family members and is confined within the home
- Unsocialised conduct disorder (ICD-10 F91.1) which occurs amongst children who persistently display aggression and violence towards other children as well as demonstrating many of the ICD-10 F91 criteria
- Socialised conduct disorder (ICD-10 F91.2) which may be found more frequently amongst adolescents and, as the name implies, is found in socialised tolerance in gang membership, group delinquency, stealing in company or truancy from school
- Oppositional defiant disorder (ICD-10 F91.3), a difficult diagnosis to apply which requires good clinical assessment as it can be seen in young children who are trying out the boundaries of behavioural acceptance by adults and peers. Severe mischievousness may not in itself be enough to be given this diagnosis. Other criteria in F91 must also be presented for the diagnosis to be applied.

The DSM-IV-TR (APA, 2000) gives three sub-types which are not too dissimilar to the ICD-10 and include Childhood-Onset Type (code 312.8), Adolescent-Onset Type (code 312.82), and Unspecified Onset (code 312.89), and grade the level of the conduct disorder as mild, moderate and severe. The DSM-IV-TR also notes that an individual must have demonstrated at least three of the behaviours during the past 12 months and at least one during the past six months.

The ICD-10 (WHO, 2007) criteria code F91 states that conduct disorder is characterised by persistent anti-social or aggressive behaviour which is more severe than mere childishness or adolescent resistance. There may also be higher than normal levels of fighting, bullying, cruelty to animals, or destruction of property, fire-starting, stealing and repeated lying. In young people other anti-social characteristics may include truancy and running away from home.

Poor frustration tolerance, temper outbursts, irritability and recklessness are associated features and it is no real surprise to learn that accident rates are higher amongst people with conduct disorder than in those without it. Day and colleagues (2008) also suggest that the homicide rate is higher amongst individuals who have anger management difficulties. In addition, suicide attempts and actual suicide rates, as well as reckless living (levels of smoking, drinking or drug-taking), are higher amongst individuals with conduct disorders than the general population.

Predisposing and precipitating factors

There is a lack of clarity regarding causative factors with the general view being that it is a combination of genetics, upbringing (especially early years), environment and socialisation which together appear to cause a lack of anger containment or lower levels of tolerance in situations most people find acceptable.

Van Goozen and Fairchild (2006) propose a genetic link, stating that alterations in neurotransmitters may be genetically inherited. Whiting (2008) also notes a genetic tendency by suggesting that low levels of stimulation cause higher than normal arousal responses resulting in extreme behaviours and risk-taking. Another argument put forward is that it may be related to early life exposure to violence or aggression in the home environment (Herrenkohl et al., 2007) which causes psychological trauma and later life aggression. Other early life experiences may also play a part, such as lack of attachment to or from a parent, abuse, neglect and bullying. This is important as verbal IQ levels and overall school performance may have been adversely affected by disruptive behaviour during childhood and adolescence, and the lack of such understanding by educationalists, health and social care staff will have a negative impact on compliance and treatment progression (NICE, 2005a). An important aspect of anger and aggression that may sometimes be missed by professional support is the role that shame plays in the individual's life. Here anger and aggression can serve the purpose of disassociating the discomfort of shame by transferring the emotions into a more acceptable outlet for the individual.

Ford, Byrt and Dooher (2010) suggest that brain trauma, alterations in brain functioning or alcohol and substance-abuse damage, may also increase the potential for aggression, although it is unclear whether this is due to loss of inhibition or frustration.

Cultural factors also appear to play a part, with societal and individual responses to ethnicity, cultural groupings, sexual orientation, religion, gender, age or disability all increasing the frustration, anxiety and anger of those who perceive that they are not understood or recognised. In some families there may be an additional tolerance for casual violence that is not accepted by the rest of society, for example where the male is typically seen as the dominant figure imposing authority through intimidation and dominance which is then perceived as an attribute for others to imitate. The same can be applied to gang culture with its emphasis on demonstrations of dominance through aggressive or violent acts.

However, all this must be kept in perspective as managing anger through aggression and violence is not a modern social phenomenon. Dolan's (1994) exploration of domestic violence between the years 1550 and 1770 found many similarities with modern times, particularly the levels of domestic crime recorded and the themes of familial traits, early childhood experiences, trauma and alcohol abuse in the perpetrators.

The cognitive view is one where there is a psychological, physical and environmental interaction which precipitates a series of response stages. These stages serve to either contain or release the emotions and thoughts which may be anger, anxiety or frustration (Westbrook et al., 2007). Usually there is a trigger which precipitates a negative automatic thought. This in turn creates emotional responses simultaneously with physiological responses. The individual's negative thought pattern perceives these somatic and affective changes as appropriate responses which in turn drives the response further and provides a rationale for the reaction and consequences (Kinsella and Garland, 2008).

Demographic incidence

Conduct disorder is the most prevalent diagnosis of both children and adolescents in hospitals and outpatient settings (Whiting, 2008), with estimated lifetime prevalence of approximately 10 per cent (12% amongst boys and 7% amongst girls). The average age of onset is around 11 years. Whilst aggression is more typically found in males, probably due to more social acceptance, it does not mean that females do not also engage in aggressive and violent behaviours. Antai-Otong (2008) noted that women with psychiatric disorders were just as aggressive as men, and whilst pre-hospitalisation behaviour indicated that men were more prone to violent attacks involving weapons, at immediate hospitalisation women were actually more prone to violence against others.

Continuum of severity

Conduct disorders may occur before pre-school age but symptoms usually appear from middle childhood to early adolescence. Onset is rare after the age of 16 years and some individuals with milder symptoms go on to have adequate social and personal adjustments in adult life, although the earlier the onset the poorer the outcome in adult life (DSM-IV-TR; APA, 2000). Poor anger management, as noted above leads to a poorer quality of life with a higher incidence of broken relationships, accidents, homicides, suicide attempts and entry into the criminal justice system

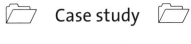

Case study

Rationale

Ben is a 16-year-old male referred to the day care unit of the local Child and Adolescent Mental Health Service (CAMHS) from the Primary Care Mental Health Team (PCMHT). This referral means that Ben will move into specialist mental health services and his care will consequently be at step 4 of the Stepped Care model. However, the care Ben receives involves CBT interventions occurring at the immediate level of negative automatic thoughts, thus the case demonstrates how low-intensity interventions, typically seen at lower levels of the care pathway, can also be applied within the specialist services.

Client

Ben is 16 years old and has been referred to the unit following an altercation with the educational psychologist, where Ben swore and became aggressive during an assessment session. He had been absent from school on numerous occasions during the last year and when he did attend he was accused of bullying and threatening other pupils. He was consequently due to be suspended but the school disciplinary panel recommended he be seen by the educational psychologist first. Ben had been increasingly violent towards his mother and his sister during the previous three months and he was a well-known member of a local gang of youths. This gang were suspected of vandalising property, threatening older residents and attacking other young people late at night, but as no one had come forward to verify this no proof had been established by the police. Ben's provisional diagnosis by the psychologist was socialised conduct disorder at moderate level (DSM-IV-TR; APA, 2000).

Assessment sessions 1–5

Initial assessment indicated that Ben lived with his mother and sister although his father visited the home occasionally. Ben's mother had stated that these visits were often a trigger for Ben's aggression as his father would come around asking for money or alcohol. After his father had left Ben would be extremely angry, and over the last few months he had become violent towards his mother and his sister after such visits.

Ben had been an 'average' pupil throughout his school years and, according to his mother, had deteriorated educationally only in the last year, since he started

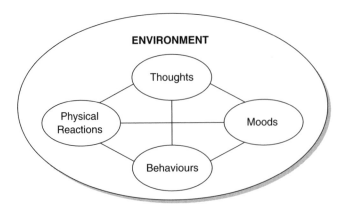

FIGURE 8.1   Five aspects of your life experience © 1986, Center for Cognitive Therapy

to 'hang out with the wrong crowd'. His school teachers found him surly and uncommunicative and were frequently catching him bullying other pupils for money or snacks, which had led to a recommendation that he be excluded. Ben had subsequently been referred to the educational psychologist to whom he was threatening and aggressive, resulting in the psychologist referring him to the PCMHT, who in turn had referred him to CAMHS due to his age.

In the first sessions Ben revealed that he mistrusted and disliked authority figures but in the main he frequently fidgeted, looked at the floor and avoided any communication. If he did reply it was with guttural utterances or mono-syllables. He slouched and exhaled heavily throughout the first three sessions and often refused to reply to any questions put to him. He was clean, well groomed and always attended on time, but he refused to complete any assess-ment scales for anxiety or depression, although he presented no observable signs of either.

In view of Ben's reluctance to engage with the therapeutic process, and concerns that he might not continue to attend the sessions, socialisation to the CBT model was paramount. At this stage the intention was to assist Ben to understand his current difficulties and their impact on his life, as well as to introduce the principles of CBT. The approach adopted was to explain the five aspects of your life experience model (Padesky and Mooney, 1990) using the example of when Ben became aggressive with the psychologist (Figure 8.1). Ben showed an interest in how situations influenced his thoughts. He could see the negative nature of his thinking and how this then activated physical and emotional responses, which in turn influenced his reactions and behaviour. This encouraged Ben to participate a little more in the assessment process. It was found that he responded well to Socratic questioning, which is a method commonly used in CBT to gather information from specific and recent exam-ples of the problem in question. An example of this is shown below:

Therapist (T):	Tell me about the last time your father visited you.
Ben (B):	I dunno … it was last week … (Shrugs.)
T:	What happened?
B:	Same old same old …
T:	I don't know what normally occurs, would you mind letting me try and see it from your point of view?
B:	He knocked on the door as usual, shouting, drunk as always. Mum opened the door and he started on her. It drives me mad that she lets him treat her like that …
T:	What did you do?
B:	What do you mean what did I do! I went out didn't I, pushed him away, threatened him … threatened to flatten him.
T:	Was this all on the doorstep?
B:	Always is. We won't let him in the house. But he just stands there shouting the odds. I have to go out but mum locks the door and … I can't get to him. (Leans forward and stares at floor.)
T:	Does he stay out there for long?
B:	F****** ages man, makes me want to kill him …
T:	So how do you calm down?
B:	(No answer for several minutes.)
T:	Ok Ben, you don't have to say anything. Let's talk about the physical effects of anger. (Therapist leads the session into psycho-educational material.)

It took several assessment sessions for Ben to feel comfortable enough to speak more openly and it was only in session 4 that enough information had been gathered to devise a conceptual presentation of his main presenting problems. The first phase of the formulation highlights the triggers and immediate presenting problems, whilst the second phase highlights the reinforcers for the original responses. These are shown in Figure 8.2, and are based on the work of Zarb (1992).

Ben did not initially accept the conceptual presentation, particularly any suggestion that he was anxious, but he did accept that his aim was to push people away and that he mistrusted authority figures. It took another session, however, before Ben was willing to discuss tasks outside the sessions.

Treatment sessions 1–3

The cognitive approach to interventions tends to follow the work of Novaco (1979, 2000) who in turn based his work on Meichenbaum's Stress Inoculation Training (1975). The model takes three stages of therapeutic input: a preparatory stage which helps the client to identify patterns of anger, triggers

Initial presenting problems

Presenting problem	Duration/frequency	Related cognition
Aggressive and threatening towards his immediate family	Last three months/after father has visited the house	Mother and sister are weak. They don't know how to stand up for the family or to the father
Aggressive towards those viewed as authority figures	Last year/almost daily	Mistrusts and is suspicious of authority. Views them as interfering and unhelpful
Animosity and aggression towards father	Last few years/continuous feeling	He is a bully and takes things the family need. Dominates and frightens his mother

Reinforcement contingencies of presenting problems

Target behaviours	NATs/emotions	Desired consequences
Shouts and threatens mother and sister	They are too weak to help me, I need to stand up for myself. (Frustration and anger)	Mother and sister leave me alone
Threaten others, particularly authority figures	They interfere and don't understand what's going on. (Frustration and anger)	They leave me alone
Shout and become violent towards father	He is a bully and hurts me and the family. (Anxiety and anger)	For the father to disappear from my life and leave the family alone

FIGURE 8.2 Main presenting problems (after Zarb, 1992)

and negative automatic thoughts (NATs) associated with the anger; a skills acquisition stage which supports the client in learning new techniques to both recognise provocation and lower the level of arousal; and an application stage wherein the client practises hypothetical situations, applies new skills and then reviews the outcome in order to learn different adaptations to anger. Novaco stressed that the approach is self-directional and the therapist role is to continue the engagement with the process as the attrition rate in anger management treatment is commonly high.

Preparatory stage

This stage had already commenced during assessment through the socialisation and Socratic dialogue, and to develop this further homework was introduced. The use of language was particularly sensitive as Ben prepared to complete exercises outside the sessions. Words such as 'homework', widely used in CBT interventions could not be ascribed to Ben's work as he may have felt disempowered and they would possibly remind him that he was back at school. Session 6 reviewed the parameters of the therapeutic process

Situation	Immediate feelings and thoughts (0/10)	Immediate behaviour	Six hours after the situation (0/10)	After a night's sleep (0/10)
Mother nags me for staying out late with friends drinking	Feel angry and tense/she is weak and irritating 8/10	Shout and threaten her until she leaves me alone	Still angry with her/want to leave home, it's a dump here 6/10	Less angry/ she's alright if she leaves me alone 2/10
Friend C disses me saying am disabled cos not in school	Very angry/he is wrong to diss me in front of others/wrong to diss me anyway! 9/10	Walked away to stop myself hitting him	Mad as anything/C will have to be hurt for what he said. He can't get away with it 8/10	Angry/C will get it very soon. He is gonna get hurt bad 8/10
Dad came round again, drunk. I pushed mum out of the way and threatened him 'til he left. He says he'll come back with his mates. Some chance.	Angry/could kill him. He's a bad man that deserves everything he gonna get 9/10	Shouted and threatened him until dad left	Not as angry/ Thinking how I can get him to stay away. Maybe visit his house? 6/10	Not bothered/he is an irritant, not worth bothering about 2/10

FIGURE 8.3 Ben's anger diary

including restating issues of confidentiality and trust, stressing that Ben could lead the speed and level of the sessions and that therapy would attempt to go at his pace. The principles of CBT were again outlined with a specific focus on the need to identify negative automatic thoughts (NATs) and their triggers. For this purpose Ben agreed to keep an anger diary, completing columns 1 and 2 only at this stage (see Figure 8.3). Also as homework, Ben was asked to look for any patterns within the diary and he identified that it was when he was criticised or controlled that he became angry, as well as when he had any contact with his father. Furthermore, he could see that it was when he had been drinking alcohol that his anger increased and that his typical NATs tended to be that his mother was weak, his friend disrespected him and that his father deserved everything he got.

In preparation for the next stage of therapy Ben was asked to continue with his anger diary but to go on to complete all columns (Figure 8.3).

Sessions 4–7

Skills acquisition stage

The aim of this phase is for Ben to learn new ways of managing his anger by challenging his negative thinking, lowering his physical arousal and changing his behaviour.

Therapy began with thought challenging, the NATs identified in the preparatory phase being the focus of this, starting with 'My mother is weak.' This commenced with an examination of the evidence for this thought and Ben responded by recalling that his mother nags him a lot and that she appears to be afraid of his father, whom she's never prevented from bothering them. Ben was prompted to consider why his mother behaved as she did, with the example of her nagging him after he's been out being used to focus the discussion. Whilst initially Ben was unable to see beyond this being a sign of weakness, he eventually started to consider the possibility that it might be because she was worried about him and that her reaction, rather than being an attempt to control, might in fact be an attempt to care.

An impromptu conversation with his mother also served to challenge Ben's belief about her weakness when between sessions he had talked to her about her behaviour towards his father. He was surprised when she disclosed that she was not afraid of his father but in fact felt pity for him 'having to come round and beg from us' and that she did not need Ben to fight for her.

It was more difficult to challenge the thoughts Ben held regarding his friend disrespecting him, as discussion identified increasing evidence for this thought but little evidence against. The conclusion reached was that it was a realistic thought and that his friend was not displaying friendship towards him.

Perhaps the most difficult thought to challenge was that his father deserved 'everything he gets', primarily because Ben became very angry at attempts to discuss this and he could not therefore articulate the meaning of 'everything he gets'. It did, however, become apparent that this NAT was supported by an underlying dysfunctional assumption that Ben should be responsible for protecting his family, although this had already been weakened by having earlier challenged the thought about his mother's weakness.

Following the thought-challenging exercises Ben was supported to develop more balanced alternative thinking. It became apparent that Ben had continued to dwell on his father's behaviour, as despite remaining angry towards him Ben was adjusting his negative thoughts away from his father deserving 'everything he gets' to thinking that his father did not deserve anything from him as he 'was not worth it' (Figure 8.4).

It was during this phase that Ben appeared to be more accepting of therapy, which was demonstrated through his commitment to his diary. Completion

Angry thought	Balanced thought
My mother is weak	My mother is stronger than I think
My friend disrespects me	My friend is not my friend
My dad deserves everything he gets	My dad deserves nothing from me – he's not worth it.

FIGURE 8.4   Balanced thought chart

Walk away from situation
Go out for a walk
Reduce alcohol intake
Use the balanced thinking chart
Sleep on it

FIGURE 8.5 Alternative behaviours

of the additional columns enabled Ben to identify an important pattern, which was that his level of arousal could dissipate over a 24-hour period in the majority of situations (Figure 8.3). This was particularly important as Ben had rejected the reading materials on physical relaxation techniques (such as breathing exercises, mindfulness methods and daily physical activities), reporting that they were unhelpful.

Ben was by now developing good awareness that his own thinking about a situation differed from that of others, but he still felt that his resulting behaviour was acceptable. His diary inserts revealed that Ben's main method of dealing with his angry thoughts was through shouting and threatening, and whilst he initially insisted that he was happy with this response further discussion began to change this. When questioned about the consequences of his behaviour Ben reluctantly admitted that it had no real long-term benefits as not only was the conflict not resolved but he knew that it was in fact worsening his relationship with others. Ben was therefore prompted to compile a list of alternative behaviours (see Figure 8.5) with a view to applying these in practice, in the form of behavioural experiments.

Sessions 8–11

Application phase

The aim of this phase is for Ben to apply and review alternative strategies to manage his anger.

Ben identified his mother's nagging as the area he would like to address first and so the initial focus was on exploring different situations in which his mother nagged him, with alternative behaviours being discussed. After exploring these hypothetical situations Ben agreed to apply alternative thinking and behaviours when his mother nagged him and to record the incidences for discussion in subsequent therapy sessions. The results of these behavioural experiments can be seen in Figure 8.6. Whilst it was clear that Ben was able to apply the new strategies in anger-provoking situations it was also clear that alcohol influenced Ben to return to his old unhelpful responses.

Situation	Initial thoughts and feelings	Behaviour	What happened after
Mum nagging because I was late home and missed tea	At it again! Feel tense	Applied balance, thought 'it's only because she cares'. Went to my room for 30 minutes to calm down	Went downstairs and watched television with mum. No falling out
Mum going on at me for not cleaning my room	Stop nagging! Irritated	Went out for a walk	Spoke to mum, said I'd clean the room next day and she said ok. No falling out
Came home drunk, mum shouted at me (again!)	Stop talking to me, stop shouting, and leave me alone!	Shouted at her and stormed off to bed	Next morning felt bad, let her down. Mum ignored me

FIGURE 8.6 Anger diary records of behavioural experiments

Following the success of the behavioural experiments Ben agreed that he would continue to apply his new anger management techniques in all situations as they arose and that he would again record these for therapeutic discussion. The excerpts indicated that Ben showed a lack of improvement regarding his alcohol consumption, but in other areas he continued to make progress, particularly in his relationship with his mother and sister. He was beginning to feel in control of situations and relationships and becoming more flexible in his responses; for example he was making efforts to come home earlier in the evenings and also to make time to eat with the family at least twice weekly. Ben had also been on a shopping trip with them although he did say that he would not be repeating that exercise as it bored him.

Regarding the friend who repeatedly disrespected him, Ben was slowly distancing himself, his diary showing that his new perception was allowing him to break away from the friendship. As a result Ben reported spending time with friends who preferred to stay indoors 'listening to music and things' rather than walk the streets as the nights grew cooler.

In relation to his father, Ben would still retreat into mumbling and would avoid eye contact if session time focused on this and his thought diary indicated that there was little progress. Therapy therefore concentrated on continuing the hypothetical exercises around this relationship, and despite his reluctance Ben went on to apply them in his dealings with his father. This proved successful, the strategies of most benefit being to instigate balanced thinking or walking away.

Treatment evaluation sessions

In the penultimate session Ben appeared with heavy bruising of the face and hands and disclosed that his old gang friends had taken against his decision to be with other friends, resulting in the gang, led by his friend C, beating him. Ben in turn had contacted several older friends and they had fought C's gang leaving them 'hurt badly'. The session therefore focused on Ben's rationale for his behaviour and reactions which he insisted were not related to NATs but which came instead from a requirement for him to assert himself in his neighbourhood and with his peers. 'You've gotta see my view ... can't let them push me around. This needed sorting and it been coming a while anyhow.'

This was a difficult session as Ben's behaviour impinged on the therapist's own personal sense of responsibility, ethics and a perception that violence is not the answer to such disputes. These views were shared with Ben who responded by stating that such morals were 'ok where you come from but in my patch you would die'.

The final session was also sensitive as Ben had to relinquish his sense of trust and support provided by therapy and to generalise these approaches towards others. Ben suggested that it was not appropriate for him to return to school but that he would consider the remainder of the year completing a work-placement curriculum and this was to be explored with his headteacher.

The evaluation of the problem presentation originally conceptualised showed that Ben had not been aggressive towards his sister or his mother for two months and was in fact beginning to enjoy their company. He had also relinquished all contact with some of his previous friends. His father still came round to the house but Ben and his mother had agreed that Ben would leave by the back door and would have no interaction with his father. He now felt that his mother could manage the situation and he did not feel the need to intervene.

Ben agreed he had developed a stronger sense of his own anger, the patterns that it tended to follow and the triggers that would instigate these strong emotions. He stated that he now had a wider skills set to lower his arousal when he was provoked. Although acknowledging that his alcohol consumption was a contributory factor for his anger he showed no inclination to change this aspect of his life.

Ben was gaining more success in managing his physiological anger arousal, mainly by walking away or sleeping on issues but he continued to resist exercises such as breathing and relaxation, stating they were 'useless' and in fact made him tenser. Nevertheless, he found the cognitive and behavioural elements of therapy useful as he developed new adaptation techniques.

Discharge strategies

Ben was discharged back to the care of his GP who was invited to make a re-referral for top-up sessions should Ben deteriorate within the next year. Beyond this timeframe consideration should be given to the most appropriate service for Ben which could be the CAMHS Team or the PCMHT. In either case, further low-intensity sessions would be relevant and these could be offered outside of specialist mental health services at steps 2 or 3. Ben was also informed that he could refer himself to either service.

Critique of case study

This case study highlights the time it takes to build up a therapeutic relationship with a client who has conduct disorder and is mistrustful of others. In such a situation much of the early sessions which would normally be taken up with homework tasks (after assessments) had to be suspended and the number of sessions increased. Equally Ben's reluctance to participate in the assessment exercises meant that therapy had to rely on the Socratic method to gain information and at times extra data had to be acquired from his mother. It might have been more appropriate for Ben and his mother to have been seen within a family therapy setting using systemic approaches, but his initial animosity towards her meant this was impractical in this case.

The language used in therapy was also important; the use of wrong terminology or words that would have negative connotations for Ben had to be avoided and this was particularly true in the issue of self-study and out of session exercises. Language and its use in psycho-educational approaches requires an understanding of the verbal and cognitive abilities of the client in order to balance the information, giving material at the right level for the client. In Ben's case several sessions were spent in reviewing and repeating exercises to support his understanding and this inevitably hindered other activities.

Ben also refused to participate in exercises that would have a beneficial effect on his physical reactions to anger, which again perhaps slowed down progress but is a realistic portrayal, and it may be that in time Ben would resort to breathing and relaxation exercises through being referred to a therapist specialising in mindfulness techniques when he is ready to do so.

Problems arising in therapy

One of the main issues in therapy is trust and the establishment of a relationship that has objectives and goals. Ben had a history of poor relationships with those he saw as authority figures and it was realistic to expect a period of adjustment to occur before Ben would begin to engage with therapy itself. It would be simpler to label Ben with an intractable conduct disorder but many individuals with the right support at the right time can lead adequate lives after therapy. Trust is entwined with confidentiality, and again therapeutic interaction in cases of conduct disorder takes time as the client begins to realise that confidentiality within sessions is maintained and actively demonstrated by the therapist.

Equally at time of discharge the issue of trust remains important. The individual with conduct disorder who has developed trust in the therapy and the therapist now has to carry on with less support and rely on learning and the acquired skills and adaptation abilities to continue the work therapy had only started. This can be difficult, for, as mentioned earlier, the attrition rate for anger management from referral to treatment end is high anyway and learning to generalise trust and coping skills outside of the sessions is therefore an integral aspect of therapy. That is why the discharge phase stresses the opportunity for the client to informally refer themselves to therapy again; it does not provide maintenance therapy support or even a dependency relationship but provides the basis for the client to feel secure that they can access support if required.

The issue of language is important. Ben needed to be treated as a young adult; in fact many issues in his life would test the abilities of many adults and he had to understand that he led the pace of therapy and the level that it could be taken to. In this case the work was around NATs and adaptations to triggers and reactions when angry, but his relationship with his father may have a direct bearing on dysfunctional underlying assumptions or even schema level functions. Yet Ben's immediate problems were of a priority when he first came to therapy and in relation to NATs immediate interventions were appropriate, whilst his youth and the duration and length of therapy prevented further work in this area of underlying assumptions at core level. This could be an area that could be explored further if Ben wished to return to therapy. Language therefore had to be targeted at his maturity level, his intellectual abilities and his perceptions of adult interaction, and much time was spent in sessions in this area because they impacted on trust and confidence building in the therapeutic process itself.

Finally there is the issue of the client's behaviour outside therapy, which may contrast strongly with the therapist's view of the world. In this case study Ben engaged in a form of gang dispute which may be accepted in his peer group and he therefore had a rationale for responding in a way that was at odds with the view of violence held by the therapist. Yet it could be argued that Ben was not reacting to NATs in that situation but was responding in a way that was considered the norm amongst his peers. This makes therapy hard as the therapist must judge several things: whether the reaction was a NATs response to triggers; whether therapy itself provided a justification for the actions; and whether therapy can continue from the therapist's perception rather than the client's. Trust, after all, works both ways. In this case therapy did continue because the therapist took the view that Ben was approaching the issues in a way that the therapist might not but the approach fitted Ben's perception of his world, albeit one which did not fit into the world view of the therapist.

Think about ...

1. On what criteria did Ben meet the diagnosis for moderate conduct disorder?
2. How was his anger pattern maintained?
3. The Socratic methods were important in this case study; how would you encourage the client to gather assessment data with you?
4. What would you have done differently to encourage the client to engage in new physiological adaptations to anger?
5. What are the issues around therapeutic trust and boundaries when treating anger management techniques?

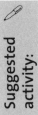

Suggested activity:

- Try and recall when you were last angry; can you identify the anger adaptation model at work?
- Keep your own thought diary for a week and measure your responses to specific situations – immediately, six hours later and the next day. This will help you understand the immediacy of certain thoughts and feelings and how many clients require some time to be free of strong emotions, especially anger.
- It takes a lot of nerve to engage in therapy. Practise different approaches to making therapy more acceptable, adapting these depending on the client and their presenting problems.

9
Client Presenting with Vaginismus

Janice Lamb

Learning objectives

By the end of this chapter you should be able to:

Describe the sexual response cycle
Explain the symptoms of vaginismus
Discuss how the vicious cycle maintains symptoms of vaginismus
Outline the main components of systematic desensitisation used in the
    treatment of vaginismus
Recognise how cultural and community values may influence treatment
    progression

Diagnostic criteria

The sexual response cycle was first proposed by Masters and Johnson (1966) as a four-stage model and although it is a highly individual physical, emotional and psychological process there are physiological stages common to healthy adults: excitement, plateau, orgasm and resolution. Kaplan (1979) outlined a three-stage model of desire, excitement and orgasm and her description of desire as a prelude to physical sexual response is widely accepted. The DSM-IV-TR (APA, 2000) follows four stages: desire, excitement, orgasm and resolution. Desire is described as the individual having fantasies about, and the desire to have, sexual activity; excitement as the subjective sense of sexual pleasure and accompanying physiological changes; orgasm as the peaking of sexual pleasure; and the final stage, resolution, as muscular relaxation and general well-being.

The DSM-IV-TR (APA, 2000) describes sexual dysfunction as a disturbance in sexual desire and in the psychophysiological changes that characterise the sexual response cycle or by pain associated with sexual intercourse, causing marked distress and interpersonal difficulty. There are nine major diagnostic categories for sexual dysfunction in DSM-IV-TR although this case study is concerned only with vaginismus, which is an exclusively female disorder.

The DSM-IV-TR, code 306.1 (APA, 2000) and ICD-10 (WHO, 2007) provide almost the same criteria, although the ICD-10 specifies a minimum duration of at least six months. Both identify the central feature of vaginismus as the recurrent or persistent involuntary contraction of the perineal muscles surrounding the outer third of the vagina when vaginal penetration is attempted. It is specifically a psychological condition or a combination of psychological and other factors and requires careful assessment. Any attempt at penetration causes marked distress or interpersonal difficulty and therefore it is important to discount any general medical condition or physical causative factors (Basson et al., 2003). Vaginismus can be lifelong (primary) or it can occur after a period when sexual function has been normal (secondary). It can also be situational, occurring only with certain partners, or generalized, occurring independent of partner or circumstances.

There is ongoing debate regarding the DSM-IV-TR (APA, 2000) classification as it does not mention pain as a criterion, or that vaginismus and dyspareunia could co-exist, though Reissing and colleagues (2004) found that women often suffer with comorbid pain. Ter Kuile and colleagues (2005) also demonstrated that a considerable percentage of women with lifelong vaginismus report vestibular pain when touched with a cotton swab. DSM-IV-TR regards persistent, involuntary spasms of the vaginal muscles to be the defining feature of vaginismus; however, Reissing et al.'s (2004) study strongly suggests that it is not.

As available research does not support either distinction between vaginismus and dyspareunia, or pelvic muscle spasm as the defining feature of vaginismus, Binik and colleagues (2002) suggest that vaginismus is better defined as a problem with penetration which extends to sexual intercourse. Basson et al. (2003) concluded that despite the woman having a wish to allow vaginal entry there were involuntary pelvic muscle contractions and avoidance due to anticipation of pain and not due to other structural or physical causes, clearly identifying the anticipation and fear of pain whilst omitting the assumed muscular spasms.

Predisposing and precipitating factors

A number of psychosocial causes have been suggested as predisposing factors; Masters and Johnson (1970) suggested the inhibiting influence of religious orthodoxy, response to a partner's sexual dysfunction, a reaction to sexual orientation concerns or prior sexual trauma, whilst Bancroft (2009) identified negative attitudes or beliefs about sex and inadequate sexual information. Wijma and Wijma (1997) add that distorted cognitive perceptions regarding external genital changes during the sexual response cycles and the spatial capacity of the vagina may also play a part, and de Jong and colleagues (2009) noted that feelings of disgust may elicit an acute response instigating a defensive reflex that evokes involuntary pelvic muscle activity, typically preventing entry of a penis, finger, sexual device, tampon or speculum into the vagina.

According to learning theory, the vaginismic response followed by pain, represents a classically conditioned fear response to sexual stimuli (Leiblum, 2000). The woman is faced with a situation or behaviour likely to lead to penetration which causes anticipatory thoughts of pain and failure; when this occurs repetitively it generates anticipatory anxiety, interrupting arousal and giving rise to contraction of the pelvic muscles. Pain confirms the anticipatory thoughts and creates a vicious circle as the contraction of the pelvic muscles occurs simultaneously with a burning sensation in the lower third of the vagina which is enough to trigger more muscular contractions leading to further burning sensations. These are often misinterpreted as physically based (Wijma and Wijma, 1997), and the fear of penetration is maintained through avoidance behaviour to preclude opportunities to disconfirm the negative beliefs (Leiblum, 2000). This type of reaction thus has similarities with the panic model described by Clark (1986).

Demographic incidence

Vaginismus is one of the most common female psychosexual dysfunctions, and although population-based estimates are 1 per cent or less (Fugl-Meyer and Sjögren Fugl-Meyer, 1999; Ventegodt, 1998), the prevalence rates in clinical settings are significant. Referrals to sexual dysfunction clinics indicate a prevalence rate of between 5 per cent and 70 per cent (Bancroft and Coles, 1976; Catalan et al., 1990; Masters and Johnson, 1970; Renshaw, 1988).

Hirst, Baggaley and Watson (1996) reported 15.5 per cent of 155 female referrals experienced vaginismus, Goldmeier and colleagues (1997) found 25 per cent, whilst Read, King and Watson (1997) reported an estimate of 30 per cent.

O'Sullivan (1979) observed differences across cultures, with the rate amongst Irish women attending a clinic as 42 per cent and Barnes (1981, 1986a, 1986b) suggested that vaginismus was the most common cause of unconsummated marriages in Ireland. The highest prevalence rate of 70 per cent was reported in Turkey (Tugrul and Kabakci, 1997), and Shokrollahi and colleagues (1999) reported that 8 per cent of a sample of 300 young, married women at a clinic in Iran reported vaginismus.

Continuum of severity

Lifelong, or primary vaginismus has a notably abrupt onset and presents during initial attempts at vaginal penetration. Acquired, or secondary vaginismus, may develop suddenly in women who have previously been able to engage in vaginal penetration or examination, but both will most typically present as a chronic condition unless treated.

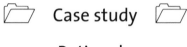

Case study

Rationale

Vaginismus can have a significant effect on relationships and the following case study demonstrates a CBT approach at immediate (NATs) level. It presents therapy carried out with a married couple, Sofya and Irfan, and as this is based in a specialist psychosexual service, intervention is at step 4 of the Stepped Care model.

Client

Sofya, 28, had informed her GP that she had experienced difficulty consummating her marriage and had consequently been referred to a female consultant gynaecologist. There she had confided that she had little sexual knowledge, was fearful of penetration and that she thought that anatomically her vagina was too small to accommodate a penis. She had additionally disclosed her worries about the impact the problem was having on her marriage, as both her husband and herself were feeling increasing pressure from their families to produce their first child.

Whilst Sofya had tolerated an examination of her external genitalia by the consultant she had became very distressed and tearful at the suggestion of an internal examination and it was at this point that a referral was made to the psychosexual service.

Assessment

In order to obtain a thorough history it is useful to interview the couple together and individually as this provides maximum opportunity for the confidential disclosure of relevant personal information and the personal views of each partner about the problem.

Date/Time	Type of sexual activity	Thoughts/ images during activity	Level of sexual arousal (0–10)	Physical sensations	Behaviours	Thoughts/ images after activity

FIGURE 9.1 Record of sexual interaction

In the initial interview, Sofya was seen with Irfan who is 31 years old; both are English-born Indian Muslims who, with their families' agreement, chose each other and have been married for four years. They have not been able to consummate their marriage as initial attempts at penile vaginal penetration caused Sofya to become distressed and experience significant burning pain.

Sofya and Irfan were both brought up within close families; however, sex was not openly discussed and sexual experiences before marriage were forbidden so neither had received any sexual education or pre-marital experience. They had a genuine affection for each other and regularly engaged in sexual intimacy, kissing, caressing and experiencing good levels of arousal. Whilst Sofya was providing Irfan with genital stimulation, she avoided any genital contact from Irfan. During the assessment phase Sofya and Irfan were asked to continue to engage in sexual activities and were asked to keep a diary which could provide valuable information which had not emerged during the assessment interview. An example of a self-recording measure is shown in Figure 9.1.

Individual assessment session with Sofya

Sofya recalled that she had been told during her early teen years that 'having a penis inside your vagina is like having a metal rod thrust inside you', and she was able to identify this as a clear precipitant. Other mistaken beliefs about her body and penetration emerged, including spatially distorted cognitions concerning the capacity of her vagina and a belief that penetration would cause significant bleeding. Sofya acknowledged she had never looked at her vulva or vagina and was very unaware of her own anatomy but she also expressed feelings of disgust about this 'worst part' of her.

It is important to gain an understanding of religious and culturally based beliefs related to sexual practice and explore these thoroughly, and Sofya explained that women from her cultural background are brought up to believe their vagina is dirty. This belief may be resistant to change and precipitate further distress if challenged at this stage of therapy.

Sofya was asked to recall the last occasion she had been sexually intimate with Irfan, during which she was prompted to identify the thoughts, emotions, physical sensations and any behaviours she was aware of at the time. Sofya described experiencing good levels of sexual desire and was aware that whilst kissing and cuddling Irfan she began to feel sexually aroused, but as the intimacy developed and she became aware of his arousal and erection, her thoughts were filled with anticipation of pain and failure.

To avoid any attempts at penetration she engaged in a number of behaviours, which included providing stimulating pleasure to distract Irfan from stimulating her. Another strategy was to wear her underwear and if she sensed Irfan moving his fingers towards that area she guided his hands back towards her breasts. However, these strategies did not provide adequate remission from her vaginismus as when he pressed his erect penis towards her body she was aware of pelvic tension and of pulling herself away. Sofya expressed feelings of distress and guilt that she could not do what she and Irfan wished sexually, as she was always fearful that things would progress to attempted penetration.

As sexual dysfunctions tend to be associated with problems of anxiety and depression, characterized by feelings of guilt, low self-esteem and personal inadequacy (Carrasco, 2001), a mood measure provides valuable information. Sofya was therefore asked to complete a Hospital Anxiety and Depression Scale (HADS; Zigmond and Snaith, 1983). Her score on the anxiety subscale was 11, in the moderate range, whilst her depression subscale score was in the normal range.

Individual assessment session with Irfan

Irfan acknowledged his frustrations at not being able to achieve penetration with Sofya. He was aware that Sofya has developed ways of avoiding penetration and he remained concerned about how his community viewed childless marriages. Irfan had very little sexual knowledge, particularly about female anatomy. He acknowledged he had never looked at or directly touched Sofya's vulval area and his beliefs about sex relationships could be attributable to common myths.

Case formulation

Having completed an initial assessment together and individually, the next step was to develop a formulation of their problem. This presented an opportunity to reconceptualise the vaginismic response as a multi-dimensional problem influenced by a variety of factors including thoughts, emotions, behaviours, physical sensations and the two people's interactions as a couple.

It was important to strike a balance between the couple in terms of their individual contribution to the sexual problem and so they were encouraged to regard the problem as a joint one.

The formulation used Williams's (2010) five areas formulation, a model based in the here and now with a focus on maintenance factors. This was developed collaboratively with Sofya and Irfan using a recent sexual experience and this presented a good opportunity to begin socialisation to the treatment approach. The formulation can be found in Figure 9.2. Their relationship was generally a happy one and they had a mutual motivation to overcome their problems and bring into focus what changes they wanted. The formulation established objectives to reduce anxiety and thus the vaginismic response to penetration, as well as highlighting the maintenance role of avoidance, and these formed the rationale for the therapeutic approach.

Sofya and Irfan identified the following goals for therapy:

1. To gain sexual knowledge, including sexual anatomy and sexual responses
2. To be able to have penetrative intercourse without fear and pain
3. To enjoy having a sexual relationship.

Treatment sessions 1 and 2

Approaches developed to treat sexual dysfunctions have acknowledged the influence of thoughts and attitudes (Kaplan, 1974; Masters and Johnson, 1970), but they have been predominantly behavioural. For vaginismus the approach continues to be exposure to the fearful situation in accordance with the principles of systematic desensitisation in vivo in combination with counter-conditioning (Hawton et al., 1989).

Sofya and Irfan attended together for the first two sessions which focused on psycho-education regarding sexual anatomy, the sexual response cycle and the impact anxiety has upon sexual responses. This began at a basic level since excessive information may cause anxiety, and care was taken when introducing diagrams to avoid offending either party. This was done in a graded way, beginning with line drawings and anatomical diagrams and building up to photographs. As spatial distortions concerning the vagina were raised during the assessment, information was provided on expansion of the vagina during sexual arousal. Psycho-educational input would later be supported by behavioural exercises in order to reinforce the effectiveness of new knowledge.

Sofya and Irfan were asked to consider the common sexual myths (see Figure 9.3) and discussed the likely thoughts and behaviours of people in imagined sexual situations who held such beliefs. They both recognised the

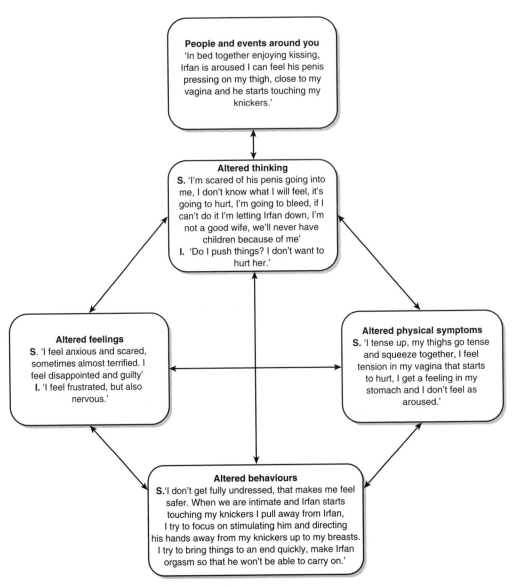

People and events around you
'In bed together enjoying kissing, Irfan is aroused I can feel his penis pressing on my thigh, close to my vagina and he starts touching my knickers.'

Altered thinking
S. 'I'm scared of his penis going into me, I don't know what I will feel, it's going to hurt, I'm going to bleed, if I can't do it I'm letting Irfan down, I'm not a good wife, we'll never have children because of me'
I. 'Do I push things? I don't want to hurt her.'

Altered feelings
S. 'I feel anxious and scared, sometimes almost terrified. I feel disappointed and guilty'
I. 'I feel frustrated, but also nervous.'

Altered physical symptoms
S. 'I tense up, my thighs go tense and squeeze together, I feel tension in my vagina that starts to hurt, I get a feeling in my stomach and I don't feel as aroused.'

Altered behaviours
S. 'I don't get fully undressed, that makes me feel safer. When we are intimate and Irfan starts touching my knickers I pull away from Irfan, I try to focus on stimulating him and directing his hands away from my knickers up to my breasts. I try to bring things to an end quickly, make Irfan orgasm so that he won't be able to carry on.'

FIGURE 9.2 Case formulation adapted from Williams's (2010) five areas formulation. Reproduced by permission of Hodder Education.

impact some of these beliefs were having on them individually. Sofya focused on 'men always want sex', stating she often thought that was all that interested Irfan. He challenged this view, stating he often wanted to caress her but did not always think about attempting sexual intercourse. The sexual interactions record was then introduced and Sofya was encouraged to note down the emotional consequence of negative thoughts and influences on sexual behaviour (see Figure 9.4).

- The only true kind of sex involves putting a penis inside someone else, anything else isn't really sex
- Having sex on your own isn't really sex
- Sex should always involve an orgasm
- If one person orgasms that has to be the end of sex
- Sex should always start with lots of foreplay
- Foreplay is for kids
- Men need an erection in order to have sex
- Sex is about putting on a good performance, not about enjoying yourself
- Men should take control of sex, they should be the ones who initiate it and determine what is done
- Men are always ready for sex
- Men always want sex
- Women rarely want sex
- Women need to be convinced to have sex
- People shouldn't need any extra lubrication in order to have sex except that produced by their bodies
- Men should be able to last all night
- Women should have sex with their partner otherwise they will lose them
- All kissing and touching should lead to sex
- It is bad to have sex on your own
- You should never have sex on your own if you have a partner
- If you fantasise about someone else you're not happy with your partner

FIGURE 9.3   Common sexual myths

Date/ Time	Type of sexual activity	Thoughts / images during activity	Level of sexual arousal (0-10)	Physical sensations	Behaviours	Thoughts/ images after activity
13.4 10.30pm	Kissing & cuddling in bed	Don't want this to go further, Irfan wants sex, if he tries to put his penis near me it will hurt	4	Tense, tightening in my body	Saying 'I'm tired', yawning, trying to turn over	I'll always be like this, I'll never manage penetration
18.4	Kissing in kitchen during visit to parents	I love him	7	Pleasure, aroused	Happy to carry on (but know it's safe)	It's not fair, want to have sex but too scared

FIGURE 9.4   Record of sexual interaction completed by Sofya and Irfan

With the therapist's guidance a therapeutic contract was agreed between both Sofya and Irfan; this focused on reducing Sofya's fear regarding penetration by giving her control over any potential penetrative situation. The contract stipulated that there would be no penetrative attempts and that Sofya would be the one that would decide what she would and could manage at any given time. This type of proscription or 'banning' of sexual intercourse was a component of the approach emphasised by Masters and Johnson (1970) in order to reduce performance demands which may contribute to sexual dysfunction.

Session 3

Sofya attended this session alone and was introduce to progressive relaxation which consists of alternatively tensing and relaxing groups of muscles in a prescribed sequence, for example, starting from the feet and moving upwards. Kegel exercises, a form of circumvaginal muscle relaxation (Spence, 1991) were also taught to enhance control over these muscles. This is generally taught before any self-examination work is done so that relaxation skills and the feeling of being in control are learnt before starting exposure to the feared anxiety-provoking situation.

An idiosyncratic hierarchy of anxiety-provoking situations was developed collaboratively with Sofya and she was asked to note positive and negative thoughts and feelings in order to discuss them during sessions. The therapeutic contract hierarchy shown in Figure 9.5 is the original version; however, revisions were made during therapy in response to difficulties which are detailed later.

It is more effective for a woman to achieve penetration if she uses her own finger during the initial stages of therapy. This enables her to experience

---

1. Practising general relaxation and relaxing the muscles of the pelvic floor
2. Using a mirror to look at the vulva and identifying own anatomy
3. Touching the labia majora with a finger
4. Touching the labia minora with a finger
5. Parting the labia minora and looking at the vaginal opening
6. Touching the vaginal opening
7. Inserting one finger slowly into the vagina and slowly withdrawing it
8. Inserting one finger into the vagina, containment and relaxation, slow withdrawal
9. Inserting two fingers slowly into the vagina and slowly withdrawing them
10. Inserting two fingers into the vagina, containment and relaxation, slow withdrawal
11. Steps 3–8 with one of Irfan's fingers – with Irfan's consent
12. Steps 9–10 with two of Irfan's fingers– with Irfan's consent
13. Touching of vaginal opening with erect penis
14. Penis slowly entering and withdrawing from the vaginal entrance
15. Penis entering more of the vagina's depth and being contained
16. Penis entering and moving in the vagina
17. Penis thrusting and allowing ejaculation in the vagina
18. Maintaining arousal, progressing the ability to have sexual intercourse in a 'technical way' into enjoying love making

---

FIGURE 9.5 Therapeutic contract hierarchy between Sofya and Irfan

her tense muscles, assess the start of the burning pain and when relaxing to recognise the muscular changes and reduction of pain. Encouraging daily exercise effectively helps to counteract avoidance of contact with the genital area and penetration and, as this is achieved in a more relaxed way, counter-conditioning takes place. Vaginal trainers (smooth, plastic, penis-shaped tubes in graduated size and length), are also frequently used in this treatment. Sofya was made aware of the trainers but chose to work with her fingers.

Sessions 4–5

Sofya's progress was reviewed at the beginning of each session and she reported she was working at level 4 of the hierarchy and was experiencing increasing positive thoughts as she became more relaxed during self-examination.

Sofya and Irfan were therefore introduced to sensate-focus exercises which are home-based tasks that provide an opportunity for a range of cognitive and behavioural techniques to be utilised, such as graded exposure, communication skills training and attention-focusing. The task assignment can also be structured as behavioural experiments through which evidence can be produced to challenge negative thoughts and dysfunctional beliefs.

Sensate focus (Masters and Johnson, 1970) has been adapted in various ways but the aims are for the couple to learn how to communicate about feelings and preferred physical contact, to focus on their partner's cues, to gain knowledge about the physical contact their partner finds most pleasurable and to achieve relaxation in the sexual situation. The first stage of sensate focus (known as sensate focus 1) begins with sensual non-sexual contact to areas of the body, with each partner engaging in attention-focusing and giving feedback. Sofya and Irfan were asked to engage in these exercises two to three times per week over a two-week period.

Communication skills for providing feedback were discussed and both were discouraged from focusing only on negative comments such as accusing or blaming comments when difficulties occur, 'mind reading' (attributing motives or intent to the other), interrupting or staying silent. They were encouraged to use self-asserting 'I' statements such as 'I feel … ', 'I would like … '. The therapy explored any reservations the couple held regarding the exercises, as these also provided support for cognitive restructuring. Sofya was further introduced to negative and unhelpful thought recording and how to challenge these thoughts by replacing them with an alternative helpful thought (Figure 9.6).

One session focused on Sofya choosing to keep her briefs on during the sensate-focus exercises and readily recognising this was being used as a safety

Date	Emotion	Situation	What were you thinking?	What would be a more helpful thought?	How do you feel now?
24/05/2011			Rate belief in thought (0–100)	Rate belief in thought (0–100)	How much do you believe original thought?
	Anxious, scared	Doing sensate exercise	I don't want to do this (100) Irfan might not stick to the rules (85) He's going to want sex (90)	I can relax (90) Irfan agreed to this and will stick to it (60) I can tell him what I am thinking (80) I can focus on my sensations, as I do this (50)	A bit better, less anxious (50) (30) (40)

FIGURE 9.6   Thought record relating to a sexual situation

behaviour. With further exploration she agreed during the next sensate-focus session to engage in a behavioural experiment in which she removed her under-wear whilst engaging in sensate-focus exercises and afterwards recording her thoughts and feelings. These understandably recorded more anxiety than usual but nevertheless they demonstrated to Sofya that she retained control of the situation.

Sessions 6 and 7

Sofya's reported that she was working at level 6 of the hierarchy. Irfan expressed irritation that the progress was slow and Sofya acknowledged she was finding it difficult to progress to level 7. She indicated that she did not know what to expect in terms of what she would feel inside her vagina despite previously successfully challenging her thoughts on spatial capacity.

Therapy therefore re-focused on these concerns by using an anatomical model and this provided an opportunity for Sofya to explore and increase her awareness. Psycho-educational techniques were also used to increase her knowledge of penetration, again using anatomical diagrams and the model. The objectives of these strategies were to increase Sofya's confidence which would support her self-penetrating exercises.

Sessions 8-10

Sofya continued to express concern that she had not been able to self-penetrate using her finger. She described not having the courage and she was reassured that it is not uncommon for women with vaginismus to have difficulty in attempting penetration. Sofya was informed that in many cases self-penetration in the presence of a female therapist improves success in the treatment of vaginismus (Ter Kuile et al., 2005) and it was therefore agreed that in the following session Sofya would engage in in-session penetration. Plans were made to have a member of the gynaecology team that Sofya had previously met to be present to assist with guidance for penetration if required.

In the session Sofya was encouraged to practise her relaxation exercises and with a well-lubricated finger began to touch her labia and vaginal entrance but on partial insertion she became anxious and withdrew it stating she didn't like how it felt and she believed it to be a dirty thing to do. The therapy therefore took into consideration Sofya's belief that a vagina is a 'dirty part' of the body, which may be difficult to challenge due to early life and culturally developed beliefs, and instead Sofya was asked to consider penetration with the smallest vaginal trainer. Whilst this raised concerns about collusion with avoidance, Sofya's beliefs had to be taken into consideration and accommodated in an idiosyncratic way. Sofya voiced her determination to achieve penetration and relaxation was again encouraged before penetration with the smallest dilator was achieved.

The hierarchy was reviewed and in place of using fingers for penetration Sofya agreed to work with the vaginal trainers. She was advised to use the smallest trainer and achieve penetration without anxiety or discomfort several times before moving on to the next size. During penetration with the trainer the Kegel exercises were encouraged to provide an opportunity to feel the tensing and relaxing of the muscles in contact with something inside her vagina.

Sessions 11–12

Sofya's confidence increased significantly after utilising the vaginal trainers and Irfan was also pleased with the progress. Sofya still described a burning sensation but had gained awareness of utilising both relaxation and positive self-statements and was therefore continuing with her exercises.

Because significant progress was being achieved during the sensate-focus 1 exercises, with Sofya now able to relax, engage in attention-focusing and enjoy the sensations without distraction from negative thoughts, sensate-focus 2 exercises were introduced. The aim of sensate focus 2 is to continue sensate focus 1 plus contact with the genitals. The initial objective is not to achieve arousal but to encourage each partner to focus on the sensations they experience and give feedback about what is pleasurable.

It was at this point that the individualised hierarchy that Sofya had been working through in parallel to the work she and Irfan had been doing in sensate-focus tasks began to dovetail. Having acquired a feeling of control with the vaginal trainers it was agreed that the exposure would continue with further collaboration with Irfan: initially genital touching in the sensate-focus 2 tasks, progressing to steps 11 and 12 of the hierarchy.

Irfan, however, stated that whilst he would touch Sofya's external genitalia he did not want to insert his finger into her vagina. They had discussed this out of session and had agreed he would participate in penetration using a vaginal trainer. With guidance in therapy the boundaries and method were agreed. Sofya would guide Irfan's hand and provide verbal assistance while he held the vaginal trainer so that she would maintain control over the moment and position of penetration, and once they were comfortable Irfan would gradually take over.

Sessions 13–17

Having achieved a high level of control of the vaginal muscles and absence of the anxiety response, Sofya and Irfan progressed on to level 13 of the hierarchy. It was agreed that Sofya would guide Irfan's penis to her vaginal entrance and Irfan would gradually take over. Irfan expressed concerns that he might cause pain and they revisited their contract and agreed that they would both cease any penetrative activity the moment any negative feedback was given, and simultaneously Sofya would use her positive self-statements.

Levels 14 to 17 of the hierarchy constitute technical training in penetration. Whilst Sofya was confident in achieving penetration, Irfan reported frustration with progress and sometimes this was affecting his arousal. Whilst he no longer had fears about hurting Sofya, he acknowledged he was thinking he should be 'more in charge'. Further exploration of this revealed Irfan was worried that their sexual life would always be the same. Therapy revealed that both wanted to establish a pattern of intercourse with enjoyment as well as the absence of fear and pain associated with penetration. However they were encouraged to continue focusing on the exposure component to establish conditioning of new responses rather than trying to develop their repertoire of sexual skills, but to further increase a sense of independence therapeutic sessions were spaced further apart.

As progress continued both were invited to discuss how they would like to develop their sexual relationship further. They explored ideas such as positional variation and whether they wanted to engage sexually at different times of day or have sex outside the bedroom, and so on, and it was agreed that when they felt comfortable with their shared ideas they would initiate more varied sexual experiences.

Treatment evaluation

In the final session, returning to the formulation led to a summation of progress. This had been positive and the session reflected on the adjustments made to the hierarchy given the difficulty they had both experienced in terms of penetration with a finger. It was acknowledged that this had to be altered due to discomfort and its undesirability based on their cultural beliefs. Sofya and Irfan had achieved their original goals and were regularly engaging in pain-free intercourse which they described as enjoyable. They were now trying to conceive but were not letting this dominate their sexual relationship.

A repeat of the original HADS (Hospital Anxiety and Depression Scale) used at assessment indicated that both Sofya's scores were now within the normal range, indicating that her anxiety had markedly decreased.

Discharge strategies

As treatment was successful, Sofya was discharged from the psychosexual service and a discharge letter sent to her GP outlining the treatment intervention and the outcome. It was not expected that Sofya would develop secondary vaginismus but the GP was alerted that anxieties regarding childbirth might precipitate a future relapse and this area of care should be monitored when relevant.

Critique of case study

Sofya and Irfan came to therapy after a number of years of attempting to cope with her vaginismus condition, and whilst it was a case of primary vaginismus it had developed into a chronic condition. The fear and anxiety regarding penetration was therefore of sufficient strength to prevent any attempts at digital self-penetration. Added to this was the complex issue of early learning and cultural taboos regarding vaginal touching and cleanliness. Therapy adapted to both by exposing Sofya to the potential use of vaginal trainers which she found an acceptable alternative to self-touching.

Another idiosyncratic therapeutic strategy was to have a supervised in-session finger penetration, which, although it failed, did raise the issue of cultural taboos and allowed Sofya to consider the use of vaginal trainers. In-session support for such an intimate behaviour differs from the more normal interventions in cases experiencing vaginismus, but Sofya's was a chronic example and research supports such an intervention with a female psychotherapist. An added sense of safety and acceptance was provided for Sofya with the presence of a gynaecologist who could give detailed anatomical guidance if required.

More work could have been done to enhance counter-conditioning strategies, particularly when Irfan expressed frustration at the slow pace of progress through the pre-agreed hierarchy, which provided an opportunity to focus more on such techniques. However, as in most cases in real life, Sofya had to go at her own pace and through graded exposure gain more control over her anxieties regarding penetration. It is possible that there would be more of a priority for counter-conditioning work to have been implemented earlier if therapy was for a shorter number of sessions, and whilst the pace of therapy had a positive outcome, in another case counter-conditioning might be introduced earlier.

Failure to reduce negative thoughts and cognitive skills deficits (such as attention-focusing skills) which contribute to dysfunctions will limit the long-term effectiveness of therapy and these had to be addressed in the early phases of treatment through the use of positive-thinking techniques for Sofya. However, this made for a particularly complicated therapeutic treatment as such work was completed in parallel with the contract hierarchy agreed between husband and wife and could be difficult for less experienced therapists working in a couples context. Another approach that could have been considered would have been mindfulness-CBT which could have been assimilated into the hierarchical contract.

Problems arising in therapy

A potentially destructive problem was Sofya's reluctance to engage in self-penetration with her own fingers. By acknowledging how difficult this was for her the therapist could have been perceived as colluding with Sofya's wish to refrain from penetration exercises and reinforce disconfirmation of beliefs. Certainly Sofya's husband raised the issue that after several sessions his wife had not gone beyond step 3 of the agreed exercises. Yet he too had a cultural aversion to touching the vaginal area and so therapy had to accommodate these beliefs, despite their potential to reinforce and maintain existing conditioning. The use of an idiosyncratic approach to therapy allowed progress to continue but it could have been a major barrier to further work, and the issues of cultural and early life influences remains a poorly researched area for CBT practitioners.

Socio-cultural factors are crucial to understanding how sexual problems are experienced. Much of the process of psychosexual therapy involves the therapist encouraging and 'giving permission' for specific forms of sexual interaction as well as more general patterns of interaction within the relationship (e.g. self-asserting). It is important to keep in mind that many of these principles are based on western middle-class values and there should be awareness, openness and discussion about contrasting values of cultural and religious origin. In this way differences can be negotiated and accommodated, even in sensitive areas such as sexuality, rather than have therapy values imposed on a reluctant client. Of particular importance is the understanding and skills to adapt problem-specific or protocol-driven formulations into idiosyncratic models that meet the needs and objectives of the individual. From socialisation to the ending phase, there are potential problem areas if the practitioner attempts to impose their particular views on different cultural and community-based values and beliefs.

1. What maintenance factors prevented Sofya seeking therapeutic interventions for her diagnosis of vaginismus?
2. What role do significant others have in psychosexual CBT?
3. How can cultural factors and community values help therapeutic interventions to change?
4. What professional considerations are important in psychosexual interventions and do they differ significantly from other interventions requiring CBT?

Think about …

• Ask friends to make a list of three issues that would stop them accessing therapy and three issues that they would find most difficult to discuss once in therapy. Can you identify the most common reasons for both? Discuss with professional colleagues how you and therapy services could help overcome the issues identified.

Suggested activity:

10
Client Presenting with Post-Traumatic Stress Disorder (PTSD)

Ian Ross

Learning objectives

By the end of this chapter you should be able to:

Identify the symptoms of post-traumatic stress disorder (PTSD) from diagnostic criteria

Understand the development of PTSD from both a cognitive and behavioural perspective

Discuss a case formulation and decide on cognitive and behavioural interventions

Plan and implement the CBT treatment interventions

Be aware of factors that may cause a relapse of PTSD

Diagnostic criteria

The DSM-IV-TR (APA, 2000) code 309.81 diagnostic criteria for post-traumatic stress disorder (PTSD) reflect the diversity of this condition. The major criteria for the diagnosis of PTSD in clients who have been exposed to traumatic events include re-experiencing, avoidance, numbing and hyper-arousal. Each of these symptoms, alone or as a group, should have a duration of more than one month and cause clinically significant distress and impairment. If the duration is less than three months then PTSD is considered acute; more than three months is chronic, while some individuals may have chronic PTSD with delayed onset if the symptoms appear at least six months after the trauma.

A traumatic event has to involve two elements: the individual experienced or saw an event(s) that involved actual or potential death, serious injury or physical harm to the self or others; and the response was fear, helplessness or horror. Afterwards the event is persistently re-experienced with intense mental and physiological distress and hyper-perception of internal or external triggers or cues about the actual event.

These experiences culminate in persistent avoidance of any cues related to the trauma or general numbness in three or more of the following areas: efforts to avoid any thinking or feelings related to the trauma including discussing the incident(s); avoidance of activities, places or other cues to the event(s); an inability to recall potentially important elements of the trauma; a noticeably significant deterioration in interest or participation in everyday activities; feelings of separation from, and difficulties in, maintaining or commencing relationships; and an associated sense that the future holds little, if any, hope for the individual.

The person often makes conscious attempts to cope with the above but with little success as hyper-arousal not present before the trauma causes two or more of the following symptoms: sleep disturbances; irritability and outbursts of anger; poor concentration; hyper-vigilance; and an exaggerated startle response, all of which prevent adequate coping strategies from being established.

Re-experiencing refers to the fact that the individual experiences vivid and disturbing recall of the traumatic situation and associated events. Clients may report distressing thoughts and images which may occur in nightmares or as flashbacks.

Nightmares will be recurrent and distressing and generally include re-experiencing of the traumatic event. Dreams in general will often be anxiety provoking and involve elements of the original event. Clients report that they wake from these dreams sweating, crying and extremely agitated.

Flashbacks are described as unexpected and vivid fleeting feelings of reliving the traumatic event. The flashbacks may be so intrusive that the client experiences sensory changes, for example the sounds, smells and images associated with the event. There may even be physiological reactions to the flashback, such as panic attacks in which the client experiences increased heart rate and shallow breathing. Flashbacks, however, tend to be rare occurrences and the more correct psychological term for these flashbacks is dissociative episodes, because the client is actually reliving rather than just simply recalling the events.

Avoidance and numbing are included together under criterion C in the DSM-IV-TR. For the client with PTSD, there is an understandable avoidance of any situation which may be similar to the traumatic event. In these situations they sense traumatic stressors or unpleasant memories of the event may be triggered. There is also a marked numbing of cognitive and emotional responsiveness of the client to everyday experiences.

ICD-10 (WHO, 2007) offers simplified but similar diagnostic criteria to DSM-IV-TR (APA, 2000). A study by Peters, Slade and Andrews (1999) concluded that the major difference between the two systems was that the DSM-IV-TR included numbing alongside avoidance. There is an argument that the avoidance and numbing should be considered as separate entities as treatment may differ for the two conditions (Taylor, 2006). Numbing with low mood, withdrawal and significantly decreased sense or awareness of pleasure mirrors depression, which is often comorbid with PTSD and may require a different therapeutic approach.

Trauma cues can provoke distressing psychological and physiological responses. These cues are stimuli arising from the traumatic event to which the client has become highly sensitised (hyper-arousal) and they evoke a classical behavioural response. An example would be a survivor of a house fire who may become extremely anxious when they smell smoke. Research with firemen established that an indicator of hyper-arousal in PTSD is the *startle response* (Guthrie and Bryant, 2005). This response is triggered by the cues or stimuli developed as a result of the traumatic event. Typically a client becomes startled by, for example, a noise associated with the trauma; they may report feeling anxious and tense and respond unpredictably to others. This is very common in victims of road traffic incidents (RTI). Examples of traumatic situations and stressors that may develop are listed in Table 10.1.

There may be some obvious exclusions from this list, for example life events such as divorce and separation; however, clients may present with symptoms of PTSD in grief, as a result of a traumatic death of, for example, a close relative.

TABLE 10.1 PTSD traumatic situations and associated stressors

Traumatic situations	Stressor or cue
Military combat operations; terrorist attack	Gunshots; explosions; smells
Violent personal assault (e.g. mugging, robbery, kidnap or hostage)	Strangers; confined spaces
Sexual assault, abuse or rape, both in children and adults	Violent outbursts; physical discomfort
Incarceration as a prisoner of war; torture	Confined spaces; restricted movement
Natural disaster (earthquake, fire, tornado, hurricane)	Lightning, thunder
Severe motor vehicle accident	Screeching tyres; fuel smells
Severe accident at work or in the home	High altitude locations; machinery
Unexpectedly observing serious injury or unnatural death of another person	Witness to accident; crowds; lifeless body

Predisposing and precipitating factors.

There are two groups who are predisposed to PTSD: the first are those who are more likely to be exposed to traumatic situations than others, for example those in employment activities such as military combat; and the second are those who have observed a traumatic or highly stressful situation by, for example, watching an incident reported on the television. It is this second group of clients that creates the most difficulty in the diagnosis of PTSD and it is these clients that are most widespread. From a therapeutic point of view there is therefore a need to understand any predisposing or precipitating factors in a client's circumstances in order to identify whether they are more or less vulnerable to PTSD.

Ozer and colleagues (2003) identified seven predictors of PTSD from a meta-analysis of 2,647 studies. The final summary list was: prior trauma; prior psychological problems and adjustment; family history of psychopathology; perceived threat to life during the traumatic incident; low post-trauma social support, low emotional responses at the time of the incident and peri-traumatic dissociation; slowing of time; unreal environment and numbness at the time of the incident. The study concluded that whilst none of these factors was sufficient on its own to cause or precipitate PTSD symptoms, the existence of peri-traumatic factors is the strongest predictor of vulnerability to PTSD.

Demographic incidence

Post-traumatic stress disorder is common (NICE, 2005b) with a lifetime prevalence of approximately 8 per cent overall. The incidence or risk of developing PTSD after a traumatic event is estimated to be between 8 per cent and 20 per cent, but there are difficulties in determining this. This is because incidence rates for PTSD can be largely influenced by the occurrence of events, for example the Iraq and Afghan wars and natural disasters such as the Asian tsunami, which will inevitably contribute to the prevalence. Also, as the NICE guidelines (2005b) note, the largest body of data on prevalence and incidence comes from the USA and Australia, so there is limited data specific to the UK from which to draw.

Some indicators of PTSD prevalence and incidence do, however, emerge from the international studies (NICE, 2005b) and these are summarised below.

- The majority of people will experience at least one traumatic event in their lifetime.
- Intentional acts of interpersonal violence, in particular sexual assault and combat, are more likely to lead to PTSD than accidents or disasters.
- Men tend to experience more traumatic events than women, but women experience higher-impact events (i.e. those that are more likely to lead to PTSD).

- Women are more likely to develop PTSD in response to a traumatic event than men; this enhanced risk is not explained by differences in the type of traumatic event.

Continuum of severity

The NICE guideline for PTSD (NICE, 2005b) ranks the severity of PTSD by both symptoms and the length of time that these have been experienced. Symptoms in the initial four weeks post trauma are often mild, with a gradual development in severity, up to three months. Beyond three months the symptoms of PTSD may gradually become worse, with increasing frequency of flashbacks and dissociation.

Clients with PTSD suffer a number of comorbid conditions, such as depression, agoraphobia and substance abuse, with clients reporting alcohol and drugs being used to 'block out' the unpleasant and distressing memories. They also report strong feelings of shame and guilt.

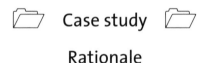

Case study

Rationale

PTSD often presents as a diverse and complex condition and this case offers an insight into level 4 of the Stepped Care Pathway, which involves one-to-one CBT therapy aimed at both the immediate and intermediate cognitive levels. The setting for this case is initially in the client's home and then progresses to trauma-focused CBT (Foa et al., 2009) within the specialist mental health services, as recommended by NICE (2005b).

Client

A young male, Adrian, aged 22 years, was referred to the local Community Mental Health Care Team for assessment by his GP, after complaining of experiencing anxiety when he left his house at night to visit friends. He had been assaulted eight weeks prior to the referral, whilst walking home from a birthday celebration at a friend's house. In the early evening he had been involved in an argument with a group of gatecrashers to the party; the police had been called and the gatecrashers removed. Adrian had left the party at around 1.00am and was walking along a well-lit pavement towards his home. He was attacked from behind and suffered a number of blows to the head and back from an unknown assailant. He fell to the ground and lay stunned for some time before staggering home and calling the police at around 2.30am. No arrests were made as the Crown Prosecution Service ruled that the police had insufficient evidence for a case. He suffered bruising and a broken rib and was off work for four weeks. At the time of the referral he had just returned to work as a shop assistant in a local clothing store, on a part-time basis. However, his boss was concerned at his erratic attendance for work.

The initial assessment by the CMHT confirmed anxiety and hyper-vigilance. It emerged during the interview that Adrian was finding it extremely difficult to leave the house at all, with thoughts of going out leaving him feeling panicky. The agoraphobia was particularly evident at night time. In addition, Adrian described vivid and disturbing nightmares of the assault, in which he saw gangs of unidentified assailants rushing at him with clubs and iron bars. He was convinced that the gatecrasher gang had waited for him to leave the party. He would awake screaming and sweating. He also described flashbacks when he experienced vivid recollections of the street on which he was attacked and the distress of lying injured on the pavement, stating 'It was as if it was happening all over again.' Adrian stated that he was angry at the inability of the police to make an arrest and distressed at what he saw as the failings of the legal system to offer him some redress.

Adrian failed to attend further sessions at the CMHT as he was unable to leave the house. A case conference was called and the decision was made to refer Adrian to level 4 of the Stepped Care model to receive one-to-one trauma-focused CBT therapy at home.

Assessment session

The assessment session took place in Adrian's home because of his agoraphobia. At the beginning of the session Adrian was made aware of confidentiality and client safety. He was advised of a potential breach of confidentiality if the therapist assessed that he was a danger to himself or others. This action was necessary as Adrian had previously described his low mood and acknowledged some suicidal thoughts, although a further assessment indicated low risk. He constantly expressed deep anger at the unknown perpetrators of the trauma and stated that he would seek revenge.

The assessment session was divided into two parts: firstly a clinical interview, and secondly completion of self-reports. The interview was structured to establish the nature and severity of the incident, symptoms and wider issues such as comorbidity, moods, avoidance behaviour and social networks.

Clinical interviews generally follow a structured format such as the Structured Clinical Interview for DSM-IV-TR (APA, 2000), which is based upon the DSM-IV-TR criteria. The reality of assessment is that it may be limited to one session, for example in legal insurance cases, but almost always continues to evolve over therapy sessions.

Adrian was asked to describe the symptoms he was experiencing using FIDO – an acronym which helps the client to record symptoms, and measures **F**requency, **I**ntensity, **D**uration and **O**utcome. Adrian reported that his flashbacks were occurring perhaps twice or three times a week, that they were intense, lasted perhaps seconds, and generally ended leaving him feeling confused and anxious.

The second activity in the assessment session required Adrian to complete a number of self-reports or questionnaires covering PTSD and comorbidity.

A number of self-report instruments for PTSD have been developed which provide this data. Frequently used self-report questionnaires are the PTSD scale (Foa et al., 1997), the Clinician Administered PTSD scale (CAPS; Weathers et al., 2001) and the Impact of Events Scale – Revised (IES-R; Weiss and Marmar, 1997). Creamer, Bell and Failia (2003) have found that the three subscales of this questionnaire (intrusion, avoidance and hyper-arousal) confirmed the validity for use of this instrument in general populations. The IES-R was used to measure Adrian's PTSD symptoms.

Depression is commonly comorbid with PTSD and so the Hospital Anxiety and Depression Scale (HADS; Zigmond and Snaith, 1983) self-report questionnaire was used to determine the level of depression and anxiety. Typically scores are represented as HADS A for anxiety and HADS B for depression. Crawford and colleagues (2001) provided normative data from the general population which confirmed that it is acceptable to also use the total score rather than the anxiety and depression subscales, because of the high comorbidity. PHQ-9 (Kroenke et al., 2001) is a specific measure of severity of depression and this too was administered. Adrian's scores on the IES-R, PHQ-9 and HADS are presented in Table 10.2. Adrian's scores on the IES-R confirmed moderate to severe PTSD and his reports of agoraphobia were supported by the scores on HADS, whilst the PHQ-9 indicated moderate depression.

At the end of the assessment session, Adrian was asked to keep a diary record of his activities, thoughts, feelings, physical sensations and emotions over the following weeks. The rationale explained to him was that the diary would help supplement the formal assessment information and provide additional examples of situations that could be used during the development of interventions. The diary could also be used by the client as a measurement of progress by, for example, the use of SUDS (Subjective Units of Distress Scale)

TABLE 10.2 Self-report questionnaire data

Questionnaire	Assessment score	Normal range
IES-R	2.8	0–1.5
PHQ-9	12	0–3
HADS	23	0–15

which uses a 1–10 scale where 1= no acute distress; 5 = moderately upset and 10 = unbearably bad (Wolpe, 1969).

When reviewing the session, Adrian expressed anxiety that he 'was going mad and was confused'. Normalisation is a useful technique to reassure the client that what they are experiencing is what any normal person would, given the abnormal situation they have experienced. This was explained to Adrian, alongside a brief description of the course of the CBT therapy process and how Adrian would learn to cope with these disturbing symptoms.

Case formulation

Conceptualisation is about making sense of the origins, maintenance and development of the client's difficulties. The therapist helps the client establish a working hypothesis for testing and verification after appropriate interventions – in effect client goals or outcomes. Conceptualisation links theory with therapeutic interventions.

At the beginning of this session, again in Adrian's home, the agenda was confirmed. This was:

1. Homework from previous session – events diary feedback on last session and discussion
2. Discussion of Adrian's goals for therapy
3. Conceptualisation of Adrian's problems
4. Homework for following session.

Adrian produced his diary, an extract of which is shown in Figure 10.1.

It was clear from Adrian's diary that he was unable to leave the house on his own and even with support from his friends found it difficult during daylight. He recognised that the choice of the DVD was not useful as this had triggered feelings similar to his own experience of street violence. This was a useful discussion point from which Adrian could increase his understanding of PTSD symptoms.

Adrian's symptoms could be conceptualised using various models and these were briefly and simply discussed as part of Adrian's psycho-education.

The Conditioning Model (Rescorla, 1988) considers a number of behavioural components in PTSD, which are conditioned fear and avoidance of trauma-related stimuli, accompanied by minimal cognitive processing. This is best described by the ABC model where **B**ehaviour occurs within the context of **A**ntecedents and **C**onsequences. Typically, *reinforcing* consequences **(C)** *strengthen* behaviour **(B)** in the presence of a given antecedent **(A)**, whereas *punishing* consequences **(C)** *weaken* behaviour **(B)** in the

Date/ Time	Situation	Physical sensations	Thoughts	Behaviour	Mood
12/6/10 8am	Decided to leave house for milk for breakfast	'Panic', sweating, heart beating SUDS 4/5	'I don't want to go out' SUDS 4/5	Hesitated at door, opened door and then slammed it and went back to kitchen SUDS 4/5	Low – angry with problem SUDS 4/5
14/6/10 6pm	Joe came around and asked me to come down to the DVD store. Thought a movie would cheer me up	Very agitated Strangers on pavement SUDS 3/5	'Not keen, but might cope having someone with me' SUDS 3/5	Walking rapidly – couldn't concentrate in store SUDS 4/5	Low – angry that this was happening SUDS 4/5
8.30pm	Watching DVD with Joe – scenes of violent attacks on hero	Again agitated SUDS 3/5	'Some of the violence made me feel as if it was happening to me' SUDS 3/5	Moved out of room – Joe upset and embarrassed as he realised the problem SUDS 4/5	Angry at the intrusion into my social life SUDS 4/5

FIGURE 10.1   Extract from Adrian's events diary

presence of a given antecedent **(A)**. Adrian has become conditioned to fear and now avoids trauma-related stimuli, for example dark streets and the sound of footsteps behind him. There is minimal cognitive processing in that the behavioural response is so powerful and overwhelming. In Adrian's case, there are several conditioning stimuli or antecedents, for example dark streets and pain from injuries, which lead to re-experiencing aspects of the assault, resulting in hyper-arousal and an increase in the PTSD symptoms. The agoraphobia that Adrian experiences, therefore, is as a result of avoidance which is reinforced safety behaviour, in response to the hyper-arousal he feels.

The Emotional Processing Model (Foa et al., 1998) considers both cognitive and behavioural components. These start with schema and negative beliefs that, for example, 'the world is a dangerous place', which then link to 'fear structures'. For Adrian these fear structures are stimuli associated with the attack, for example darkness and strangers on the street, to which he responds with appropriate behaviour such as trembling and hyper-arousal. This behaviour is also reinforced by cognitive interpretation of the meaning of this information, for example that the street is a dangerous place. Whenever Adrian attempts to leave his house, therefore, the

1. Agoraphobia – not wanting to go out, threat of danger but also dealing with the shame of hyper-arousal and anger when with friends.

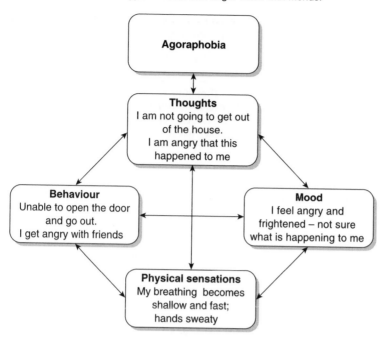

Goal for therapy – be able to leave the house in both daylight and after dark, on my own and with friends.

FIGURE 10.2 Conceptualisation of agoraphobia adapted from Williams's (2010) five areas formulation. Reproduced by permission of Hodder Education.

incoming stimuli activate sensory networks and evoke fear and anxiety. He quickly recognises that his response is different to everyday experiences, but seeks instead to avoid the situation of leaving the house and to stay in the safety of his home.

Adrian confirmed that he understood the conceptualisation process and identified three areas and goals for therapy, which he considered most difficult for him. The therapist worked with Adrian to conceptualise these using the five areas model (Williams, 2010). Please see Figures 10.2, 10.3 and 10.4.

Adrian agreed to continue his events diary and conceptualise any new situations as he had done in the session. He was given copies of the conceptualisations previously worked on, as well as a supply of blank sheets. It was also agreed that as Adrian had been able to go to the DVD store with his friend, he should attend the next session at the therapy centre and record his thoughts and feelings on a five areas chart.

1. PTSD flashbacks, nightmares – anxiety, hyper-arousal and vigilance

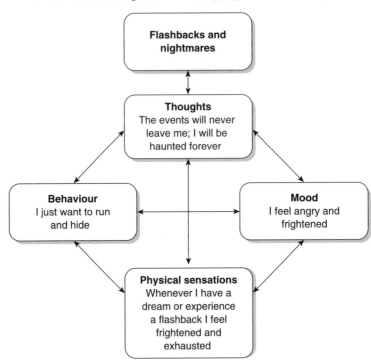

Goal for therapy – understand the symptoms of PTSD and learn how to manage them so that they do not have such an impact on my daily activities.

FIGURE 10.3 Conceptualisation of flashbacks adapted from Williams's (2010) five areas formulation. Reproduced by permission of Hodder Education.

Treatment sessions 1–2

Adrian had a friend walk with him to the therapy centre and his thoughts and feelings about this were discussed in the session, the agenda of which was:

- Homework – review the situations diary
- Goals for therapy and interventions
- Psycho-education
- Emotional regulation.

Adrian reviewed his worksheet and noted that whilst he had felt anxious about walking to the centre it had not been as bad as he had initially thought. Discussion of this led to the proposal of a programme of interventions, the first of which would be designed to allow normalisation of Adrian's daily activities and build on his recent excursions from his house. The core interventions agreed with Adrian are listed in Table 10.3.

As a first intervention, psycho–education is useful to help with the normalisation of the confusing and often disturbing symptoms of PTSD. Adrian had

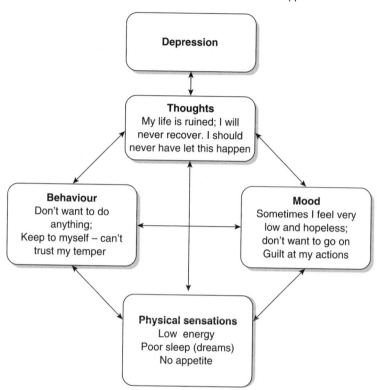

Depression – should have not allowed this to happen.

Goal for therapy – be able to manage my low moods and feel less guilty.

FIGURE 10.4   Conceptualisation of depression adapted from William's (2010) five areas formulation. Reproduced by permission of Hodder Education.

TABLE 10.3   Core interventions

Priority	Interventions	Activity	Sessions
Normalisation	Psycho-education	Information sourcing	3
Agoraphobia	Emotional regulation	Breathing retraining and relaxation	3
	Exposure	Situational	4
PTSD symptoms	Exposure	Reliving	5, 6
Depression	Cognitive rationalisation Behavioural activation	Thought diary Pleasure and mastery report	7, 8, 9

little or no understanding of PTSD and he needed to be informed and have confidence in his ability to manage his condition. Following the explanation, Adrian was relieved to hear that the memory losses and poor concentration that he experienced after the assault were common to trauma clients and not due to some major injury to his brain. Despite brain injury having been ruled out when he underwent investigations after his admission to A&E, Adrian had remained particularly disturbed by the flashbacks and vivid nightmares, associating these with some imagined non-recoverable brain injury. Adrian was therefore presented with information leaflets and recommended to sites on the internet to educate himself more about the symptoms of PTSD and he said that he already felt much more reassured.

Emotional regulation is helpful when the client experiences uncomfortable or distressing feelings. Early introduction allows the client to recognise that they have tools that they are able to use to manage situations, thus increasing the feeling of empowerment and normalisation. The first exercise with Adrian was focused on breathing retraining and applied relaxation, to help Adrian become more aware of his physical sensations and experience ways in which he could manage his arousal. The conceptualisation diagrams produced in session 2 highlighted the interaction between physical arousal with thoughts, emotions and behaviour. A handout was made available, which described the exercises, and Adrian agreed to practise these as homework.

One of the drawbacks of relaxation and breathing exercises is that the client may well use them to develop avoidance strategies, for example using the relaxation to avoid thinking about a particular stressor, rather than allowing engagement with the sensations the stressor produces or using breathing to reduce the resultant arousal. An awareness of this is therefore paramount, as is monitoring of the way in which these exercises are applied.

Exposure is also an important PTSD intervention and takes two forms: situational exposure (safe, harmless external stimuli) and imaginal 'reliving' (a systematic, repeated and prolonged exposure to traumatic memory). Along with psycho-education and emotional regulation, exposure has been shown to be effective in reducing the severity of PTSD symptoms (Foa et al., 2009).

Session 3

This session commenced with situational exposure and a series of experiments were devised to allow Adrian to experience leaving his home. He had already demonstrated progress in this area and now the goal was for him to attempt the exercise on his own. These experiments would be graded: each time he would first stand at the open door in daylight and observe his surroundings and on becoming aware of his feelings he would then walk to the chosen destination. Adrian was able to differentiate between feelings of vulnerability as a result of the assault and the less disturbing feelings of vulnerability when standing on the street. After each exposure Adrian was encouraged to use his

Goal	Details	SUDS before	SUDS after
1. Go out of the house alone during daylight	Make one journey a day to the local shops; once a week to therapist's office		
2. Go out and meet friends in daylight	Perhaps link it to above – go somewhere else close by		
3. Meet friends at night but take taxi	This will need planning		

FIGURE 10.5   Graded situational exposure chart

breathing and relaxation to reduce his arousal. A chart of the graded exercises was drawn for Adrian to use for homework. This is shown in Figure 10.5.

At the end of the session Adrian confirmed that he had understood and was comfortable with his activities for the week ahead.

Sessions 4–6

The aim of these sessions was to continue work on Adrian's second therapeutic goal: the symptoms of the PTSD. The session started with a discussion of Adrian's homework and an acknowledgement of his success in that he was able to report reduced SUDS after the exercise to a level of 2 or 3.

Exposure techniques, coupled with emotional regulation, are central to PTSD treatment as they allow the client to relive and process the mass of sensory information from the traumatic incident (Foa et al., 2009). Reliving the trauma can be a very distressing activity and the client needs to be allowed to work at their own pace. In some circumstance the session content may be recorded on an audiotape for the client to play back and listen to between sessions. PTSD creates confused memories and misunderstood emotions, thoughts and behaviour. Traumatic memories tend to be stored as perceptual and affective states, with little verbal representation, and learning to tolerate the memories of intense emotional experiences is a critical part of recovery. The reliving process involves translating the non-verbal dissociated traumatic memory into secondary mental processes, in which words can provide meaning and form, thereby facilitating the transformation of traumatic memory into narrative memory.

A typical imaginal exposure activity will last up to 45 minutes and this process is illustrated in the dialogue with Adrian below:

Therapist (T):   Sit back, close your eyes and describe to me in as much detail as you can remember, what happened on that night after you left the party.

Adrian (A):   I remember leaving the house. It was a warm evening and I walked out onto the pavement.

T: Did you notice any particular sounds, sights or smells?

A: The pavement was reasonably well lit and it was very quiet, there were no cars around. But it did cross my mind that the hedge of the next door house was overgrown and cast some curious shadows.

T: OK … I am getting a picture now of you walking along – what were you thinking at that moment?

A: My mind had turned to the incident earlier on with the gatecrashers and I did wonder if they might come looking for me.

T: As you think about that now on a SUDS scale of 0 to 5, how does it make you feel?

A: Not good – about a 3.

T: So the earlier incident had made you nervous.

A: Yes.

T: Ok let's go back to your walk home. You noticed the shadows and reflected on the gatecrashers. What else were you aware of?

A: Not much, until I felt this terrible blow to the right side of my neck and a searing pain.

T: Right now how do you feel?

A: Very anxious – at a 5. I feel bad – it was so shocking and painful.

T: OK would you like to do some steady breathing that we practised earlier to allow yourself to calm down.

Adrian proved to be cooperative and over the period of three sessions carefully related the events leading up to, during and after the assault. He listened to the tape as a homework assignment and wrote down any other details that he recalled. It was significant that during reliving Adrian became aware of very strong emotions of anger at the assailant and guilt at letting down his friends by not being able to socialise after the incident. These additional insights were written down in a thought diary, so that they could be used in cognitive restructuring exercises in later sessions. Adrian reported a sense of relief after each session and commented on the feelings of release. He had not, until then, had the opportunity to fully explore the events of the assault in a non-judgemental atmosphere. He also reported that the flashbacks, whilst still prevalent, seemed less threatening as did the vivid dreams.

Sessions 7–9

The third of Adrian's goals was depression, which was addressed in sessions 7–9. Adrian had kept a diary since the first session and made notes each day about the various situations, thoughts, emotions, feelings and behaviour he became aware of. During reliving Adrian had become aware of negative thoughts such as 'I should have not allowed this to happen', 'I was stupid'

Situation	Thought	Associated Mood	Alternative thought	Rate new mood
What were you doing?	Describe and categorise: negative/ catastrophic/black and white/self blame	Rate 0 low–10 high		Rate 0 low–10 high
Friends visited me at home	I am no good to my friends as I am so limited in what I do	Low, feel guilty 3	I am pleased I have such good supporting friends who understand that I have been through a difficult time	Less guilt 6

FIGURE 10.6 Adrian's thought diary

and 'I have let my friends down as I am not able to visit them.' Many of the thoughts fitted the descriptions of Beck and colleagues (1979) as being cata-strophic, black and white and self-blaming. A selection of these thoughts was discussed with Adrian who was encouraged to seek alternative explanations (Figure 10.6).

Depressed clients such as Adrian cease involvement in pleasant activities, partly as a result of their agoraphobia. Behavioural activation (Dimidjian et al., 2006) exercises were therefore introduced with Adrian once he was able to leave the house. At least one activity each week that was pleasurable was planned with Adrian, as well as one that offered a sense of achievement. The activities should ideally build upon each other to reinforce the pleasure and sense of mastery.

Treatment evaluation session

After nine sessions of therapy, an evaluation was undertaken to establish the extent of the diagnostic criteria that had contributed to the diagnosis of PTSD at the initial assessment. Adrian also re-completed the PHQ-9, BAI and PTSD scales. The questionnaire data before and after therapy are summarised in Table 10.4. In addition, the DSM criteria for PTSD were reassessed and Adrian was asked to rate his initial symptoms of PTSD, for example disturbed sleep, nightmares and flashbacks, against his present experience using SUDS.

TABLE 10.4 Self-report scores

Measures	Before therapy	After therapy
IES-R	2.8	1
PHQ-9	12	3
HADS	23	9

It was evident from all measures that Adrian no longer met the criteria for PTSD or depression and at a month follow-up he reported that he had returned to work full-time and was in the process of slowly restoring his social network.

Discharge strategies

Due to Adrian's successful treatment he felt confident to be discharged at the end of therapy. It was agreed that there appeared to be no current clinical basis for Adrian to enlist any further support from local agencies, but he agreed to approach his GP should his needs change. The GP was informed of Adrian's discharge and invited to make a re-referral should the need arise.

Critique of case study

PTSD is a complex condition encompassing symptoms in mood, cognition and physiology, and therefore assessment should be comprehensive and global. It can be enticing for the therapist to identify symptoms in one modality (e.g. cognition) such as flashbacks or acute anxiety attacks and initiate treatment without observing other issues such as the debilitating effects of poor sleep on concentration or memory.

In the assessment phase it can take some time to discern the various symptoms and then prioritise the immediate problem issues. PTSD symptoms cannot therefore be contained within a 'single' condition, but should be viewed from a psychotherapeutic perspective as a complex presentation requiring a number of different approaches.

Finally, individuals with the condition are apt to develop comorbid depression and subsequent frequent relapses which cause enduring PTSD if interventions are not provided early. Enduring and chronic PTSD requires case formulations and treatment interventions, at intermediate, and in some instances, core belief levels.

Problems arising in therapy

The paradox with PTSD is that an otherwise cognitively engaging client may at first assessment be seen to be unsuitable for therapy because of their lack of cooperation and engagement in the process. The PTSD associated hyper-vigilance and hyper-arousal create dysfunctional thinking and distressed emotions, plus clients often have an anxiety about engaging in a therapy that will revisit the trauma they have experienced. This may show in unwillingness to cooperate with reliving activities, including homework. Some clients may find the over-whelming emotional reactions to the reliving experience intolerable and fall back into the established patterns of avoidance.

The apparently successful therapy for PTSD may reveal wider issues of comorbidity, for example long-standing depression and substance misuse. The traumatic incident may also have resulted in injury, and once therapy has con-cluded the client may need physical rehabilitation.

In instances of domestic violence and sexual abuse and rape, clients may experience continued anxiety in dealing with relationships with the perpetra-tors of their trauma, particularly when the relationships have been close, for example within families.

Dissociation and numbing are key criteria in the diagnosis of PTSD and therefore, may be experienced by the client in the course of therapy. The therapist needs to be alert to the onset of these conditions and to be able to reassure and work with the client in managing these.

1. Depression is frequently comorbid with PTSD. How would you differentiate a client's depression from PTSD?
2. Reliving sessions with clients can often result in vicarious traumatisation of the therapist. What does this mean and how would a therapist manage this?

Think about ....

- Think about a time you experienced a frightening event; make a note of the thoughts, emotions, physical feelings and behaviour that this induced. Conceptualise this information in the five areas diagram and see if the model helps you to make sense of the event.

Suggested activity:

11
Client Presenting with Chronic Bulimia Nervosa

Mike Thomas

Learning objectives

By the end of this chapter you should be able to:

Identify bulimia nervosa from the diagnostic criteria
Describe the development of the condition
Identify the range of assessment tools leading to case formulation and
  treatment
Understand the interventions at core belief level

Diagnostic criteria

The diagnostic criteria for bulimia nervosa (BN) using DSM-IV-TR 307.51 (APA, 2000) states that the individual experiences recurrent bouts of binge eating that clearly includes larger amounts than normal and is eaten within a specific short timeframe. The bingeing episode itself may be described as uncontrollable by the individual, although if interrupted the bingeing will stop and this may explain the reason for bingeing to be viewed as a secret activity by the individual. In an attempt to manage any weight gain the individual will engage in compensatory behaviours more than twice a week, up to three months, including behaviours such as self-induced vomiting and laxative abuse (purging BN). Alternatively the individual may stop eating for a period of time in between bingeing or may over-exercise (non-purging BN).

The DSM-IV-TR (APA, 2000) goes on to state that individuals experiencing BN will usually be distracted to a great degree by their weight and shape and will normally incorporate such thinking into their overall schema of the self, their attitudes towards others and how they interact with the world.

Compensatory behaviours to lose or control weight gain are always found in bulimia nervosa. Excessive use of laxatives is more common than self-induced vomiting, though both are more common in purging sub-types. Over-exercising is a trait in non-purging sub-types but some individuals will engage in both behaviours during bingeing periods. Most individuals with BN are slightly over- or underweight but within normal paradigms, but individuals with BN have an excessive emphasis on body shape and weight in relation to their own self-concept, which leads to a heightened sense of anxiety and episodes of depression.

Approximately one-third of individuals diagnosed with BN engage in substance misuse and over one-third also meet the criteria for borderline personality disorders (Murcia, 2006). Frequent purging leads to electrolyte imbalances, dental problems, stomach and oesophageal ulcers and dependency on laxatives. In severe cases there may be oesophageal tears, ruptures and cardiac arrthymias (Robinson, 2009). Self-harming behaviour is not uncommon and scars can develop on these sites which can maintain poor self-body image.

Differential diagnoses are important to prevent poor intervention. Physical conditions should be discounted as should BN symptoms found in primary anorexia nervosa where bingeing/purging may occur. Some BN symptoms can manifest themselves as chronic depression and the therapist should be alert to comorbid conditions including personality disorder and obsessive compulsive disorders (Engel et al., 2007; Murakami et al., 2002; Thornton and Russell, 1997).

Predisposing and precipitating factors

The aetiology of BN is poorly understood, although there is agreement that it is a combination of bio-psycho-social factors. Some individuals are thought to have a genetic predisposition to the condition with a pre-determined susceptibility to negative beliefs about their body. If such individuals are then subject to childhood trauma or negative experiences within the familial and socio-cultural environment these beliefs could be reinforced, thus increasing the probability of the condition forming. Studies on hypothalamic–pituitary–adrenal disturbances suggest this possible genetic predisposition (Castro et al., 2008), whilst others see a crossover between a complex psychological and physiological adaptation or maintenance of mood through the effects of foodstuffs (Goodwin, 1990).

There remains a great deal of interest in the socio-cultural aspects of eating disorders with views ranging from those situated in economics to feminism. For example, BN has normally only been seen in modern capitalist countries but the rate is rising in growing economies such as India and China. Feminist theory argues that the increase in BN is influenced by the beauty/fitness/media industries. They argue that a society dominated by images of 'ideal' shaped bodies creates an undue influence on the individual's self-concept and for some individuals the pressure to conform to such images is taken too far and culminates in eating disordered conditions (Fallon et al., 1994; Malson and Burns, 2009). There are also studies which indicate that familial influences and early traumatic experiences (such as sexual abuse) may precipitate eating disorders in adolescence (Guilfoyle, 2009; McGowan et al., 2009).

Cognitive approaches suggest that poor self-esteem precipitates dysfunctional locus of control and an over-evaluation of body shape and image (Cooper and Shafran, 2008). NICE guidelines (2004) state that CBT is the treatment of choice.

There is a lack of consensus regarding 'recovery' and the treatment today is aimed at maintenance support and self-management using a variety of face-to-face CBT sessions, support groups and online treatment such as e-CBT.

Demographic incidence

BN can now be found amongst other economies, with emerging data for prevalence in Africa, India and China, and it is more prevalent among all social and ethnic groups. The DSM-IV-TR (APA, 2000) suggests approximately 1 to 3 per cent of adolescent females experience BN, whilst Cooper, Todd and Wells (2000) suggest it is approximately 1 to 2 per cent of young females, with a higher prevalence amongst professions which focus on body shape and weight such as dancing, modeling, acting and athletics. Older females also experience BN, although it is unclear whether this is due to an underlying chronic BN or a spontaneous onset. The condition is viewed as unusual amongst males with figures ranging from one-tenth of the female rate (DSM-IV-TR; APA, 2000) to 'extremely rare' (Fairburn and Beglia, 1990), although more males are now self-referring.

Continuum of severity

Bulimia nervosa is a serious condition, viewed as lifelong. It can be in remission but recur during stressful life events, or remain as a chronic and persistent condition. Self-harm is often an accompanying behaviour and suicide is a risk factor, particularly with repeated failure of treatments or recurrent depression. Mortality rates are higher amongst individuals with eating disorders than with any other mental health condition (Birmingham et al., 2000). Outcomes vary, with more positive results tending to occur during early onset phases. The level of comorbidity worsens as BN continues to a severe and enduring condition (Berkman et al., 2007; Thomas, 2000), and less than half of all individuals with an enduring condition show any lasting signs of recovery (Wilson and Fairburn, 2007). It is treated through developing self-management and coping mechanisms, whilst maintenance therapy is helpful for individuals with severe and enduring BN. Comorbid conditions add to the complexity of self-management, particularly for clients with accompanying disorders such as chronic anxiety or depression.

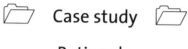

Case study

Rationale

This case study follows the care of Jane, a 24-year-old woman with a seven-year history of bulimia nervosa, complicated by comorbidity and a range of complex conditions. In line with NICE recommendations (2004) the care Jane receives is CBT and the venue for this is the outpatient department of the local mental health hospital, where she is seen by a psychological therapist. As care takes place within the specialist mental health services, and the CBT interventions are aimed at core level the case study is an example of treatment at step 4 of the Stepped Care model.

Client

Jane has had BN since the age of 17. She is well known to the mental health services, having been referred to a range of these in the past. Jane's referral, as usual, came from her GP who stated that Jane was bingeing daily, was inducing vomiting digitally and was taking laxatives to ensure her system was 'totally cleared'. She had been complaining of a lack of energy, tiredness and low mood and that she was uninterested in her daily life. Jane had reported trouble sleeping and that she was weeping frequently for no apparent reason.

Jane had admitted to running four miles a day and spending an additional hour on her exercise bike. At weekends she was drinking alcohol to excess and usually had a hangover lasting 'for days'. She reported thinking about food constantly, which she finds distressing, and that she is preoccupied with her body shape and weight.

Jane is in a stable relationship although she lives by herself due to finding her boyfriend too 'messy'. He is aware that Jane has BN.

Assessment sessions 1–5

As Jane was known to the mental health services it was not necessary to repeat a full historical assessment; instead this information was contained in her case notes which were reviewed at the assessment. Had Jane been new to the services, however, the assessment would have covered pertinent information such as when she first became bulimic, any known triggers, early-life events, significant illnesses, familial links and support, school career, significant events or friendships, traumas, and past diagnosis, treatments and outcomes,

A problem-based assessment was carried out to gain information regarding Jane's main immediate problems. This included asking about her general physical health, her mood state and gradually more detailed questions regarding her eating, bingeing and purging patterns. Jane was also asked specifically if she could identify any particular triggers for the current recurrence of her bulimic symptoms and how she viewed her body, weight and her perception of others towards her. This involved questions regarding her current maintenance strategies for managing her symptoms, including her mood states, motivation, self-harming behaviours, compensatory activities and substance use. The assessment interview then continued to her immediate relationships with others, her leisure activities and her mood states over the past weeks.

Jane has a history of sexual abuse carried out by a male family friend. This began when she was seven and stopped when she was 12. The relationship was manipulative with the abuser 'spoiling' Jane, treating her as the favourite amongst her siblings. Jane has grown up believing she was an accomplice to the relationship due to her role in keeping this as 'their secret' and this consumes her with guilt and anger. At 12 Jane exhibited signs of aggression and withdrawal and the abusive relationship abruptly ended when the family friend moved away.

Jane continued to deteriorate and at 14 she informed her mother of the abuse. There then followed a period of family tension and fractures, with accusations and counter-denials, and it was when Jane became progressively more depressed that her mother spoke to social services. Jane subsequently began to skip school and after claims that she was bullied she was moved to another school. Although Jane was viewed as bright she left school with no qualifications. At 16 her parents began divorce proceedings and for a while Jane lived with her grandparents away from her sisters and brothers. She was first diagnosed with bulimia nervosa and comorbid depression at age 17. Jane remembers constantly feeling let down by adults. She lost confidence, became withdrawn and was more obsessive about her diet and exercise.

At present Jane has very little contact with her family. The abuser has never been found or prosecuted.

At 22 Jane met her current partner which is a supportive relationship for her. She is currently unemployed, largely due to her regular bouts of depression

- Eating Attitude Test-26 (Garner et al., 1982), contains 26 questions related to eating disorder symptoms. Replies are across a spectrum of: always (scores 3); usually (2); often (1); sometimes (0); rarely (0); and never (0). The cut-off for an eating disorder is 20. Jane scored 33 due to her current bulimic symptoms, which is regarded as high.

- Eating Disorder Examination (Fairburn and Beglia, 1990), a semi-structured interview schedule profiling the elements of bulimia, restraint, eating concern, shape concern and weight concern. Scores can be compiled as high, moderate or low. Jane scored significantly high in all categories except restraint where she reported a lack of control once bingeing starts; and a preoccupation about food and weight to an obsessive degree.

- Beck Depression Inventory II (Beck et al., 1996), a 63-item questionnaire regarding mood. Jane scored 24, indicating moderate depression.

- Anxious Thought Inventory (AnTI) (Wells, 1997), a 22-item anxiety questionnaire across a spectrum of: almost never (1); sometimes (2); often (3); and almost always (4). It provides a measure of social, health and meta-anxiety (worry). Jane scored significantly for both social and meta-anxiety but not for health anxiety.

- Dysfunctional Thought Record-OCD (Wells, 1997), which notes triggers for intrusive thoughts, feelings and behaviours: the emotional intensity (scored 0 to 100); and the anxiety about the intrusion, the response to the anxiety and the emotional intensity of the outcome (scored 0 to 100). Jane recorded frequent distressing thoughts about food and the compulsion to binge (intensity of 95) culminating in a binge/purge episode which gained an outcome score of 70 signalling emotional relief. However, this relief was short-lived and intrusive thoughts would soon return causing a response of either more bingeing or exercising.

- Jane was also asked to complete a food diary and bingeing log in order to compile information regarding possible triggers, frequency and duration of bingeing and purging patterns. Alongside the log were an exercise diary and a sleep diary. This information was collated (see Figure 11.2) using the diagnostic criteria of the DSM-IV-TR (APA, 2000) and the ICD-10 (WHO, 2007).

FIGURE 11.1 Initial assessments undertaken by Jane

which serve to increase her bingeing behaviour. She has difficulty 'connecting' to other people, being wary and mistrustful of their motives. She consequently has a restricted social circle and her current episode of bingeing was precipitated by attempts to widen her social circle following encouragement from her partner.

Jane is currently supported by the Community Mental Health Team but over the last seven years she has had four inpatient episodes and a number of attempts at CBT.

To complement the information derived from both the case notes and the clinical interview Jane was asked to participate in a number of assessment tools, some in between sessions, and the results are shown in Figure 11.1.

Following a thorough assessment it became clear that Jane was currently experiencing symptoms of severe and chronic bulimia nervosa with comorbid depression, OCD symptoms and moderate anxiety. This was fully discussed with Jane before her agreement was sought to conceptualise this information in a case formulation.

Jane binges daily by eating a large meal followed in the same period by crisps, ice-cream, porridge, chocolate, cake, biscuits and cola drink of up to one litre. This is usually in the evening but may also occur at lunchtime and evening. The binge can last from 15 minutes to nearly one hour and once she starts to eat Jane states that she has no control over her abilities to stop and ceases only when she feels uncomfortably full and bloated.

Jane induces vomiting digitally and over-uses laxatives after vomiting. She runs daily and cycles for one hour every night; when particularly stressful she will cycle for up to three hours or go for a late-night run. Jane has been bingeing and over-exercising in this way for many years in an attempt to prevent gaining weight.

Jane bases her self-worth on how much she weighs or how she presents to others. Although she has a BMI of 24 she is convinced that she is obese and that certain areas of her body are 'ugly'. Her stomach and thighs are believed to be 'wobbly' and she wears jeans, leggings and loose tops to cover these areas. She is constantly preoccupied by thoughts of getting fat and frequently engages in crash diets and 'de-toxifying' programmes. Jane experiences severe anxiety at the thought of getting fat. She feels overwhelmed by the constant thinking about food which causes her to feel helpless and tearful.

Jane has no history of anorexia nervosa and in assessment discussions states that she has no desire to be 'that thin', although she has thought about wanting to lose weight to be below BMI of 17.

Jane meets the criteria for purging type as she engages in the misuse of laxatives and induces vomiting every day.

FIGURE 11.2   Collation of Jane's diary

Case formulation

Although Jane had previously experienced CBT and was knowledgeable about interventions for BN she was still provided with information about conceptual models illustrating links between thoughts, feelings and behaviour and was given self-help handouts. She responded by stating she knew about the therapeutic milieu, her condition and that her self-management techniques were currently not working. Jane explained that she would like to reduce her negative thoughts about herself and the resultant anxiety.

It was felt that a problem-based case formulation (Cooper et al., 2009) should be utilised which identified links and patterns between obsessive intrusive thoughts, anxiety levels and bingeing triggers. This was presented in diagrammatical form demonstrating one incident from Jane's food diary (Figure 11.3). Jane participated in the formulation process, identifying where she thought links might occur.

Jane's food diary (Figure 11.2) indicated a pattern of negative responses in social situations as well as confirming the criteria for purging sub-type bulimia nervosa. It was not difficult for Jane to understand that the trigger for her alcohol over-indulgence was fear that she would make a poor first impression. Another trigger was the fear that she might let her best friend down. Jane therefore had good insight into the NATs triggering her embarrassment but

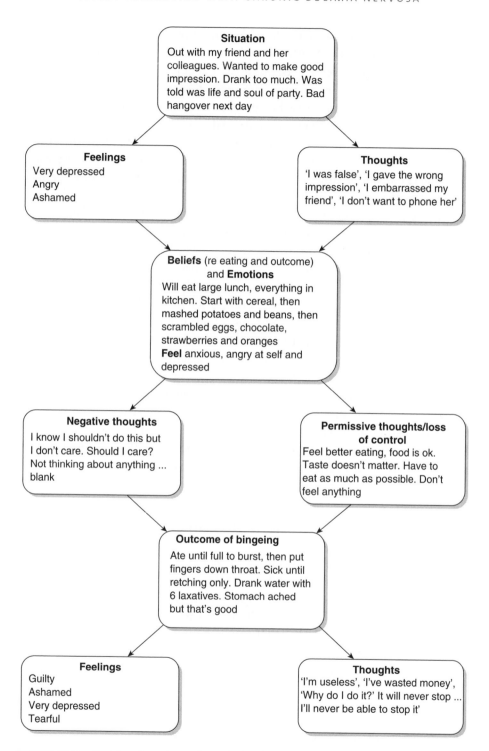

FIGURE 11.3   Problem-based case formulation (Cooper et al., 2009)

did not have good self-awareness to understand how she could have prevented the behaviour originally. Neither could she see that the 'life and soul' image might have some positive aspects. In this area of core beliefs she lacked insight.

Jane had worked on her negative automatic thoughts and her dysfunctional underlying assumptions in past therapies but now wished to explore her core beliefs and whether these were the potential source of her assumptions.

Core beliefs are difficult to work with and uncomfortable in therapy, as attempts to deal with them lead to temporary exacerbation of symptoms. Working at core levels, however, can be helpful to the client as the work in therapy reinforces positive beliefs by reinterpretation, alterations in dysfunctional underlying assumptions and elimination of NATs (Kinsella and Garland, 2008).

Jane could see that her dysfunctional assumptions suggested that whatever she did was going to go wrong anyway and her NATs led to over-presenting herself as a character she was not. She was cautious around other people and could not immediately warm to a group in a social setting and Jane stated that this was due to her experience of abuse earlier in life. The session explored memories of the abusive relationship and how it could have left feelings of mistrust. Jane recounted how this early life event was followed by her family's inability to cope with the abuse, and her experience of social care interventions which increased her negative beliefs about other people.

Jane began to question whether her sense of guilt about the abuse, the family breakdown and insensitive interventions by statutory services could have led to the formation of current views held about herself and others. It was agreed that treatment would commence with exploration at core level of her negative self-beliefs and their impact on her assumptions about herself and others.

Treatment sessions 1–7

There are different views with regard to schematic interventions. Duker and Slade (1988) and Freeman and Dattilio (1992) argue that there should be a restructuring of the self based on discarding old dysfunctional beliefs and adopting new positive beliefs. Duker and Slade refer to the effects of harmful schematic beliefs as 'fragmenting the self' because the individual tries without success to adapt different aspects of their personalities to any given situation. The overwhelming anxieties and depression lead to assumptions that in the end it does not matter anyway as any strategy inevitably fails. Freeman and Dattilio discuss discarding old schemas and rebuilding new ways of thinking and believing. Both approaches are considered by other therapists as long-term interventions.

Cooper, Todd and Wells (2009) and Kinsella and Garland (2008), however, prefer reinterpretation, where existing beliefs are viewed as positive or the individual learns new coping skills to contain the destructive elements of such beliefs (Robinson, 2009). Jane decided that she would try to manage existing schemas in a more positive manner so the reinterpretation approach was adopted.

The first stage of reinterpretation is developing a coping strategy to deal with the expected worsening of Jane's symptoms as she implements new ways of tackling her belief structures. A psycho-educational approach explained the phenomenon of symptomatic deterioration and stressed its temporary effects. It also involved explaining to Jane how her thought processes worked, and using the cognitive triad she was able to see how her relation between herself, others and the world was influenced by her early life experiences. Jane agreed to monitor her progress by keeping a diary of her anxiety levels and mood states and recording all bulimic/bingeing episodes (noting triggers, behaviours and effects on mood and thinking). She also agreed to increase her medication as a short-term measure and to use the telephone support services offered by the Community Mental Health Team. Raising her awareness of symptom deterioration also helped to reinforce positive beliefs that change was occurring.

To begin work on her core beliefs Jane was asked to choose an incident from her diary and she chose the same one that was used in the case formulation, which had evidently impacted on her. This was explored using Socratic dialogue (Padesky, 1993), the aim being to identify the meaning behind the incident and hence identify any underlying beliefs:

Jane (J):   I get very drunk quite quickly and really embarrassed myself. Talked too much, laughed too loudly … I cringe when I think about it.

Therapist (T):   What does being drunk mean to you? After all, people get drunk at parties, celebrations, weekends and so on.

J: Being drunk is horrible, you see people stumbling about late at night, people shouting and being gross. It's not a good place to be and I say such rubbish when I'm drunk … exaggerate what I do or what I think … people see the wrong side of me.

T: So what would be so bad about that Jane? You can correct wrong impressions can't you? Maybe people are more tolerant than you think?

J: It's not that simple. When I'm drunk … when I'm nervous, I drink too much and people think I'm a bit of an idiot anyway, with being bulimic and so on.

T: So how do you think people see you normally?

J: People tend to see me as a bit high maintenance or perhaps a bit shallow. I don't really think about that. I'm all over the place with watching what I eat, bingeing a lot, watching my weight …

T: But if you had to talk about it what do you believe others think about you?

J: Well ... one is I'm definitely not in control of my life, the bulimia controls me and everything I do, people who know me are aware of that. And I guess because I'm like I am people don't like me.

T: So do you think there may be two beliefs here which perhaps support your assumptions that people think you are shallow or being false; you are not in control of your life and that people don't like you?

J: I never thought about it like that ... I can see how it fits so yeah I do think I have no control and that people don't like me ... I can see where these affect what I think even before I meet someone ...

Following the dialogue the information was transferred into the diagrammatic form of the downward arrow technique, partly to reinforce what had just been discovered but also to demonstrate how Jane could utilise this technique herself. This can be seen in Figure 11.4.

In the next session Jane completed a positive belief questionnaire and scored a mean of 2.75 overall, indicating poor positive self-belief. The session concentrated on the two lowest scores which were 1s for 'I can generally control my own life' and 'I am a strong person', the former reinforcing the core belief previously identified.

Of the three core beliefs identified – people don't like me, I am weak, and I am not in control – Jane thought that the last two were of equal importance, rating her belief in each as 80 per cent. It was these that Jane therefore wanted to challenge.

Situation
I got very drunk in front of potential new friends

Negative automatic thoughts
It's bad to be drunk, not socially acceptable and it's also not who I really am
(What does that say about me?)

↓

That I lie and manipulate others; I'm shallow. I might be an alcoholic
(What's so bad about that?)

↓

Well, people won't like me, will they, and also I don't think I'm in control
(What does this say about me?)

↓

Core belief
That I am not in control and that other people don't like me

FIGURE 11.4   Downward arrow

Belief: I am weak

Evidence for	Evidence against
I binge almost every day I have had BN for over seven years I cannot stop eating when I binge I avoid people	I have had BN for seven years without it killing me! I have a boyfriend so maintain a relationship

Belief: I lack control over my life

Evidence for	Evidence against
I cannot fight the compulsion to binge I avoid others because I'm anxious Dieting controls me I can't plan anything	I can attend therapy!

FIGURE 11.5   Evidence for and against core beliefs

Jane was asked to examine her view that living with BN and self-managing for seven years was compatible with loss of control or weakness. She began to see the mental resilience required to live with a debilitating condition and how BN controlled but did not destroy her life. Using hypothetical exercises, therapy continued by exploring the worst that could have happened as a result of the bulimia, which highlighted that Jane had in fact reduced its effects through a certain level of control. Through these exercises Jane began to explore a different view of bulimia as a chronic condition. She started to see the condition as a chronic health condition requiring management similar to arthritis or diabetes. Following this, Jane compiled a list of activities she could do to maintain optimum daily life and tentatively began to question whether bulimia could be controlled by her rather than it control her.

Once she had started to reframe her thinking about her management of her condition Jane was asked to begin recording both the evidence for and against her core beliefs. To start this process an evidence chart was drawn up and populated in the session for each belief and as homework Jane was asked to give thought to any further evidence, particularly against. These charts can be seen in Figure 11.5.

The next session reviewed her bingeing and eating diary and it was apparent that bingeing episodes were becoming more frequent. Jane complained that she was thinking even more about food and the urge to binge was almost constant. Jane therefore had to explore how she could develop a coping strategy to deal with the worsening of her symptoms as she implemented new ways of tackling her belief structures. Therapy revisited earlier information about the temporary worsening of symptoms; however, Jane decided that core work would continue for two more weeks and if symptoms continued then a reformulation and different treatment approach would be adopted.

Belief: I am weak

Evidence for	Evidence against
I binge almost every day I have had BN for over seven years I cannot stop eating when I binge I avoid people	I have had BN for seven years without it killing me! I have a boyfriend so maintain a relationship I have established and kept a good friend I can take care of my daily needs I can shop and cook and manage my own money I have opinions about issues I can cope with the bingeing urges a bit better

Belief: I lack control over my life

Evidence for	Evidence against
I cannot fight the compulsion to binge I avoid others because I'm anxious Dieting controls me I can't plan anything	I can attend therapy! I attend therapy and arrange my day around the appointment I have a diary with tasks to do which I complete on the day I attend appointments with my GP I live by myself through choice I choose when I go to bed, get up, go out and so on I live within my means

FIGURE 11.6   Thought-challenge chart

As therapy progressed Jane continued to collect evidence against her two core beliefs of being weak and having no control in her life, and as this increased her belief level reduced. Jane was now rating her belief that she was weak as 65 per cent and as lacking control at 70 per cent as she still binged and remained anxious. The objective was to keep reinforcing positive evidence for the two core beliefs and challenging negative assumptions until Jane was scoring below 50 per cent; at which point she would begin to consider alternative replacement beliefs. The thought-challenge evidence chart can be seen in Figure 11.6.

In the next session Jane provided her diary notes which indicated that bingeing was lessening and her mood and anxieties were lifting. Jane talked about her growing awareness of bingeing triggers and had started to tell herself that these were feelings she knew and were controllable. It did not stop her feeling anxious but she had started to see how bingeing was her method of reducing such feelings in the short term. Jane's positive belief questionnaire achieved an increased score of 3.75 with a score of 2 each for controlling her own life and being strong, which reinforced the view that change was occurring.

Jane then discussed how her boyfriend and friend view her in social situations compared to how she perceives herself. Hypothetical situations were used to demonstrate these differences. The exercise helped Jane to see how her own behaviours, her own beliefs about bulimia and her interaction with others were part of a pattern arising from her own beliefs, dysfunctional assumptions and NATs. Her rating of both was now 50 per cent and therapy thus started to support Jane to develop alternative thoughts about the same situation in her original case formulation.

Sessions 8–12

As Jane continued to gather evidence for the core beliefs, therapy moved on to look at childhood experiences, at which point she talked about her belief that she was to blame for the abuse. A hypothetical exercise to consider Jane's beliefs around a child being manipulated by an adult helped her to focus on how difficult it was for a child to have a defence against such behaviour, which started the process of challenging this belief. Jane also explored the thinking behind the actions of the adult and began to discuss how the adult could be guilty of harm done whilst the child is innocent due to lack of maturation and socialisation. Jane began to reframe her beliefs about her own guilt and collusion in the abusive relationship she experienced. She broke down several times and needed constant reassurance and sensitivity when returning to and revisiting previous points.

When revisiting her childhood experiences Jane began to question how the effects of her adolescent traumas had impacted on her ability to trust others, and slowly she began to collect evidence which supported new beliefs and reframed old beliefs with more positive meanings. Some core beliefs were also extinguished by exploring her guilt around the abuse and she eventually viewed these feelings as a result of manipulation and not her fault. By reframing feelings in an adult context she began to view bingeing and laxative abuse as containment behaviours rather than self-harming activities to control her anxieties and to 'punish' herself.

Only after she was confident that she had fully explored her original abuse did she revisit the original case formulation and her example of the Friday night out. Jane could now discuss the view that others present that evening could have been anxious about meeting a new person and she could provide some alternative thoughts about this incident, taking evidence from her friend and her own increasing confidence. She stated she could now see that being the 'life and soul' of the gathering might have actually lessened the anxieties of others (see Figure 11.7). Her friend had mentioned what a good night it was and that others thought Jane a 'laugh'. Jane suggested that she might take up her offer to have another evening but would discuss her strategy in the therapeutic sessions beforehand so she could be more herself. In this way Jane began to develop reinforcement strategies for her new beliefs, and therapy explored hypothetical situations which would continue such reinforcements.

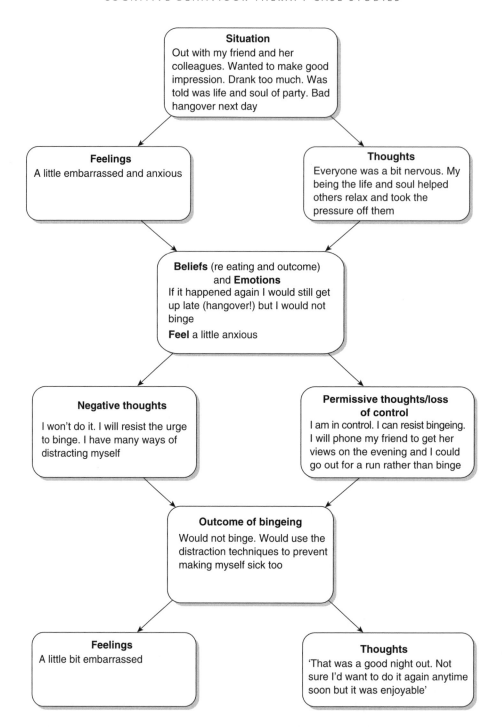

FIGURE 11.7   Review of original case formulation using critical incident

The final three sessions with Jane focused on positive thinking incidents from her diary. Jane had collected episodes where she had demonstrated positivity and these were explored in the context of external validation for core beliefs and underlying assumptions, particularly when they challenged contrary beliefs such as mistrust of others or supported new beliefs about herself.

Treatment evaluation sessions

At the end of therapy Jane's scores on anxiety and mood scales had increased before the final session approached, despite the fact that other scores were lower. Jane stated she was not ready to be independent of therapy and believed she would relapse very quickly without support. This was despite her scores around being weak and not feeling in control coming down to 40 per cent and 35 per cent respectively. Other results showed her goals to increase positive thinking and her relationship with food had also significantly improved, with bingeing down to once a week and use of laxatives much less. On the positive self-evaluation scale she was now achieving a mean score of 6.2 and her compulsion to eat when she felt anxious had become so manageable she was now anxious about weight gain.

The focus therefore centred on how Jane would monitor her own condition and use self-assessment sheets so that she could alert her care co-ordinator if her condition worsened. Therapy discussed future potential triggers such as her upcoming night out with colleagues and how hypothetically Jane would manage the situation beforehand and afterwards, based on the work she had done in previous sessions.

Discharge strategies

Jane was not symptom-free. She was considered to be in remission and the chances of relapse were significant. Her request to join a BN users group was supported with a referral. Jane also attended regular Care Programme Approach (CPA) meetings organised by her care co-ordinator within the Community Mental Health Team to which she invited her partner and which provided another monitoring tool for her progress.

Critique of case study

Jane presented with complex issues involving severe and enduring BN alongside comorbid depression, anxiety and obsessive-compulsive traits. Several assessment tools had to be utilised to prioritise intervention. This appeared to be bingeing episodes brought about by anxiety and overwhelming compulsive urges. Other symptoms such as low mood affected her motivation, particularly during the first few sessions when symptoms worsened, and her anxieties increased as each particular trigger was identified.

Core work is difficult. It requires revisiting of earlier sessions so can appear slower than work with NATs or dysfunctional assumptions. Also the worsening of symptoms has to be managed, whilst treatment still needs to be focused on core beliefs.

As core beliefs are reframed the dysfunctional assumptions are destabilised and the negative automatic thoughts can consequently have no roots. They free float within conscious awareness of the individual until redeployed upon other concerns. This can mimic generalised anxiety disorders and non-specific phobias and runs the risk of increasing negative symptoms. The importance of client involvement to clarify and validate observations cannot be overstated.

Therapy at core level means returning to assessment tools, comparing results pre- and post-sessions, revisiting the case formulation and connecting patterns and events in early childhood to a present context. Supporting the client to manage free-floating dysfunctional assumptions and NATs is difficult and takes time. Twenty to 24 sessions should therefore be considered the norm for this type of therapy (Cooper et al., 2009).

Jane was not an uncommon case study. Reduction in bingeing episodes and stronger levels of management were achieved as a result of the therapy, but it was also accepted that progress continues with the support of others outside the therapeutic sessions. The work done in CBT sessions acts in this case as a base upon which Jane can continue to improve her self-management of a complex, severe and enduring condition through self-help groups locally.

Problems arising in therapy

The main issue in this case study was the worsening of symptoms during the early stages of therapy. These are frequently experienced when working at core level and for many clients the impact on motivation is negative. This can in turn lead to poor non-attendance rates and a perception that therapy does not work. Early awareness and implementation of a management strategy is the most constructive method of dealing with clinical deterioration. However, risk assessment needs to be heightened too as the occurrence of increased self-harming behaviours and suicide attempts also increases. The follow-up of non-attendance is therefore paramount.

The rise in physiological symptoms in severe and enduring eating disorders is common and can destabilise therapy. Symptoms can mask underlying but emerging conditions, so close observation to ensure that presentations are not masking underlying physical illnesses is needed. These physical illnesses can affect attendance rates and the client's responses in therapy, for example opportunistic infections preventing attendance and dental conditions which can affect speech. In Jane's case her partner was supportive but familial sabotage is not unknown as the individual increases in self-confidence and symptom control. Undermining strategies can also occur within relationships, particularly if there is co-dependency or the partner has a vested interest in maintaining the 'caring' role. Changes in self-confidence or body image can lead to more social interaction and opportunities to develop other friendships which can be viewed with concern by family members, particularly if existing relationship dynamics change. The individual in therapy and those closest to them experience the anxieties of change, and resistance and resentment can easily be blamed on the therapy.

Setting goals too high can mean a lack of achievement which can in turn reinforce negative core beliefs. If Jane had already thought that she would fail and then did not reach pre-set goals it would make it more difficult to work with her core beliefs in future. Ambitious goals are therefore counter-productive at core level work. Goals need to be realistic and small at the commencement of therapy because of the increase in negative presenting symptoms which sap energy and the increased low mood which saps motivation. Attainment is important as it reinforces change and commences a process of reframing existing core beliefs, or introducing new beliefs, and for this reason goals are better met sooner rather than later.

Think about …

1. A resurgence of negative symptoms is not uncommon when working at core level. How would you support a client to self-manage during this aspect of therapy?
2. What would influence your decision regarding prioritising problems when working with a client with a complex condition?
3. Severe and enduring bulimia nervosa is often entrenched in personality traits. What would be your therapeutic goal when working on the symptoms of bulimia itself and when would you decide that a referral to support and self-help groups would be appropriate?
4. Does maintenance therapy play a useful role in managing conditions or does it encourage a dependency relationship with CBT therapy? What is the rationale for your answer?

Suggested activity:

- Observe the social interaction between your peers and friends over one week and see if you can identify the role eating and food plays in their communication. For instance do they meet at mealtimes, breaks, go out to eat at weekends? Think about what impact such social activity would have on someone who was shy or withdrawn; do food and eating habits help or hinder socialisation?

12
Client Presenting with Anorexia Nervosa

Mike Thomas

Learning objectives

By the end of this chapter you should be able to:

Identify the symptoms of anorexia nervosa
Describe the cognitive perspective for anorexia nervosa
Discuss a cognitive formulation which addresses dysfunctional underlying assumptions
Outline a cognitive and behavioural treatment programme which takes account of the physical and psychological aspects of anorexia nervosa
Recognise the treatment length for severe and enduring anorexia nervosa

Diagnostic criteria

Anorexia nervosa (AN) can best be described as a syndrome condition wherein a number of symptoms occur together causing particular and observable outcomes. The DSM–IV–TR (APA, 2000) 307.1, diagnostic criteria states that the person experiencing anorexia nervosa refuses to maintain body weight, their weight is less than 85 per cent of that expected for their age and height and yet the person holds an intense fear of weight gain despite being very underweight. There is usually a marked disturbance in self-image which is predominantly influenced by weight and shape and denial that low weight is a serious condition.

- Retarded growth and delayed maturation in the young (appearance is younger than chronological age)
- Intolerance of cold
- Abdominal discomfort
- Bloating
- Slow heart rate (bradycardia)
- Hypotension
- Dental enamel erosion
- Cardiac arrhythmia
- Fine body hair (lanugo)
- Reduced bone density
- Reduced white blood corpuscles (leucopoenia)
- Oedema of the lower limbs

FIGURE 12.1   Physical symptoms of AN

Amenorrhea (loss of menstruation consecutively for three months or more) is common amongst females old enough to menstruate and there are a number of serious physical conditions associated with anorexia nervosa.

The DSM-IV-TR classifies anorexia nervosa into two specific types: restricting and binge-eating/purging. With the former the individual engages in reduced intake of food and nutrients but does not engage regularly in binge-eating or purging behaviours, whilst with the latter the individual engages in a restrictive intake and binge eats and/or purges using self-induced vomiting, laxatives, diuretics or enemas. As over-exercising is a common feature it should also be considered a form of purging behaviour.

Alongside low weight, physical presentations often include some, or all, of the symptoms found in Figure 12.1. Differential diagnosis of anorexia nervosa should always include the possibility of physical and psychological causes of weight loss.

Predisposing and precipitating factors

There is some evidence that early childhood experiences may alter the brain function. McGowan and colleagues (2009) report that early childhood abuse alters hypothalamic-pituitary-adrenal stress responses, whilst other studies have found a link with early life viral infections (Parkes et al., 1995; Sokol, 2000). There is also the suggestion that individuals with anorexia nervosa have lowered serum activity (Maes et al., 2001).

Twin and family studies suggest a possible genetic bias but these are balanced by other studies which indicate that family dynamics may play a part. The view that controlling parents and dieting mothers influence the daughters' adoption of an eating disorder remains prevalent, although many feminists have highlighted the gender imbalance in such an approach (Gremillion, 2004; Moulding, 2009; Ryan et al., 2006).

Green (2009) suggests that up to 50 per cent of young people with AN have a history of sexual abuse, compared to up to 30 per cent of the general population and that they may engage in anorectic behaviours to forestall pubescence and emerging adult sexuality. This is a view supported by Zimmerman (2008), who suggests that the intense fear of gaining weight and body image disturbances may be due to fear of the person's own emerging sexuality.

Because the aetiology of anorexia nervosa remains unclear the dominant view is one where the condition arises due to interaction between genetics, family dynamics, culture, trauma and personality factors.

The cognitive approach views the maintenance of AN as occurring through interaction between learning, experience and the development of fixed patterns of behaviour. Personality factors do appear to have some general presentations which include resistance to acknowledging AN as a problem, conformity to authority, social introversion, emotional narrowness and inflexible thinking, although it is unclear whether this is cause and effect or alternatively the effects of AN on the personality. Cognitive behavioural therapy focuses on reframing patterns of thoughts and behaviours which maintain the condition. AN is perceived as a condition which provides the individual with a means to avoid unpleasant or distressing life events, and the idea of surrendering such maintenance is itself highly anxiety provoking. Cognitive intervention involves helping the individual to identify problems and the coping strategies that they would prefer to adopt to tackle the problem. Evaluating progress and achieving goals attempts to reframe dysfunctional cognitive processes to break the maintenance cycle.

Demographic incidence

Whilst AN can be found amongst the younger and older generations, it is predominantly an adolescent condition with most people presenting between the ages of 14 to 18. However, this is the age when individuals present with marked symptoms so the condition may have been hidden for some time beforehand and may therefore have an earlier onset than medical epidemiology suggests.

In industrialised societies AN is considered to affect approximately 1 per cent of women, with a much lower incidence in men. In fact it is estimated that only 10 per cent of all diagnoses of AN are male (Walsh and Cameron, 2005) but the figure for both is rising worldwide and the full figure is unknown. The difficulty is that not only do many people not come forward with the condition but it is also often misdiagnosed, predominantly as a symptom of another mental health condition or simply as disordered eating behaviour.

There is general agreement that anorexia nervosa is more prevalent in industrial countries where there is an abundance of food and the social perception of attractiveness (especially for women) is to be thin. Cultural norms also appear to play a part in at least sustaining anorexia nervosa, with a combination of the media, the beauty industry, clothes designers and health and fitness interests having a strong influence on individuals' self-perception. Group norms around food, weight, shape and social behaviour also impact.

Continuum of severity

Without intervention death will occur, and unfortunately does in around 15–20 per cent of those with a long-term condition (Green, 2009). Anorexia nervosa therefore remains the mental health condition with the highest level of mortality. With early onset and intervention a return to normal weight is the goal, but the condition itself can be chronic, severe and enduring. Robinson (2009) points out that individuals may have the condition for 8, 10 or even 20 years before recovering but the condition may also be lifelong. Such chronicity supports the development of complex psychological and physical presentations, and prolonged specialist mental health and other agency support is often required, including admissions to prevent death.

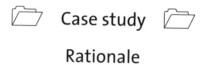

Case study

Rationale

The following case study demonstrates the care of Alison who has severe and enduring anorexia nervosa. Severe and enduring eating disorders are embedded in the core beliefs about the self and support dysfunctional underlying assumptions and negative automatic thoughts. Due to the complexity of the condition intervention takes place within a specialist eating disorder unit at step 4 of the Stepped Care model, and in line with NICE guidelines (2004) involves CBT at both intermediate and schema level within an integrated care team approach.

Client

Alison is aged 39 with a history of restricted eating since age 16 and a diagnosis of anorexia nervosa since age 19. She has a Body Mass Index (BMI) of 15 and is a client within the specialist inpatient eating disorder unit (EDU) of her local mental health trust. Alison is known to the team, having had several admissions. She is monitored closely with regular laboratory investigations as there have been three admissions to the local critical care unit within the last two years due to potassium levels being below 3mmol/l. She has been in the EDU for three weeks, having been transferred from the intensive care unit and has now been referred to the psychotherapy team for CBT intervention. She has a diagnosis of anorexia nervosa purging sub-type.

The information provided by the intensive care unit revealed that Alison's physical and mental condition had been so poor that her GP, contacted by her boyfriend, had immediately admitted her to the coronary care unit until her potassium had stabilised. Alison could not recall her admission to hospital and because her memory and concentration had been so poor she was transferred to the EDU for additional support. Alison stated that being in the EDU was helping her towards recovery and she understood the need to be an inpatient again.

Alison lives with her boyfriend who knows about her anorectic condition and who supports her, though he reports concern over her frequent illnesses. Alison dismisses his concerns as overly worrying. Physically Alison is 155cm tall (just over 5 foot 1 inch) and has a tendency to wear jogging clothes with a body warmer over her hooded top. Her lips and fingernails are bluish in colour and her skin pallid and pale. As she speaks she wipes frequent bubbles of frothy spittle from the corners of her lips and her hair is flat and brittle against her scalp. It is frequently observed on the EDU that Alison refuses any offers of refreshments and that she speaks slowly and quietly, avoiding eye contact in favour of looking at the floor. This was how she presented during the assessment.

Assessment sessions 1–2 (week 3 of stay)

Stage 1 – formulation development

Because of the complex nature of this condition it may be of more benefit if the assessment is viewed as a process. Assessment needs to take account of its primary function which is to elicit data to help identify diagnosis, develop formulation and guide treatment interventions, but in AN there is also the added complexity of comorbid and related conditions and the dominance of other symptomologies which can impact on the treatment. Furthermore, a number of different assessment tools (for example laboratory results) will elicit data over a number of sessions, which may reveal other aspects impacting on formulation or re-prioritising objectives. Nevertheless the assessment stage takes into account the two common CBT methods, interviews and measuring tools.

The assessment interview took into account Alison's past clinical and psychotherapeutic case notes, which revealed that Alison was raised by her mother and father (now a retired director of clinical services and a senior police officer respectively). There is no known history of early childhood trauma or illness and the family unit appears to have been close. Alison was considered very bright in school and was expected by staff and family to go to university. She was slightly overweight as an adolescent but was not unduly concerned until she dated a boy for several months. This relationship ended abruptly when she was 15. Alison's case notes record that this was due to his attempts to instigate a sexual relationship, which she resisted, which was followed by the boy spreading rumours that he had finished with her because he was repulsed by her body fat. Alison was shocked and became acutely sensitive to how others might view her. Over the next year she became withdrawn and began to restrict her food intake and she adopted an excessive exercise routine and laxative use, believing she was less anxious when her weight kept falling. At age 16 she was taken to her GP who referred her to a dietician to adopt a healthier eating pattern. Over time, however, this did not work and Alison was referred to the mental health services, her first admission to hospital being at the age of 19.

Over subsequent years Alison has had several periods of remission interspersed with interventions which included psychotherapy and nutritional (dietician) support. She has a history of several inpatient stays, both in mental health and acute physical care for low BMI, low potassium, low phosphate levels, deteriorating bone structure and low urea levels.

Alison lived with her parents until the age of 33 when she moved into an apartment on her own. This ended when she was found collapsed by a neighbour, following which she decided that it was too hazardous for her to live alone and she moved in with her present partner. That was six years ago.

Following the clinical assessment a number of self-report measures were administered to attain more specific information about the impact of the anorexia nervosa. These included the following:

- The Eating Attitude Test-26 (Garner et al., 1982) which is a widely used measure of symptoms and characteristics of eating disorders. At a score of 37.1 Alison was higher than the cut-off point of 20 and demonstrated significant scores in the dieting subscale and preoccupation with weight.
- The Eating Disorder Belief Questionnaire (Cooper et al., 2009) which has 32 questions and rates, on a scale from 0 to 100, the level of beliefs in four subscales: negative self-beliefs, acceptance by others, self-acceptance and control over eating. Each subscale score is totalled and divided by the number of questions in each and although utilised by its developers for bulimia nervosa it was nevertheless useful to gain some information regarding Alison's approach to beliefs about herself and her weight. Alison achieved the following scores:

- o Negative self-beliefs 530 divided by 10 = 53
- o Acceptance by others 340 divided by 10 = 34
- o Self-acceptance 495 divided by 6 = 82.5
- o Control over eating 354 divided by 6 = 59.1

- The results suggested that Alison had an average score for negative self-beliefs with a strong view that she was able to manage her anorectic condition by herself. She did not feel that she was unacceptable to others and in fact prided herself on befriending and supporting the younger residents in the unit. She felt that she had little control over her eating whilst in the unit, as this was controlled by others, but would normally have scored higher in this category if she was at home.
- An Eating Disorder Examination (Cooper and Fairburn, 1987) which uses four subscales related to eating disorder symptomologies: restraint, eating concern, shape concern and weight concern. This was used to gain a measure of severity. Globally Alison scored 53 divided by 12 = 4.41 (3 in this instance used as the median line), indicating severe restricting of intake during the past month. The score would, however, have been higher had the measurement been taken prior to her admission.

Other assessment tools such as a food diary, weight and physiological tests were not used and neither was Alison's BMI, as these were monitored by the dietician and ward staff and were disseminated during the weekly case conference meeting, which included Alison.

Case formulation

Due to Alison's long anorectic condition the case formulation took a maintenance approach to treatment. From a cognitive perspective this approach had a number of advantages. Cooper and Shafran (2008) suggest that the negative impact on continuing failure to achieve control and weight/shape goals impact on self-evaluation and create a cycle which maintains the eating disorder. Low self-esteem is therefore a difficult and entrenched area to overcome in treatment as it reinforces a sense of hopelessness when therapy is viewed as failing. For this intervention Cooper and Shafran's (2008) transdiagnostic cognitive behavioural formulation for the maintenance of eating disorders was utilised (Figure 12.2).

Despite stating that she recognised that being in the EDU was helpful, the assessment results and case formulation completed with Alison indicated that she resented and resisted the idea of being in the unit. She now revealed that she felt that staff either did not understand her or gave the wrong advice. She felt that as she physically improved her sense of self was being lost and that weight gain made her feel 'fat' and 'ugly'. She was getting increasingly angry about her loss of control which impacted on her core self-esteem and how she would normally manage her low weight. Alison expressed surprise and disappointment

	Dysfunctional scheme	for self-evaluation
	Over-evaluation of control over eating, shape or weight	**Over-evaluation of achieving 'perfectionism'**
	I think that being thin is good for me and hate the idea of weight gain *I dislike the fact that others presently control my eating* *I am anxious*	*I present a good but false presentation that I do not set high goals* *I hide this from others* *(see below)*
	Core low	**self-esteem**
L **I** **F** **E**	**Strict dieting/weight-control behaviour**	**Achieving in other domains**
	I maintain a strict restricted diet *I believe I am ugly if not thin* *I believe I know my best weight* *I'm struggling to understand how my body is letting me down* *I resist the idea of others controlling my weight*	*I want to be liked. Hate idea that others think poorly of me* *I think staff in the unit do not understand me* *I can be dominant with partner and family and will always push my own views*
	Binge-eating *I do not eat enough and never binge*	**Low weight** *I take pride in maintaining low weight and resist help from others* *I get easily depressed and have difficulty concentrating*
	Mood	**Intolerance**
	Compensatory vomiting/laxative use *Overuse of laxatives*	**'Starvation' syndrome** *Easily irritated and angry* *Fatigued emotionally* *Hiding feelings from others*

FIGURE 12.2 Cooper and Shafran's transdiagnostic formulation. From Cooper, Z. and Shafran, R. (2008) Cognitive behaviour therapy for eating disorders. *Behavioural and Cognitive Psychotherapy* 36: 713–722 © British Association of Behavioural and Cognitive Psychotherapies, published by Cambridge University Press, reproduced with permission.

that her body was not coping well with a low BMI but believed that the recurrent low potassium was a problem she could 'survive'. The case formulation also demonstrated that she would not openly challenge staff in case they thought badly of her. Alison had insight into the fact that her own strong drive for a low weight and restricted diet distressed others so her goal was to be discharged so she could self-manage, which had been a successful strategy in the past.

A decision was made to have intensive sessions of two a week as she was expected to stay in the unit for 12 weeks and had already been in for four. These sessions would focus on the links between controlling her weight and food intake, her mood states and her low self-esteem.

Treatment sessions

A severe and enduring eating disorder requires longer periods of treatment. This would usually adopt an approach along a continuum, from initial self-esteem work to locus of control (decision-making), before working on eating patterns and self-management. Thomas's five-stage approach (Thomas, 2000) has been found to be particularly useful, but this takes a multi-method approach, with CBT techniques being utilised alongside other interventions, whereas this case study, though taking a similar approach, uses CBT methods only. The approach it follows is Cooper and Shafran's (2008). They identify three aspects in therapy requiring extra therapeutic vigilance and support, these being: motivational enhancement; weight gain to get out of 'starvation' state; and the involvement of significant others in treatment. Alison identified her boyfriend.

Cooper and Shafran's treatment approach incorporates 20 sessions in four stages moving from two sessions per week to fortnightly sessions over a period of four months. In this case this was not realistic as Alison was in the unit for only 12 weeks, and a decision was made to have all sessions twice weekly. The stages include formulation development, psycho-educational approaches and introducing regular eating and weight gain in stage one. The next is a transitional phase comprising joint review of progress, identifying barriers to change, modifying the formulation and planning stage three. This stage concentrates on reframing barriers which prevent change and addressing the key elements that maintain the disorder. The final stage evaluates treatment progress and prepares plans to prevent future relapses.

In the weekly care programme conference it was decided that stage one of the approaches had been completed. Alison had been in the unit for nearly four weeks and the monitoring of Alison's eating and weight had been carried out by the nursing staff, whilst a pattern of regular eating had been implemented with the unit dietician. As an assessment had already been carried out and a case formulation developed with Alison, it was decided that therapy would move into stage 2 for two sessions. The first session would focus on her relationship with significant others to identify barriers to change.

Sessions 1–2 (week 4)

Stage 2 – identifying barriers to change

These sessions centred on a situational mood diary which identified incidents where Alison had felt anxious or low in mood following interactions with others. The three main barriers identified within Alison's diary are presented in Figure 12.3.

The sessions focused on each of the above in turn with individual incidents being linked back to the case formulation. Alison was asked if she would

1. Admission to the Coronary Care Unit for potassium uplift made me angry for two reasons (scoring 95 out of 100); that my body was letting me down and that I felt the attitude of the staff on the CCU was judgemental once they discovered I had a history of anorexia. Although I did not care if I lived or died their attitudes made me feel ashamed to be there and I complied with all that they asked so I could be discharged quickly.

2. Nursing staff on the EDU make me feel very anxious (80 out of 100) all the time as I feel they are watching my behaviour closely and particularly during mealtimes I feel that I am treated like a young girl. I am escorted at all times and have to spend an hour 'sitting around' after each meal. The diet planned with the dietician depresses me (90 out of 100) as I loathe the content, taste and texture of what I am eating. I feel bloated and fat all the time and cry in the night at the thought of my body storing fat. I am constipated and miss my laxatives. I hate being weighed and feel trapped every time I am asked to get on the scales. I don't believe in the care strategy adopted and feel I am going through the motions to please the consultant, dietician and nursing staff. I feel drained by this pretence but at the same time don't want to upset the staff as they appear to care a lot and obviously want me to improve.

3. Feel that Anthony is the only person who understands me. He is supportive of my early discharge and has implied that I don't look good in the Unit and would be better off at home. I believe he will continue to support my wish to be discharged. Felt anxious when he left the Unit (60 out of 100).

FIGURE 12.3 Situational mood diary

like to talk about the impact of the staff attitudes on her sense of shame and low mood but she replied that it no longer mattered and was not worth going over. However, the case formulation indicated that this might be related to the judgements given by others in her early teenage experience. Then she had responded by isolating herself, which seemed not too dissimilar to the response taken by her in the Critical Care Unit. This appeared to be an important potential barrier to change for Alison and therapy explored the relationship between core beliefs, dysfunctional assumptions and negative automatic thoughts. Alison agreed that this could be an area to explore further in stage 3 of therapy.

Time was also taken to explore how her own beliefs about the potential responses that would be made by the unit staff if she spoke her mind, was closely related to her feelings of self-esteem and competence. Alison believed that she knew more about anorexia nervosa than the unit staff and this was reinforced by other residents to whom she often gave advice. Alison was giving similar advice as the staff but felt that she reinforced their information in a more powerful way by giving herself as an example. She felt compromised when other residents observed her complying with staff requests and she coped with her feelings by informing them, in strict confidence, that she was only complying to get an early discharge.

Socratic dialogue therapy very gently explored these areas. This included whether she felt her own behaviour undermined the work of the staff, or whether her adoption of a position as a 'senior' resident sent out a confusing message to others by 'only going through the motions'. Alison believed that if staff knew how she really thought they would think badly of her. Links back to the case formulation suggested that this area may be related to Alison's view of her self-esteem, of needing to be liked, of personal achievement in maintaining her anorectic lifestyle and of her consequent sense of failure because she required the input of others.

Despite Alison's diary indicating that her relationship with her boyfriend appeared to be maintaining her anorectic status, Alison did not want to discuss her relationship with Anthony, believing he did not feature as a barrier to change.

For stage 3 Alison identified her attitude and feelings during her current residency as the highest priority and it was therefore agreed that this would be addressed first.

Sessions 3–15 (weeks 5–10)

Stage 3 – reframing barriers to change

The next 12 sessions occurred over six weeks and were intensive one-hour Monday and Thursday appointments with time outside spent on self-completing exercises.

The first session focused on hypothetical exercises assessing the impact of different scenarios if she disclosed to various staff her thoughts about the care programme. Eventually it was agreed that with support of her care co-ordinator Alison would raise her opinions in the weekly care programme planning meeting. Subsequent sessions consisted of rehearsing Alison's approach to the meeting, following which she expressed surprise that the staff had been enthusiastic and positive regarding her views.

Despite this apparent improvement in the care programme Alison still felt anxious and resented their 'interference' in her self-management. The strength of her feelings was confusing her. Whilst her depression score went from 90 to 80 her anxiety went from 80 to 90, a reverse of the scores in stage 2. This indicated that despite a decrease in depression her anxiety had in fact increased, which Alison agreed might be due to her beginning to relinquish control of her anorexia to the staff. The subsequent sessions therefore focused on her core beliefs regarding her own management of anorexia nervosa and how these were incorporated into her sense of self. For example, Alison frequently measured her life against her weight and shape and lived an anorectic life rather than a life without anorexia.

Situation	Negative Automatic Thoughts *(Thought to be challenged)*	Evidence for thought	Evidence against thought
Dietician goes through menu	She'll make me fat *She's trying to control me*		She gave me the choice of which foods to include. She said it's my decision whether I follow it or not
Staff weighing me	They don't trust me *They'd like me to be fat*	They praise me when I put on weight	My target is BMI 16, less than they would like The staff treat fat people – so they see that as a health risk too

FIGURE 12.4 Negative automatic thought diary

Over the sessions her anxieties increased, as did her low mood and she began to refuse to eat the food agreed with her dietician. Further sessions revealed a core belief of Alison's which was that to overcome anorexia meant that the disorder had beaten her, whilst, paradoxically, maintaining anorexia meant that she had beaten it. Therapy revisited the case formulation and explored the pattern between her core beliefs around anorexia and how these supported many dysfunctional assumptions. Such beliefs drove her to self-manage her condition and mistrust others who tried to help, as was evident through her negative automatic thoughts. Alison was asked to keep a negative automatic thought diary, which showed that there was little evidence to support her thoughts and that in fact she had more control over her care than she had believed. An extract from her diary can be seen in Figure 12.4. These were intense sessions which fatigued Alison and it was agreed that the next sessions would explore these unhelpful thoughts, their relationship to her early teenage experiences and the maintenance of core beliefs.

With the support of the physiotherapist, deep breathing and gentle stretching exercises were incorporated into mindfulness exercises and Alison's anxiety began to drop. She began to connect the shame and hurt caused by her teenage boyfriend and the development of constant body checking, weight and shape. She remembered how the physical manifestations of puberty and womanhood caused her great anxiety and being very underweight was more desirable. Gradually over time she focused more and more on low weight and she remembered low weight as a competitive game with herself to 'see how far she could go'.

During adolescence and early adulthood she became dominated by her over-appraisal of weight and body shape and believed 'fat' was a failure in will and personal habits and was in a deep sense 'ugly'. Alison began to see how the deep rejection, pain and humiliation caused during her adolescence had developed a core belief around self-protection and denial of her own developing body. In turn dysfunctional underlying assumptions around the worth of others and self had impacted on social interaction and negative automatic thoughts. These involved false impressions and negative views of the self and others in terms of behaviours and responses. This included her dysfunctional assumption regarding a sense of rejection and shame if she felt that others thought badly of her.

The final sessions in stage 3 focused on her relationship with Anthony, who was sceptical about her real motivation to change. Her underlying dysfunctional assumptions about weight and shape and her degree of control were being reinforced by Anthony's perception and it was therefore agreed that Anthony should be included in her plan of maintenance support.

Treatment evaluations: sessions 16–18 (week 11)

Stage four – evaluation and maintenance

These sessions examined realistic expectations for self-management of her anorectic condition. Alison had gained weight during her time in the unit and had improved physically. The first session reviewed her case formulation and although she was still low weight she had in fact exceeded her target (BMI 16.4 from 15) and her mood had improved. The final session reviewed her scores on the original assessments carried out prior to case formulation and a comparison of pre- and post-therapy scores can be found in Table 12.1.

It was clear that Alison retained an anorectic approach to living but that she had improved in several areas and had gained insight into the impact of core beliefs on her daily life. Excerpts from her diary also indicated that Alison had undertaken some reframing of her negative automatic thoughts; she now stopped to consider whether her own attitudes and thoughts influenced her

TABLE 12.1   Pre- and post-therapy assessment scores

Measurement tool	Pre-therapy scores	Post-therapy scores
Eating Attitude Test-26	37.1	23.1
Eating Disorder Belief Questionnaire:		
Negative self-beliefs	53	43
Acceptance by others	34	29
Self-acceptance	82.5	83.4
Control over eating	59.1	53
Eating Disorder examination	4.4	3.6

approach with others, and as a maintenance exercise was recording 10 positive thoughts about herself each day and five positive thoughts about others in her life.

Anthony remained sceptical and frequently asked Alison if she was only pretending to change so she could quickly revert back to self-starvation as soon as she was home. Such comments distressed Alison and hampered her positive thinking exercises because they made her think more about her own control of eating and weight.

Alison spent the final session developing a short-term plan for the first few weeks following her imminent discharge from the inpatient unit. She would continue the positive thinking log and her mindfulness exercises and agreed to join the local eating disorder self-help group.

Discharge strategies

It was agreed that Alison would continue to have maintenance interventions through the EDU day clinic. These sessions would build on the reframing and core schematic work, develop further maintenance strategies for self-care and plan tactics to minimize future relapses. The care programme would be planned and monitored by Alison and her care co-ordinator.

Critique of case study

Alison was admitted to the EDU from a coronary care unit and her first three weeks in the unit were spent building up her physical health. Therapy could not be started because Alison's poor physical health had such a negative impact on her cognitive functioning. Cooper and Shafran's model (2008) therefore had to be truncated and the longer periods of reflection and reframing could not be timetabled into a treatment plan. This is the reality in many specialist units and therapy needs to be adapted to suit the situation.

Despite her long experience with anorexia nervosa and past CBT treatment Alison still required socialisation into principles, conceptualisation and introduction to the formulation model. Using a different case formulation from one she may have used previously allowed a different perception and the level of intervention at core and intermediate levels provided a clear analytical pattern to be observed.

Her adolescent trauma had instigated a core belief system which, throughout subsequent years, had developed dysfunctional assumptions and NATS, serving to maintain her anorectic sense of self. Core work at such an intense rate was anxiety provoking, and as her dysfunctional underlying assumptions became detached from core beliefs she experienced low mood and fatigue. This is not uncommon in core interventions and it requires additional support and even suspension of treatment objectives until these areas return to levels where cognitive and affective functioning can sustain further interventions at these levels. This meant that in therapy some sessions were spent revisiting past treatment sessions, carrying out reassessments and reinforcing areas that had been previously thought to have been addressed. Core work is sensitive and delicate because of the fluctuations in mood and cognitive state instigated by reframing or developing new core beliefs. Therapeutic observations and good recording of data can help with refocusing on past work and in this case the care programme team approach and mindfulness exercises provided further support for Alison as she dealt with issues outside the therapeutic sessions.

Problems arising in therapy

Alison did not want her partner Anthony involved in the care team and he remained outside the therapeutic environment despite the fact that he was identified as a barrier to change. This would be an area explored in her CBT sessions via the day clinic.

Her relationship with fellow residents was a major barrier to successful treatment and it is not uncommon for the sub-culture of residential care to develop its own values which may be at odds with the organisation's aims and objectives. In this case Alison believed she could develop a better relationship with fellow residents than with the staff and she reinforced this belief through her interactions. This caused a clash between her dysfunctional assumptions and the expected compliance with care programmes. The use of the care programme approach, the care co-ordinator and speaking about this in the programme team meeting helped to manage the situation. It can, however, have a detrimental effect on therapy, as demonstrated by Anthony's continuing scepticism regarding Alison's acceptance of the staff in her own maintenance programme.

For individuals with severe and enduring AN, the issue of planning time, numbers of sessions and length of residential stay has the potential to cause problems for and during therapeutic treatment. For example, Alison's three weeks gaining better physical health did mean time lost for CBT interventions and her motivation fluctuated throughout, requiring more time in treatment sessions. This meant other issues could not be addressed until they could be revisited in day care sessions after discharge.

1. Which criteria did Alison meet for the anorexia nervosa purging sub-type?
2. What impact did her adolescent experience have on dysfunctional underlying assumptions and how did they support her anorexic life?
3. How does the care environment impact on therapeutic interventions with clients?
4. Why would intervention at NATs level have little impact on Alison's maintenance of her anorexic life?

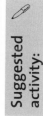

Suggested activity:

- Ask a friend if they would join you in keeping a diary of your food intake for one week and consider how your diet helps you in your day-to-day activities.
- Discuss whether keeping a food diary would lead to a raised awareness of food and eating and consider what impact this raised awareness would have.
- Discuss the physical aspect of mental health problems and list them in priority with a rationale for each. Now think about what issues would prevent interventions to help.

13
Client Presenting with Dependent Personality Disorder
Mike Thomas

Learning objectives

By the end of this chapter you should be able to:

Identify the criteria for dependent personality disorder
Understand the need for risk assessment at first presentation
Discuss how core beliefs develop underlying dysfunctional assumptions and the impact on presenting problems
Outline a treatment strategy for treatment of dependent personality disorder
Recognise the boundary issues arising in therapy

Diagnostic criteria

The DSM-IV-TR (APA, 2000) identifies criteria for 10 specific personality disorders clustered into A, B and C groups. Cluster A includes personalities that can be viewed as odd or eccentric and often present with blurring psychosis-like symptoms. Cluster B includes people who present with over-dramatic presentations and are often blatantly or erratically emotional, whilst cluster C is concerned with individuals who present predominant symptoms of anxiety. A further criterion is given for individuals who meet more than one specific type, or have traits of specific types, but who also have additional traits not included in the DSM-IV-TR criterion.

The criteria for dependent personality disorder (DPD) falls into the cluster C (301.6) and the DSM-IV-TR (APA, 2000) states that the individual with dependent personality disorder demonstrates an excessive neediness and anxiety about separation which begins in early childhood and usually contains at least five of the following. There may be difficulty with everyday decisions unless constantly directed and reassured by others; a refusal to take on responsibilities for aspects of one's own life; a fear of loss of support from others, causing acquiescence with their views in case a contrary view leads to rejection; and voluntarily undertaking tasks which others would be pushed to carry out in order to gain acceptance. There may also be an exaggerated fear that the individual would not be able to cope alone, and although displaying normal levels of activity there is usually an absence of solitary pursuits due to lack of self-confidence. The person may present with an unusually high preoccupation that they may be abandoned and left to cope alone and so, despite possibly having a record of volatile relationships, they display a tendency to seek and achieve another relationship quickly once one relationship ends. This makes the individual susceptible to manipulation and abuse.

Personality traits are enduring and entrenched and whilst this is true for everyone the difference is that individuals with personality disorders have traits that are so inflexible and maladaptive that they cause significant distress and functional impairment. The DSM-IV-TR states in its general diagnostic criteria that deviation from the individual's culture is manifested in two or more of the following: cognition (in the way a person perceives and thinks about themselves, others and events); affectivity (across the range of intensity, lability and appropriateness of responses); and interpersonal functioning and impulsive control. The criterion goes on to state that onset of any pattern should be traced back to early childhood or adolescence, hence the importance of good history-taking in assessment. Equally, it must be confirmed that the personality traits are not better accounted for by other mental disorders or due to the direct physiological effects of substance misuse, medications or toxic intake, or due to a direct medical condition such as brain trauma.

Whilst cluster A appears to have some relationship with psychosis and the learning disabilities spectrum, and cluster B appears to be on a continuum of anxiety and self-esteem, in cluster C there appears to be more leaning towards social inhibition and inadequacy. Dependent personality disorder traits have some things in common with borderline personality criteria in that there is excessive fear of abandonment, but the fear is so overpowering that relationships are seen as a balm to the fear of loneliness and the belief that the person cannot possibly take care of themselves. Any relationships therefore tend to be suffocating and clinging and when one ends there is frantic activity to gain another. Inevitably, for many individuals a settled relationship is one where they are meek, submissive and in some cases bullied or abused as there is great reluctance, and even inability, to disagree with others.

Predisposing and precipitating factors

There may be genetic links which influence infants' abilities to adapt, learn, be motivated and acquire deferred gratification skills. Green (2009) proposes that poor bonding may influence over-development of extroversion or introversion. For example, an individual may base their self-esteem and self-concept on the admiration from others, or through dysfunctional over-reliance and over-confidence in their own abilities.

Labelling is a powerful tool for social control and a cultural view of personality disorder would argue that the condition is a manifestation of poverty, poor social conditions, low educational attainment, work stress or lack of social mobility opportunities which causes unacceptable behaviour, either anti-social or disengagement (Goldstein and Rosselli, 2003).

Young (1987) and Padesky (1988) suggest a cognitive approach where early development of maladaptive schemas cause fixed and unconditional beliefs such as worthlessness, a view that one has poor coping skills or that one cannot be loved. Unconditional beliefs are more difficult to change than conditional beliefs as it is harder for external validation to be presented as evidence to reframe schematic beliefs. Linehan and colleagues (1987) propose that there may be underlying deficiencies in problem-solving abilities which creates tension and anxiety and a potential for parasuicidal behaviour, whilst Horowitz and colleagues (1984) posit the view that it may be an issue of how individuals with dependent personality disorder prioritise. They suggest there may be an inability within such individuals to process all domains of thinking, feeling and behaving in certain situations and that as a result they prioritise only one – predominantly, feeling. This results in the downgrading of the importance of the other domains.

Studies indicate that interventions can be successful in certain situations (Bateman and Tyrer, 2004) and that following therapy some individuals from the criminal justice system have a decreased reoffending pattern (Skeem et al., 2002).

Demographic incidence

The Office for National Statistics (ONS, 2010) states that the prevalence of personality disorders occurs in 54 per every 1,000 men and 34 per 1,000 women. The prevalence of individuals with a diagnosis of personality disorders that access mental health services is higher than general population figures and DSM-IV-TR (APA, 2000: 723) states that dependent personality disorder 'is among the most frequently reported personality disorders encountered in mental health clinics'. Jones and colleagues (2006) point out that research into personality disorders is predominantly in secondary and tertiary care and that the number of individuals who access primary mental health care is not always taken into account. Given their suggestion that up to 50 per cent of counselling referrals may actually meet the diagnosis for personality disorder, it would seem that current figures may fall short of the true incidence.

Continuum of severity

Personality traits and characteristics are viewed as fixed and enduring, so personality disorders are likewise viewed as entrenched and lifelong. The condition has the potential for complex diagnosis and comorbidity is high. Suicidal acts and premature deaths are significant (up to 10 per cent). Recognisable traits and characteristics usually present themselves in adolescence or early adult life and for some specific types, such as obsessive-compulsive, dependent and schizotypal personality disorders, remain enduring over a lifetime. Others, such as anti-social and borderline personality disorders, however, appear to become less dominant with age.

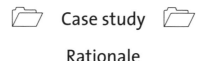

Case study

Rationale

As this is an enduring and complex presentation, intervention will be provided at step 4 of the Stepped Care model, within the specialist mental health services. It will demonstrate CBT interventions at the intermediate and core level, taking place at the outpatient department of a Mental Health Trust. Julie, a female in her mid-twenties, has a diagnosis of dependent personality disorder and this places her amongst the most frequently reported group of individuals with personality disorder who present for treatment in a mental health setting (APA, 2000).

Client

Julie is aged 26 and was first referred by her GP to the primary mental health team when she was 18 years old, following a suicide attempt. She has had several referrals to a variety of mental health services since then, including two episodes of inpatient care. At the age of 20 she was diagnosed with a dependent personality disorder. Julie's most recent referral is to the psychotherapy team based in the outpatient unit of the Mental Health Trust which has posed the question of whether CBT would be a suitable intervention for Julie at this time.

Assessment sessions 1–5

Upon initial introductions Julie interrupted straightaway to talk about her current relationship status, saying that she was in between relationships due to a recent break-up with her boyfriend. She stated that she felt 'lost' without him and that her life was empty and meaningless to the degree that she was contemplating ending her life. She reported constant thoughts of driving her car at excessive speed until she 'hits a motorway bridge' and stated that since the break-up three weeks ago she had taken excessive cocaine on a nightly basis to help her sleep and block the invasive thoughts of her boyfriend. She went on to say that she jumped between desperately wanting him back and extreme rage at the pain he had caused and that she texted or rang his mobile phone throughout the night, alternating between weeping and threatening him. Julie then disclosed that it was actually her that had ended the relationship, stating that she had she felt that her partner was too clingy and that she was uncomfortable because he was hinting that he would like to have children with her in the near future.

It was following this initial deluge of information that the format of the assessment could be explained to Julie, which was that a clinical interview would be conducted initially, the aim of which was to gain an understanding of Julie's main difficulties. This would be followed by the completion of a number of self-report measures which would both complement the clinical interview and gather more specific information about her identified difficulties.

Julie indicated that she slept very poorly, was tired all the time, took cocaine and alcohol every night, smoked excessively, engaged in no exercise and ate irregularly. She was weepy, irritable, felt 'depressed' and regularly fantasised about different ways to kill herself which were often violent and public.

Her past history indicated that Julie had been physically abused by several men since early childhood. These men were transient 'boyfriends' of her mother who was also a victim of physical abuse but never spoke out and would actually become distressed when they left. Her mother had a stable job as a personal assistant to an executive working in the railway industry with whom she had had a past affair. Julie has three brothers all older than her who she now only saw at family gatherings.

Julie was expelled from one school at age 12 for fighting and disruptive behaviour and then 'got in with the wrong crowd', who passed their time vandalising local amenities, taking drugs and drinking to excess, resulting in an anti-social behaviour order (ASBO) at the age of 16 and a short spell in a young offenders institution. She felt she was clever but she disliked the regime of schools and was often absent. At the age of 17 she got a part-time job in a shop but was caught taking alcohol for her friends within the first week.

She was sexually active by the age of 14 but did not like sexual contact and only participated because 'that's what boys wanted and I wasn't that bothered anyway'. She could not recall a time when she had not had a relationship, and her boyfriend whom she had recently asked to leave had been with her for just under a year. At the age of 18 one boyfriend ended the relationship, which was so devastating that she took an overdose. Julie made the emergency call 'just before I lost consciousness'. Since then she had made regular suicide attempts and was known to the local A&E department.

There was a lot of detail from the interview and to help Julie to bring this together and to make sense of the information Williams's five areas model was utilised (Figure 13.1). Julie had undertaken a number of CBT sessions in the past and so was familiar with formulations but nevertheless it still proved to be an effective way of re-introducing the CBT approach.

To gather more specific information regarding Julie's current difficulties the following assessment tools were used:

- Self-completing mood questionnaire which rated her mood on an hourly basis throughout the day. It was rated on a score of 1 to 10, 1 being very low and 10 being very elated. Julie scored mostly 3s throughout the day and never went above 4.
- Events diary wherein Julie gave an account of situations throughout the past week which she felt were important to her and scored them up to 10 for contentment. An example of this can be found in Figure 13.2, which shows a result of 36 from a possible 140 with no single result above 5.

Julie raised the issue of whether her diagnosis of DPD was contributing to her situation. This was a sensitive area of the session as the therapist did not want to either reinforce existing core beliefs (i.e. Julie may have thought that she was bound to react in the way she had because she had a 'personality disorder') or reinforce low self-esteem through labelling the condition. Time was spent in the session working through the criteria for DPD (DSM-IV-TR 301.6; APA, 2000) and Julie could see that she met seven out of the eight criteria, although she disagreed that she was 'clinging' or 'submissive' in her relationships.

It was agreed that Julie would contact the clinic if suicidal thoughts were becoming so strong that she felt compelled to act them out. She was also

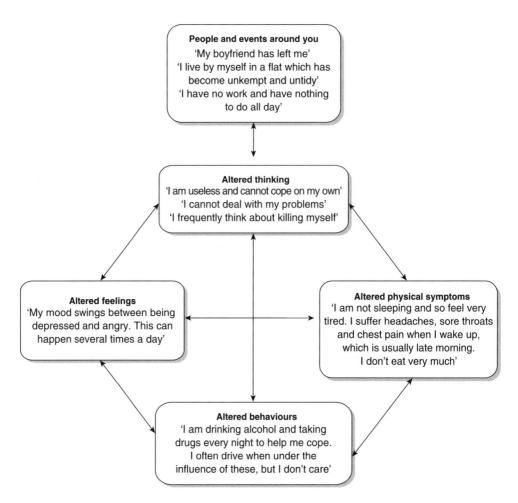

FIGURE 13.1 Initial maintenance formulation adapted from Williams's (2010) five areas formulation. Reproduced by permission of Hodder Education.

Event	Emotions	Thoughts	Response	Outcome	Results total
Missing boyfriend badly in the evenings (1)	Sad (2) Scared (4)	Wish he was here (4) It's my fault he's gone (1) He made me do it (2)	Cried (1) Texted him every 10 minutes threatening him (4) Drank (4) Took cocaine (4) Texting boyfriend when drunk and asking him to get in touch (3)	Shouted and swore down the phone on his message board (2) Got drunk and high (2) Cried (1)	36 from a possible 140 and no single result above 5

FIGURE 13.2 Events diary measuring contentment

referred to her GP for a physical assessment with regard to the pains in her chest and the headaches.

A week later Julie returned with the results of her diary which indicated a poor sleep pattern and confirmed that she had a persistent low mood. She had contacted the clinic once feeling depressed and suicidal but had been reassured after an hour's telephone discussion. Her GP had stated that her chest pain was possibly due to her lifestyle and had referred Julie to the smoking cessation programme. The GP had put Julie's headaches down to a hangover and had suggested that if she continued to drink and take cocaine then she would recommend she be seen by the drug and alcohol team. Julie also stated that she had a new boyfriend (her supplier) and was therefore 'over' her previous boyfriend, but would still like to continue CBT for her other lifestyle issues.

Case formulation

Beck, Freeman, Davis and Associates (2007) point out that the relationship interplay between the therapist and the client is often more important with a client diagnosed with a personality disorder. The interpersonal turbulence in the individual's life is played out within therapy and provides opportunities for observation of coping mechanisms and techniques. This means that the therapeutic relationship itself can model new adaptations and challenge existing interactions, which could then be practised outside the therapy. It also provides a way to demonstrate trust if there is explicit and transparent acknowledgement of the difficulties with interpersonal interactions and the effects on the self and others.

A good example was when some time was spent in the session revisiting the effects produced by Julie's break with her previous boyfriend. Julie acknowledged that she was upset and depressed when he left but insisted that it was his fault and that she had tried to get him back but he had shunned her. Her current boyfriend had been supportive and even this early on in the relationship Julie felt he could 'be the one'.

This was a delicate situation to manage. Earlier assessment priorities were no longer current for Julie and therapy would need to be reviewed. Yet Julie's dependency issues could have led to her assuming she was being rejected and the therapeutic strategy could reinforce dysfunctional assumptions. Her contentment record results from previous sessions were used to demonstrate her dependency needs and insecurities and it was agreed that Julie would try to contain her impulse to gain a deeper commitment from her new partner as therapy continued.

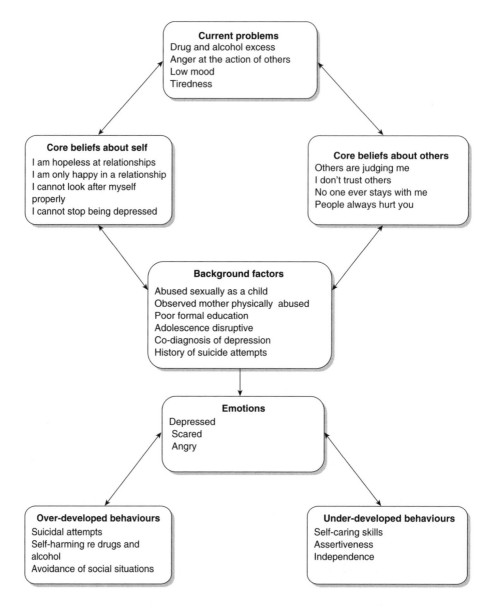

FIGURE 13.3   Julie's formulation based on Davidson's schematic cognitive formulation
model (2008)

The case formulation followed Davidson's schematic cognitive model
(Davidson, 2008). This approach emphasises cognitive dysfunctional core
beliefs and takes into account an individual's history and their emotions,
behavioural problems and environmental factors. The model attempts to discern the patterns between core beliefs and dysfunctional assumptions in the
context of present problems (Figure 13.3).

Over-developed (dysfunctional) behaviours are considered by Davidson to be reinforced and thereafter maintained throughout childhood and adolescence at the expense of more adaptive and therefore under-developed (functional) behaviours. Julie could see the relationship within the case formulation between her current problems, her core beliefs, the effect on emotions and how these interacted with her behaviours. Julie agreed that treatment would begin by working on her behaviours with a review of progress after four sessions.

Treatment sessions 1–5

Julie's original objectives were to reduce suicidal behaviour and increase her self-caring skills, and the sessions commenced with an assessment of Julie's current suicidal ideation. She reported, however, that her general feelings of helplessness and low mood were currently held at bay due to the excitement of her new relationship and felt that she would like to concentrate on self-reliance instead.

A series of exercises was initiated so that Julie could gain a baseline measurement from which she could compare any progress as therapy continued. The first exercise consisted of identifying her level of independence and her reliance on others in her daily life (Figure 13.4). The statements were marked 0 to 10 with scores above 5 indicating dependence and those below showing independence. Julie scored 41 out of a possible 50 (negative). By referring to her original formulation Julie could see how she quickly formed a dependency on others, even for simple daily tasks, and therefore therapy focused on Julie identifying those tasks that she felt could be performed independently.

	Independence (0–10)	
I can take care of all my needs	8	I need others to take care of me
	Relationships	
I never need anyone	9	I always need someone
	Trust	
I always trust everyone	8	I never trust anyone
	Confidence	
I am always sure of myself	10	I never believe in my own abilities
	Self-concept	
I always like myself	6	I rarely like myself
	Total: 41 out of 50	

FIGURE 13.4   Independence vs reliance scores

The first exercise was for her to compile a shopping list and go out to purchase the items. Her second task was to try relaxation exercises when her boyfriend went out and she was alone in the evenings or all night. She also continued to bring to sessions incidents she felt important from her contentment events diary.

Review of progress in the areas of under-development (self-caring skills and independence) showed an increase in her self-reliance skills. Her independence versus reliance scores were now 7, 9, 7, 8 and 6, giving a reduced negative score of 37 from a previous 41. Julie also stated that other people were noticing the changes in her behaviour with comments from her boyfriend that she appeared much calmer. Her contentment scores were steadily increasing as her behaviour became less dependent; for example she was more tolerant of her boyfriend staying out. She further reported that she had cooked a small meal for them both twice in the last week as well as sorted out her laundry.

Julie still, however, continued to take alcohol daily but cocaine was now used only through the weekends as this was for 'recreational' use. She stated her mood overall appeared to be brighter and she had not had any suicidal thoughts in the last week. It was therefore agreed that therapy would continue by exploring her under-developed area of assertiveness alongside the continuation of her behavioural alterations in the other two identified areas (see Figure 13.3).

Sessions 6–15

The first of these sessions concentrated on Julie's belief that she could not function without having a relationship in her life and the original case formulation was revisited. The underlying beliefs related to abandonment were examined regarding how these feelings could be related to her early life experiences, the abuse she endured and her developing view during adolescence regarding men and relationships. To enhance her under-developed behaviours Julie was asked to keep a diary record of her interaction with her current partner, focusing specifically on decision-making and planning their daily activities.

In the following sessions the diary indicated that although Julie believed she made no decisions in the relationship, in fact she often made suggestions regarding where they should go or do, when they should eat and what she should do with her time while her partner was out. However, Julie had also observed that her relationship was deteriorating and that there were more arguments and tension, which in turn was making her feel anxious and depressed and she was wondering whether to stop challenging this area of assertive under-development.

One of the traits found amongst individuals with personality disorders is a lack of tolerance of dysfunctional states for more than a few days. It is easier to revert to known coping mechanisms and the sensitivity in this area is acute. This is not uncommon in core schematic therapy in general but for individuals with personality disorders it can be so oppressive and distressing that non-attendance at therapy sessions is a frequent avoidance strategy. Julie was provided with psycho-educational sessions on mindfulness techniques which helped to focus on the events and actions in her life rather than attempt to stop the feelings she was experiencing during these events.

Julie repeated her contentment records which indicated a continuing improvement, although she reported that her mood was dropping and her anxiety was increasing. Nevertheless Julie continued to monitor her self-caring behaviours and her interpersonal interaction and a review session indicated that she was regularly bathing and did all her own laundry, her sleep patterns had improved (except for the nights she put down to post-cocaine use) and she ate more home-cooked meals. She experienced difficulties with her boyfriend who appeared to be resenting the change in Julie and had become more verbally aggressive towards her. Despite these negative aspects, Julie asked to continue therapy exploring new perspectives regarding her core beliefs.

Sessions 16–25

The following sessions focused on how Julie's core beliefs about trust triggered underlying dysfunctional assumptions about others and impacted on her emotions and thinking, and in turn her reactions and behaviours. As the sessions continued Julie began to reflect more on her over-developed behaviours and their relation to her emotional state and the under-developed behaviour of assertion that she still wanted to improve.

To work with her on assertiveness, psycho-educational sessions were carried out so that she could learn to differentiate between hostility, aggression and assertion. These sessions included attempts to understand how other people reacted to her behaviours and attitudes, exploring and rehearsing different strategies in scenarios chosen by Julie.

Julie continued to record incidents she found relevant or upsetting, but exploration in session tended to focus on the underlying beliefs and their relation to her under-developed behaviours. Julie felt her anger at others had become more manageable and she went shopping for food and household goods without feeling anxious or self-conscious. Her alcohol intake remained a problem and she reported that she binged about four times a week and drank in the afternoons if she was bored, as well as continuing her cocaine habit. Her relationship with her boyfriend was still deteriorating and she began to consider asking him to leave as he had become physically threatening.

Towards the end of therapy, when a progress review had indicated that discharge should be considered, her mood markedly deteriorated and she reported being despondent, unable to concentrate, feeling angry and once again considering ending her life. Beck and colleagues (2007) commented on the deterioration of symptomatic presentation towards the end of therapy amongst many individuals with personality disorder diagnosis, an observation supported by Davidson (2008). This is a particularly difficult area of therapy in this context as it is easier to suggest a continuation of therapy to minimise the distress experienced by the client. However, such a course often reinforces core beliefs regarding abandonment and presages a dependency relationship within therapy itself. In this case the therapy adopted a problem-focused approach and supported Julie through revisiting her original case formulation and the connections between her core beliefs about abandonment, the underlying dysfunctional assumptions and her over-developed coping behaviours in this area. Reinforcement and encouragement were also provided for the improved under-developed behaviours and two sessions focused solely on mindfulness approaches, examining the feelings she was experiencing and the scenario of ending therapy.

Treatment evaluation sessions 1 and 2

These were not particularly happy sessions for Julie. She had been assaulted by her boyfriend, who had left her, but two weeks later was asking to resume the relationship. Julie had stopped shopping, washing and eating. She had not slept well for several nights, was drinking heavily and was continuously fantasising about different methods of suicide. She blamed herself, the therapy (and the therapist) for the breakdown of her relationship and believed she had pushed her partner into the reaction when she was 'changing' and 'getting on his nerves'. Therapy again adopted a problem-focused approach which guided Julie through her original events diary showing her response to her previous relationship breakdown. This then led on to discussion of the schematic formulation and how much progress she had made on her under-developed behaviours over recent months. Julie could see that her original objectives of increased self-caring skills and decreased suicidal thoughts and her previous over-developed behaviours had altered positively.

The penultimate session used Socratic dialogue to explore abandonment beliefs in the context of her current relationship. During this period she had re-established the relationship with her partner who had moved back into her flat and her mood had lifted.

The final session discussed the dependency Julie felt she required in therapy and her desire to continue the sessions, with further exploration of core beliefs and their relation to other under-developed behaviours.

Discharge strategies

The therapist held the view that further developments would not require core level interventions which was shared with Julie alongside concerns that a continuation would lead to dependence. Whilst Julie reluctantly agreed that a period outside therapy might help her to establish her coping abilities in a more realistic manner she did not think that this would provide a full resolution. The discussion therefore led to maintenance support where it was agreed that Julie would be referred to a local service users support group. Monthly meetings would also be held with her care co-ordinator whom Julie would contact if she had suicidal thoughts, and a letter would be sent to her GP recommending she be referred for assessment of alcohol and drug usage.

Critique of case study

Julie presented with a diagnosis of dependent personality disorder compounded by low mood, anxiety and excessive alcohol and drug intake. She also had a history of suicide attempts and so the first assessment sessions had to prioritise risk assessment and the support mechanisms required to prevent self-harming behaviours.

Once this was managed, the focus on her presenting problems helped her understand her immediate experiences, although such insight did not lessen their impact. Careful assessment, observation and analysis were required throughout this phase of therapy and of particular usefulness to help prioritisation was the utilisation of Williams's five areas formulation (2010).

Soon after therapy commenced Julie was involved in a different relationship and her low mood and suicidal intent became less urgent. However, had her low mood continued and suicidal intent increased then therapy would not have continued and Julie would have to have been considered for inpatient admission.

Julie had experienced several periods of therapy in the last few years yet it was important for the therapist to re-emphasise the principles of CBT so that Julie was better able to consider the patterns presented in Davidson's schematic cognitive formulation model (2008), particularly her over-developed behaviours and their impact on her daily living.

Setting boundaries and limiting the therapeutic focus to the objectives was important as they enabled Julie to practise assertive scenarios in a safe environment and acted as a buffer against the several attempts made to move therapy into a dependent relationship. Most practitioners see boundary setting when working with clients as a normal aspect of the therapeutic contract and may take a flexible approach to boundary changes as therapy progresses, but it is essential to maintain an awareness of consistency regarding prior agreements when working with individuals who present with personality disorders as the distress arising out of ending a trusting relationship is painful. If boundaries are poor and continually broken they can reinforce negative over-developed behaviours and inhibit the emergence of more adaptive behaviours.

Working on attainable objectives as soon as therapy commenced allowed Julie to experience early positive feedback and was the first step towards understanding her negative behaviours. It was only after she was more confident in behaviour alteration that therapy continued into dysfunctional core beliefs. By then Julie had experienced change and was more motivated, yet this phase resurrected comorbid symptoms and her dependency on others influenced her progress.

The final stages were particularly sensitive and therapy had to focus on Julie's previous records and scores to demonstrate where she had made progress. This did not prevent her anxieties continuing but they were more manageable.

It is accepted that therapeutic interventions in personality disorders takes time and requires many sessions to impact on a small number of dysfunctional core beliefs but therapy needs to end at an agreed point to prevent dependency issues arising. The use of support groups and a care co-ordinator provided a framework within which Julie could practise her under-developed behaviours, to gain a more positive adaptive strategy in her daily life.

Problems arising in therapy

A problem encountered in therapy can be sudden changes to existing relationships, and in this case study Julie commenced therapy due to the breakdown of her existing relationship. Her history indicated severe dependency issues and fear of abandonment but therapy began with a crisis approach identifying any necessary risk assessment and prioritisation to prevent self-harm.

Increased abandonment anxiety allayed by a desperate rush into a new relationship is not uncommon amongst individuals with a diagnosis of dependent personality disorder. Therapy has to alter to account for such changes in relationships and when necessary work in previous sessions may have to be abandoned. For instance, Julie was initially exploring her dysfunctional responses to her previous relationship but then decided not to explore this area as she was happy with her new partner. Despite some early assessment data being abandoned, progress continued by the use of her case formulation, which was used to demonstrate how her over-developed (dysfunctional) behaviours were impacting on her new partner.

The level of distress caused by abandonment issues easily overwhelms any therapeutic inroads in early therapy and sudden changes of strategy and direction are often required for therapy to continue. Early assessment information can, however, provide an insight into a person's normal over-developed coping behaviours and may therefore be of use later in therapy.

Relations with others can become strained during therapy, as can be seen by Julie's partner becoming a focus for later therapeutic problems. He enjoyed the early improvements in Julie's behaviour but became hostile and violent as she practised assertiveness techniques. Julie's beliefs about abandonment then began to dominate any emerging new beliefs in her own abilities to maintain a less dependent relationship. Such occurrences may require an increase in the number of sessions to support any new beliefs and prevent them from being discarded.

In this case study the improvement within the relationship may have helped Julie during closure of therapy. However, the likelihood is that the relationship will continue to encounter difficulties without longer-term therapy to fully address this aspect of reliance and dependence.

Continuation of alcohol consumption and drug use is not conducive to therapy. Julie was often tired or resistive to exploring the results of her homework. Sessions had to be booked in late afternoons as Julie rarely rose before lunchtime and they had to be mid-week as she often carried a two-day hangover from the weekend. Therapy in this context requires perseverance and good teamwork. Therapy needs to prioritise objectives with the client's agreement and these should be within an agreed therapeutic contract on how and when therapy will be carried out.

Julie was not atypical of an individual presenting with personality traits; therapy took time and required frequent reinforcement of boundary limits, and in the time available she met several of her objectives. Her other issues – alcohol and drug use and maintaining a more positive relationship – would be explored within the maintenance support offered by the users group as well as through monitoring by her care co-ordinator and her GP.

1. Why were Julie's main presentations indicative of the criteria for dependent personality disorder?
2. How did Julie maintain her over-developed behaviours?
3. What would you do to ensure that Julie was kept aware of therapeutic boundaries?
4. How would you discuss diagnostic labelling with a client?

- Look at the DSM-IV-TR (APA, 2000) criteria for personality disorders and think about your own and your friends' attitudes and behaviours. Try and distinguish between socially and culturally accepted interactions and those outlined in the criteria.
- Think of the impact of living in a society where cultural and social interactions make you excessively anxious, afraid or dependent on others. Discuss with a colleague how a person would react and behave in such situations and what type of support they would require.

Appendices
Appendix 1

Anger diary 1 (to be used when collecting information to inform treatment)

The client selects incidents that have caused anger and scores the level of anger arousal from a total of ten, immediately after the incident, six hours later and the next day.

Situation	Immediate feelings/thoughts (0–10)	Immediate behaviour	Six hours after the situation (0–10)	After a night's sleep (0–10)

Appendix 2

Anger diary 2 (to be used to collect information throughout treatment)

Usefully employed as a record of behavioural experiments.

Situation	Initial thoughts and feelings	Behaviour	What happened after

Appendix 3

Balanced thought chart (used in conduct disorder interventions)

Angry thought	Balanced thought

Appendix 4

Behavioural experiment record

Thought	
Prediction	
Experiment	

Date	Situation	Outcome	Evidence (for and against)

Appendix 5

Events diary (for use with individuals with personality disorder)

This is used to measure satisfaction and contentment. A score of 50 can be reached for events viewed as satisfactory and providing contentment. The lower the score towards zero the lower the level of perceived satisfaction and contentment.

Event Score up to 10	Emotions Score up to 10	Thoughts Score up to 10	Response Score up to 10	Outcome Score up to 10	Results total Score up to 50

Appendix 6

Events diary (can be used across a variety of conditions)

SUDs – Subjective Units of Distress. Rate on scale of 0–10 where 1 = no acute distress, 5 = moderately upset and 10 = unbearably bad.

Date Time	Situation	Physical Rate using SUDS	Thoughts Rate using SUDS	Behaviour Rate using SUDS	Mood Rate using SUDS

Appendix 7

Evidence chart

Thought : _____

Evidence for	Evidence against	Balanced thought

Appendix 8

Graded exposure chart

Can be used to record exposure experiments

Goal	Details of experiment (outcome)	SUDS before	SUDS after

Appendix 9

Hierarchy example 1

Arrange in order of most achievable first and most difficult last

Steps:	Goal:	Date achieved
1		
2		
3		
4		
5		
6		

Appendix 10

Hierarchy example 2

Activity	Anticipated difficulty 1–10	Date commenced	Date completed	Actual difficulty 1–10

Appendix 11

Negative thought record example 1

Situation What were you doing?	Thought Describe and categorise: negative/ catastrophic/black and white/ self-blame	Associated mood Rate 0 low – 10 high	Alternative thought	Rate new mood Rate 0 low – 10 high

Appendix 12

Negative thought record example 2

Date	Emotion	Situation	What were you thinking? Rate belief in thought (0–100)	What would be a more helpful thought? Rate belief in thought (0–100)	How do you feel now? How much do you believe original thought

Appendix 13

OCD diary

Situation date	Time	Trigger	Thoughts at time of trigger	Intensity 0 = acceptable 5 = extreme discomfort	Activity Describe what you did	Thought, feeling mood after completing activity

Appendix 14

Panic diary

Date Time	Situation (when, where, who with)	Physical (sensations/ symptoms)	Thoughts (what were you thinking/ what images came to mind)	Behaviours (what did you do)	Severity of attack (0–10)	Duration (how long did the attack last)

Glossary

Activity assignment/activity hierarchy   A series of tasks agreed in therapy to be carried out by the client outside of therapy sessions and which can have graded levels of difficulty and achievement. Sometimes used interchangeably with homework.

Autonomic arousal   Automatic physiological responses to stimuli, for example increased heartbeat, perspiration, salivation, etc.

Avoidance   Refraining from situations or experiences which may cause distress.

Behaviour activation   Re-establishing positive reinforcing activities by developing and maintaining social interactions which enable contact with reinforcers.

Behavioural experiments   There are two potential types: one which involves activities undertaken by the client to demonstrate no or poor support for their dysfunctional assumptions or negative automatic thoughts; or the second, which involves demonstrating support for new emerging and more positive assumptions or thoughts.

Between-session tasks   See homework.

Case conceptualisation   Refers to the phase after early or initial assessment and is used to describe the process by which the therapist and the client make sense of the origins, development and maintenance of the client's current difficulties. Sometimes confused with case formulation and both terms are sometimes used together although they are different.

Case formulation   Usually the demonstration of the conceptualisation using pictorial or diagrammatic form. Case formulations can be protocol-based (tested in practice and problem-specific), generic (i.e. Padesky and Greenberger's five aspects model) or idiosyncratic (a combination of generic or problem-specific based models in conjunction with the clients' particular or complex presentation).

Chronicity   The length of time the client has had the presenting condition. Can also be used to describe severity as in 'chronic and severe' conditions, or used interchangeably with the words 'severe and enduring'.

Cognitive reframing   See cognitive restructuring.

Cognitive restructuring   Techniques which support the client to alter their underlying beliefs or dysfunctional assumptions. The client's underlying beliefs or negative assumptions are explored and replaced with more positive and helpful beliefs or perceptions.

Cognitive triad   The person develops a negative view of themselves, their current experiences in the world and of their future.

Co-morbidity   When a client presents with symptoms that suggest two or more diagnostic criteria are met and covers both physical and mental health conditions. Sometimes used interchangeably with complex presentation.

Complex presentation   A client presenting with symptoms indicating one or more dominant diagnostic criteria but with additional factors which complicate the management of daily life.

Continuum of severity   The gradient from mild to moderate and severe symptoms and presentations and usually refers to the progression or regression of the client's diagnosis.

Core beliefs   The beliefs held about the self, others, the world and the future. Sometimes used interchangeably with schema.

Diagnostic criteria   A validated or agreed formula which outlines specific symptoms and presentations and leads to a diagnosis of a named disorder or condition.

Diary   A record of events, incidents, thoughts or other issues. Used as an assessment and monitoring tool.

Dysfunctional   A term used in conjunction with a domain not appearing to work as effectively as normal, resulting in the individual developing new and erroneous ways of coping.

Dysfunctional assumptions   Erroneous conclusions based on wrongly perceived thinking or experience.

Dysfunctional behaviour   Reacting in inappropriate ways which cause the behavioural problems to be maintained or worsen.

Dysfunctional thinking   Reaching erroneous conclusions based on incorrect perceptions or assessments of situations.

Exposure   One of two approaches is generally utilised in therapy: situational exposure which refers to exposure to external stimuli; and imaginal exposure which refers to either hypothetical situations or the reliving of traumatic memories (see imaginal).

Hierarchy   A list of activities graded in order of difficulty.

Homework   A series of tasks agreed in therapy to be carried out by the client outside of therapy sessions and related to specific areas of development.

Hypotheticals   Rehearsing potential responses to imagined situations or experiences.

Idiosyncratic   The term used in CBT for individualisation.

Imaginal   A guided therapeutic technique which supports the client to re-experience traumatic memories and translate these into words and meaning organised in a chronological sequence.

Incidence   Number of new occurrences of a disorder; usually presented in a ratio of number per thousand.

In vivo   Refers to exposure that is 'in the situation'.

Maintenance therapy   A therapeutic intervention used more widely with clients presenting with chronic, severe or enduring conditions. There are two common approaches: one in which the client accesses the relevant therapeutic support as and when they feel it is warranted; or a more structured approach where the client continues to have one session several weeks apart. In between sessions there is the utilisation of e-CBT, text or telephone support.

Measures (tools or scales)   Instruments used to assess or calculate the degree or level of severity of conditions.

Mental state examination   An assessment of an individual's mental health status.

Mindfulness   A technique which encourages clients to take on a less self-focused perspective on their thoughts, bodily sensations and moods and helps the client to recognise that when change is not possible then acceptance can be therapeutic.

Modalities   Term used in CBT for aspects or area of the self; most commonly they include thinking, feeling, physical sensations, behaviour and environment.

Modifiers   Approaches that exacerbate or reduce symptoms.

Negative automatic thoughts (NATS)   The immediate, sometimes sub-conscious, unhelpful thinking as a reaction to events, situations or stimuli. The thinking attempts to make sense of incoming data and has its roots in underlying dysfunctional assumptions.

Normalising   Supporting the client to reframe experiences within the boundaries of social acceptance.

Precipitating factors   An event(s), incident(s) or perception(s) that is (are) the catalyst for the onset of a mental health disorder, dysfunction or condition.

Predisposing factors   Background or historical factors which have the potential to influence the onset of a disorder, dysfunction or condition.

Prevalence   Total number of reported cases at a particular point in time and covering both old and new cases; usually presented in a ratio of number per thousand.

Psycho-education   Individuals' use of different sources of information to better understand their current difficulties aided by tutorial/mentoring sessions to plan information gathering, provide guidance in the levels of complexity of the knowledge being sought and support therapeutic goals.

Psychophysiological   Used to describe either both psychological and physical symptom presentation; or to describe the impact that a psychological condition has on the body.

Reattribution   A range of techniques aimed at producing effective cognitive-behavioural change.

Remission   A period when signs and symptoms of a disorder are not present.

Response prevention   Following exposure the client is supported not to engage in covert or overt rituals that minimize appraised catastrophes.

Safety behaviour   Behaviour employed to prevent feared catastrophes, for example sitting down to avoid fainting.

Scales   Units, tables or measuring tools which provide information regarding specific conditions, and which support the assessment phase of therapy or provide guidance regarding therapeutic progress. Scales are usually specific measuring tools for particular presenting symptoms such as anxiety or depression but can be more generalised to mood, sleep, eating, exercise, and so on.

Schema   The framework or structure which supports core beliefs formed in early childhood and influenced by genetic and environmental factors. Sometimes used interchangeably with core beliefs.

Self-consciousness   A term used to describe the perception of self-image in a performance situation.

Self-focus   A term used to describe hyper-awareness of the self at the expense of the awareness of others.

Social dysfunction   Responding inappropriately in social situations, or avoiding social situations in order to prevent the inappropriateness occurring.

Socialisation   A term used in CBT to describe the process whereby the client is introduced to the concepts and treatment interventions within CBT and is given the opportunity to decide whether it is an appropriate intervention for them.

Socratic dialogue   An interviewing technique taking the form of a focused question and answer to allow the client to perceive a specific point related to their difficulties or to gather further assessment information.

Somatic   Referring to the physical body.

Systematic desensitisation   A guided step-by-step approach aimed at lowering arousal through graded exposure.

Thought diary   A form of homework where the client maintains a record of their thoughts focused on a pre-set situation discussed in therapy sessions. The usual format is for the client to record the time of occurrence, their thoughts before an incident, during and after.

Vicious cycle model   Demonstrates the inter-relationships between events in the environment and thoughts, feelings, physical sensations and behaviour.

References

Abramson, L.Y., Metalsky, G.I. and Alloy, L.B. (1989) Hopelessness depression: A theory-based subtype of depression. *Psychological Review* 96: 358–372.

Abramson, L.Y., Seligman, M.E.P. and Teasdale, J.D. (1978) Learned helplessness in humans: Critique and reformulation. *Journal of Abnormal Psychology* 87: 49–74.

Albano, A.M. and Detweiler, M.F. (2001) The development and clinical impact of social anxiety and social phobia in adolescents. In: Hoffman, S.G. and DiBartolo, P.M. (eds), *From Social Anxiety to Social Phobia*. Boston, MA: Allyn and Bacon.

Alwahhabi, F. (2003) Anxiety symptoms and generalised anxiety disorder in the elderly: A review. *Harvard Review of Psychiatry* 11(4): 180–193.

American Psychiatric Association (APA) (2000) *Diagnostic and Statistical Manual of Mental Disorders* (4th edn) *Text Revision*. Washington DC: APA.

Antai-Otong, D. (2008) *Psychiatric Nursing: Biological and Behavioural Concepts* (2nd edn). New York, NY: Thompson/Delmar.

Ballenger, J.C., Davidson, J.R., Lecrubier, Y., Nutt, D.J., Borkovec, T.D., Rickels, K., Stein, D.J. and Wittchen, H.U. (2001) Consensus statement on generalized anxiety disorder from the International Consensus Group on depression and anxiety. *Clinical Journal of Psychiatry* 62 (Supplement 11): 53–58.

Bancroft, J. (2009) *Human Sexuality and its Problems* (3rd edn). London, UK: Churchill Livingstone.

Bancroft, J. and Coles, L. (1976) Three years' experience in a sexual problems clinic. *British Medical Journal* 1: 1575–1577.

Barbui, C., Motterlini, N. and Garattini, L. (2006) Health status, resource consumption, and costs of dysthymia: A multi-center two-year longitudinal study. *Journal of Affective Disorders* 90(2–3): 181–186.

Barnes, J. (1981) Non-consummation of marriage. *Irish Medical Journal* 74: 19–21.

Barnes, J. (1986a) Primary vaginismus (Part 1): Social and clinical features. *Irish Medical Journal* 79: 59–62.

Barnes, J. (1986b) Primary vaginismus (Part 2): Aetiological factors. *Irish Medical Journal* 79: 62–65.

Basson, R., Leiblum, S., Brotto, L., Derogatis, L., Foucroy, J., Fugl-Meyer, K., et al. (2003) Definitions of women's sexual dysfunction reconsidered: Advocating expansion and revision. *Journal of Psychosomatic Obstetrics and Gynaecology* 34: 221–229.

Bateman, A.W. and Tyrer, P. (2004) Psychological treatment for personality disorders. *Advances in Psychiatric Treatment* 10: 378–388.

Beck, A.T. (1976) *Cognitive Therapy and the Emotional Disorders*. New York, NY: International Universities Press.

Beck, A.T. (1987) Cognitive models of depression. *Journal of Cognitive Psychotherapy* 1: 5–37.

Beck, A.T., Brown, G., Steer, R.A. and Weissman, A. (1991) Factor analysis of the Dysfunctional Attitudes Scale in a clinical population. *Psychological Assessment* 3: 478–483.

Beck, A.T., Emery, G. and Greenberg, R. (1985) *Anxiety Disorders and Phobias: A Cognitive Perspective*. New York, NY: Basic Books.

Beck, A.T., Freeman, A. and Associates (1990) *Cognitive Therapy of Personality Disorders*. New York, NY: Guilford Press.

Beck, A.T, Freeman, A., Davis, D.D. and Associates (2007) *Cognitive Therapy of Personality Disorders* (2nd edn). New York, NY: Guilford Press.

Beck, A.T., Rush, A.J., Shaw, B.F. and Emery, G. (1979) *Cognitive Therapy of Depression: A Treatment Manual*. New York, NY: Guilford Press.

Beck, A.T., Steer, R.A. and Brown, K. (1996) *Beck Depression Inventory. Version 2. Psychological Corporation*, San Antonio, TX: Harcourt Brace.

Beck, J.S. (1995) *Cognitive Therapy: Basics and Beyond*. New York, NY: Guilford Press.

Beekman, A.T.F., Bremmer, M.A., Deeg, D.J.H., Van Balkom, A.J.L.M., Smit, J.H., de Beurs, E., Van Dyck, R. and Van Tilburg, W. (1998) Anxiety disorders in later life: A report from the longitudinal aging study, Amsterdam. *International Journal of Geriatric Psychiatry* 13: 717–726.

Berkman, N.D., Lohr, K.N. and Bulik, C.M. (2007) Outcomes of eating disorders – a systematic review of the literature. *International Journal of Eating Disorders* 40(4): 293–309.

Bienvenu, O.J., Samuels, J.F., Riddle, M.A., Hoehn-Saric, R., Liang, K.-Y., Cullen, B.M.A, Grados, M.A. and Nestadt, G. (2000) The relationship of obsessive compulsive disorder to possible spectrum disorders: Results from a family study. *Biological Psychiatry* 48: 287–293.

Binik, Y.M., Reissing, E.D., Pukall, C., Flory, N., Payne, K.A. and Khalifé, S.M.D. (2002) The female sexual pain disorders: Genital pain or sexual dysfunction? *Archives of Sexual Behavior* 31: 425–429.

Birmingham, C.L., Su, J. and Hlynski, J.A. (2000) The mortality rate from anorexia nervosa. *International Journal of Eating Disorders* 538: 143–146.

Brown, T.A., O'Leary, T.A. and Barlow, D.H. (2001) Generalized anxiety disorder. In: Barlow, D.H. (ed.), *Clinical Handbook of Psychological Disorders,* (3rd edn): *A Step-by-Step Treatment Manual*. New York, NY: Guilford Press.

Burns, D. (1999) *The Feeling Good Handbook*. New York, NY: Plume.

Cameron, I.M., Crawford, J.R., Lawton, K. and Reid, I.C. (2008) Psychometric comparison of PHQ-9 and HADS for measuring depression severity in primary care. *British Journal of General Practice* 58: 32–36.

Carrasco, M.J. (2001). *Disfunciones sexuales femeninas*. Madrid, Spain: Sintesis.

Carter, R.M., Wittchen, H.-U., Pfister, H., Inf, D. and Kessler, R.C. (2001) One-year prevalence of subthreshold and threshold DSM-IV generalized anxiety disorder in a nationally representative sample. *Depression and Anxiety* 13: 78–88.

Castro, F.J., Deulofeu, R., Baeza, I., Casulai, V., Saura, B., Laizaro, L., Puig, J., Toro, J. and Bernado, M. (2008) Psychopathological and nutritional correlates of plasma homovanillic acid in adolescents with anorexia nervosa. *Journal of Psychiatric Research* 42(3): 213–220.

Catalan, J., Hawton, K. and Day, A. (1990) Couples referred to a sexual dysfunction clinic: Psychological and physical morbidity. *British Journal of Psychiatry* 156: 61–67.

Clark, D. (1986) A cognitive model of panic. *Behaviour Research and Therapy*, 24: 461–470.

Clark, D. (2004) *Cognitive Behavioral Therapy for OCD*. New York, NY: Guilford Press.

Clark, D.M. (1989) Anxiety states: panic and generalised anxiety. In: Hawton, K., Salkovskis, P.M. Kirk, J. and Clark, D.M. (eds), *Cognitive Behaviour Therapy for Psychiatric Problems. A Practical Guide*. Oxford, UK: Oxford University Press.

Clark, D.M. and Wells, A., (1995) A cognitive model of social phobia. In: Heimberg, R.G., Liebowitz, M.R., Hope, D.A. and Schneier, F. R. (eds) *Social Phobia: Diagnosis, Assessment and Treatment*. New York, NY: Guilford Press.

Cooper, M., Todd, G. and Wells, A. (2000) *Bulimia Nervosa – A Cognitive Therapy Programme for Clients*. London: UK: Jessica Kingsley Publishers.

Cooper, M., Todd, G. and Wells A. (2009) *Treating Bulimia Nervosa and Binge Eating: An Integrated Metacognitive and Cognitive Therapy Manual*. London, UK: Routledge.

Cooper, Z. and Fairburn, C.G. (1987) The Eating Disorder Examination: A semi-structured interview for the assessment of the specific psychopathology of eating disorders. *International Journal of Eating Disorders* 6: 1–8.

Cooper, Z. and Shafran, R. (2008) Cognitive behaviour therapy for eating disorders. *Behavioural and Cognitive Psychotherapy* 36: 713–722.

Cooper-Patrick, L., Crum, R.M. and Ford, D.E. (1994) Identifying suicidal ideation in general medical patients. *JAMA* 272: 1757–1762.

Crane, R. (2009) *Mindfulness-Based Cognitive Therapy*. London, UK: Routledge.

Crawford, J.R., Henry, J.D., Crombie, C. and Taylor, E.P. (2001) Brief report: Normative data for the HADS from a large non-clinical sample. *British Journal of Clinical Psychology* 40: 429–434.

Crawley, S.A., Beidas, R.S., Benjamin, C.L., Martin, E. and Kendall, P.C. (2008) Treating socially phobic youth with CBT: Differential outcomes and treatment considerations. *Behavioural and Cognitive Psychotherapy* 36: 379–389.

Creamer, M., Bell, R. and Failia, S. (2003) Psychometric properties of the Impact of Events Scale – Revised. *Behaviour Research and Therapy* 41: 1489–1496.

Curwen, B., Palmer, S. and Ruddell, P. (2008) *Brief Cognitive Behaviour Therapy*. London, UK: Sage.

Daniels, J. and Wearden, A.J. (2011) Socialisation to the model: The active component in the therapeutic alliance? A preliminary study. *Behavioural and Cognitive Psychotherapy* 39(2): 221–227.

Davidson, K. (2008) *Cognitive Therapy for Personality Disorders: A Guide for Clinicians* (2nd edn). New York, NY: Routledge.

Day, A., Howells, K., Mohr, P., Schall, E. and Gerace, A. (2008) The development of CBT programmes for anger: The role of interventions to promote perspective-taking skills. *Behavioural and Cognitive Psychotherapy*, 36(3): 299–312.

De Jong, P.J., Van Overveld, M., Schultz, W.W., Peters, M.L. and Buwalda, F.M. (2009) Disgust and contamination sensitivity in vaginismus and dyspareunia. *Archives of Sexual Behavior* 38: 244–252.

Dimidjian, S., Hollon, S.D., Dobson, K.S., Schmalling, K.B., Kohlenberg, R.J., Addis, M.B., Gallop, J.K., Atkins, D.C. and Dunner, D.L. (2006) Randomized trial of behavioral activation, cognitive therapy, and antidepressant medication in the acute treatment of adults with major depression. *Journal of Consulting and Clinical Psychology* 74: 658–670.

Di Nardo, P.A., Brown, T.A. and Barlow, D.H. (1994) *Anxiety Disorders Interview Schedule for DSM-IV: Lifetime Version (ADIS-IV-L)*. San Antonio, TX: Psychological Corporation.

Dolan, F.E. (1994) *Dangerous Familiars; Representations of Domestic Crime in England 1550–1700*. London, UK: Cornell University Press.

Drake, M. (2008) Efficiency, efficacy and acceptability: An evaluation of a stepped care model against the government's benchmark. Unpublished master's thesis, University of Lancaster, UK.

Dugas, M.J., Ladouceur, R., Leger, E., Freeston, M.H., Langlois, F., Provencher, M.D. and Boisvert, J.-M. (2003) Group cognitive-behavioural therapy for generalized anxiety disorder: Treatment outcome and long-term follow-up. *Journal of Consulting and Clinical Psychology* 71(4): 821–825.

Dugas, M. and Robichaud, M. (2007) *Cognitive-Behavioural Treatment for General Anxiety Disorder: From Science to Practice*. London, UK: Routledge.

Dugas, M.J., Schwartz, A. and Francis, K. (2004) Intolerance of uncertainty, worry and depression. *Cognitive Therapy and Research* 28: 835–842.

Duker, M. and Slade, R. (1988) *Anorexia Nervosa and Bulimia: How to Help*. Milton Keynes, UK: Open University Press.

Ellis, A. (1977) The basic clinical theory of rational-emotive therapy. In: Ellis, A. and Grieger, R. (eds), *Handbook of Rational-Emotive Therapy*. New York, NY: Springer.

Engel, B., Reiss, N. and Dombeck, M. (2007) Eating disorders – co-morbid (co-existing) conditions. Available at: http://www.mentalhelp.net/poc/view_doc.php?type=doc&id=11761&cn=46.

Essau, C.A., Conradt, J. and Petermann, F. (1999) Frequency and comorbidity of social phobia and social fears in adolescents. *Behaviour Research and Therapy* 37: 831–843.

Evans, C., Mellor-Clark, J., Margison, F., Barkham, M., McGrath, G., Connell, J. and Audin, K. (2000) Clinical outcomes in routine evaluation: CORE-OM. *Journal of Mental Health* 9: 247–255.

Fairburn, C.G. and Beglia, S.J. (1990) Studies in the epidemiology of bulimia nervosa. *American Journal of Psychiatry* 147: 401–408.

Fallon, P., Katzman, M.A. and Wooley, S.C. (eds) (1994) *Feminist Perspectives on Eating Disorders*. New York, NY: Guilford Press.

Fennell, M.J.V. (1989) Depression. In: Hawton, K., Salkovskis, P.M., Kirk, J. and Clark, D. (eds), *Cognitive Behavioural Therapy for Psychiatric Problems*. Oxford, UK: Oxford Medical Publications.

First, M.B., Spitzer, R.L., Gibbon, M. and Williams, J.B.W. (1996) *Structured Clinical Interview for DSM-IV Axis I Disorders, Clinician Version*. Washington, DC: American Psychiatric Press, Inc.

Flint, A.J. (2005) Generalized anxiety disorder in elderly patients. *Drugs and Aging* 22(2): 101–114.

Foa, E.B., Cashman, L., Jaycox, L. and Perry, K. (1997) The validation of a self-report measure of posttraumatic stress disorder: The Posttraumatic Diagnostic Scale. *Psychological Assessment* 9(4): 445–451.

Foa, E.B., Keane, T.M., Friedman, M.J. and Cohen, J. (2009) *Effective Treatments for PTSD: Practice Guidelines from the International Society for Traumatic Stress Studies*. New York, NY: Guilford Press.

Foa, E.B., Kozak, M.J., Salkovskis, P.M., Coles, M.E. and Amir, N. (1998) The validation of a new obsessive compulsive disorder scale: The Obsessive Compulsive Inventory (OCI). *Psychological Assessment* 10: 206–214.

Foa, E.B, Liebowitz, M.R., Kozak, M.J., Davies, S., Campeas, R., Franklin, M.E., Huppert, J.D., Kjernisted, K., Rowan, V., Schmidt, A.B., Simpson, H.B. and Tu, X. (2005) Randomized, placebo-controlled trial of exposure and ritual prevention, clomipramine, and their combination in the treatment of obsessive-compulsive disorder. *American Journal of Psychiatry* 162(1): 151–161.

Ford, K., Byrt, R. and Dooher, J. (2010) *Preventing and Reducing Aggression and Violence in Health and Social Care.* Keswick, UK: M & K Publishing.

Free, M.L. (2000) *Cognitive Therapy in Groups.* Chichester, UK: John Wiley and Sons Ltd.

Freeman, A. and Dattilio, F.M. (eds) (1992) *Comprehensive Casebook of Cognitive Therapy.* New York, NY: Springer.

Fresco, D.M., Mennin, D.S., Heimberg R.G. and Turk C.L. (2003) Using the Penn State Worry Questionnaire to identify individuals with generalized anxiety disorder: A receiver operating characteristic analysis. *Journal of Behavior Therapy and Experimental Psychiatry* 34: 283–291.

Fugl-Meyer, A.R. and Sjögren Fugl-Meyer, K. (1999) Sexual disabilities, problems and satisfaction in 18 to 74-year-old Swedes. *Scandinavian Journal of Sexology* 2: 79–105.

Garner, D.M., Olmsted, M.P., Bohr, Y. and Garfinkel, P.E. (1982) The eating attitude test: Psychometric features and clinical correlates. *Psychological Medicine* 12: 871–878.

Gelder, M.G. (1989) Foreword. In: Hawton, K. Salkvoskis, P.M., Kirk, J. and Clark, D.M. (eds), *Cognitive Behaviour Therapy for Psychiatric Problems −A Practical Guide.* Oxford: Oxford University Press.

Goldmeier, D., Kean, F.E., Carter, P., Hessman, A., Harris, J.R. and Renton, A. (1997) Prevalence of sexual dysfunction in heterosexual patients attending a central London genitourinary medicine clinic. *International Journal of STD and AIDS* 8: 303–306.

Goldstein, A.J. and Chambless, D.L. (1978) A re-analysis of agoraphobia. *Behaviour Therapy* 9: 47–59.

Goldstein, B. and Rosselli, F. (2003) Etiological paradigms of depression: The relationship between perceived causes, empowerment, treatment preferences and stigma. *Journal of Mental Health* 12(4): 551–564.

Goodwin, G.M. (1990) Neuroendocrine function and the biology of eating disorders. *Human Psychopharmacology*, 5: 249–253.

Grant, A., Townend, M., Mulhern, R. and Short, N. (2010) *Cognitive Behavioural Therapy in Mental Health Care.* London: Sage.

Green, B. (2009) *Problem-Based Psychiatry* (2nd edn). Oxford, UK: Radcliffe Publishing.

Gremillion, H. (2004) Unpacking essentialisms in therapy: Lessons for feminist approaches from narrative work. *Journal of Constructivist Psychology* 17(3): 173–200.

Guilfoyle, M. (2009) Therapeutic discourse and eating disorders in the context of power. In: Malson, H. and Burns, M. (eds), *Critical Feminist Approaches to Eating Disorders.* New York, NY: Routledge.

Guthrie, R. and Bryant, R. (2005) Auditory startle response in fire fighters before and after trauma exposure. *American Journal of Psychiatry* 162: 283–290.

Haddock, G. and Slade, P.D. (eds) (1997). *Cognitive-Behavioural Interventions with Psychotic Disorders.* London: Routledge.

Hartman, L.M. (1986) Social anxiety, problem drinking and self awareness. In: Hartman, L.M. and Blankstein, K.R. (eds), *Perceptions of Self in Emotional Disorder and Psychotherapy*. New York, NY: Plenum Press.

Hawton, K., Salkovskis, P.M., Kirk, J. and Clark, D. (eds) (1989) *Cognitive Behavioural Therapy for Psychiatric Problems*. Oxford, UK: Oxford Medical Publications.

Hayden, E.P. and Klein, D.N. (2001) Outcome of dysthymic disorder at 5-year follow-up: The effect of familial psychopathology, early adversity, personality, comorbidity, and chronic stress. *American Journal of Psychiatry* 158(11): 1864–1870.

Henning, E.R., Turk, C.L., Mennin, D.S., Fresco D.M. and Heimberg R.G. (2007) Impairment and quality of life in individuals with generalized anxiety disorder. *Depression and Anxiety* 24: 342–349.

Herrenkohl, T.I., McMorris, B.J., Catalano, R.F., Abbot, R.D., Hemphill, S.A. and Toumbourou, J.W. (2007) Risk factors for violence and relational aggression in adolescence. *Journal of Interpersonal Violence* 22: 386–405.

Hettema, J.M., Neale, M.C. and Kendler, K.S. (2001) A population-based twin study of generalized anxiety disorder in men and women. *Journal of Nervous and Mental Disease* 189: 413–420.

Hirst, J.F., Baggaley, M.R. and Watson, J.P. (1996) A four-year survey of an inner-city psychosexual clinic. *Sexual and Marital Therapy* 11: 19–36.

Hodson, K.J., McManus, F.V., Clark, D.M. and Doll, H. (2008) Can Clark and Well's (1995) cognitive model of social phobia be applied to young people? *Behavioural and Cognitive Psychotherapy* 36: 449–461.

Hollon, S.D. and Kendall, P.C. (1980) Cognitive self-statements in depression: Development of an automatic thoughts questionnaire. *Cognitive Therapy and Research* 4(4): 383–395.

Horowitz, M., Marmar, C., Krupnick, J., Wilner, N., Kaltreider, N. and Wallerstein, R. (1984) *Personality Styles and Brief Psychotherapy*. New York, NY: Basic Books.

Huffman, J.C. and Pollack, M.H. (2003) Predicting panic disorder among patients with chest pain: An analysis of the literature. *Psychosomatics* 44: 222–236.

Inskip, H.M., Harris, E.C. and Barraclough, B. (1998) Lifetime risk of suicide for affective disorder, alcoholism and schizophrenia. *British Journal of Psychiatry* 172: 35–37.

Jones, S., Burrell-Hodgson, G., Tate, G. and Fowler, B. (2006) Personality disorder in primary care: Factors associated with therapist views of process and outcome. *Behaviour and Cognitive Psychotherapy* 34: 453–466.

Jordanova, V., Stewart, R., Goldberg, D., Bebbington, P.E., Brugha, T., Singleton, N., Lindesay, J.E.B., Jenkins, R., Prince, M. and Meltzer, H. (2007) Age variation in life events and their relationship with common mental disorders in a national survey population. *Social Psychiatry and Psychiatric Epidemiology* 42: 611–616.

Kaplan, H.S. (1974) *The New Sex Therapy*. New York: Brunner/Mazel.

Kaplan, H.S. (1979) Hypoactive sexual desire. *Journal of Sexual and Marital Therapy* 3: 3–9.

Kendall, P.C., Safford, S., Flannery-Schroeder, E. and Webb, A. (2004) Child anxiety treatment: Outcomes in adolescence and impact on substance use and depression at 7.4-year follow-up. *Journal of Consulting and Clinical Psychology* 72: 276–287.

Kendler, K.S., Walters, E.E., Neale, M.C., Kessler, R.C., Heath, A.C. and Eaves, L.J. (1995) The structure of the genetic and environmental risk factors for six major psychiatric disorders in women. *Archives of General Psychiatry* 52: 374–383.

Kessler, R.C. (2000) The epidemiology of pure and comorbid generalized anxiety disorder: A review and evaluation of recent research. *Acta Psychiatrica Scandinavica* 102 (Supplement 406): 7–13.

Kinsella, P. and Garland, A. (2008) *Cognitive Behavioural Therapy for Mental Health Workers*. London, UK: Routledge.

Koerner, N. and Dugas, M.J. (2008) An investigation of appraisals in individuals vulnerable to excessive worry: The role of intolerance of uncertainty. *Cognitive Therapy and Research* 32: 619–638.

Kroenke, K.S. (2002) The PHQ-9: A new depression diagnostic and severity measure. *Psychiatric Annals* 9: 1–7.

Kroenke, K., Spitzer, R.L. and Williams, J.B. (2001) The PHQ-9: Validity of a brief depression severity measure. *Journal of General Internal Medicine* 16(9): 606–613.

Kuyken, W., Padesky, C.A. and Dudley, R. (2008) Process issues: The science and practice of case conceptualization. *Behavioural and Cognitive Psychotherapy* 36 (6): 757–768.

Kwon, S.M. and Oei, T.P.S. (2003) Cognitive change processes in a group cognitive behaviour therapy of depression. *Behavior Therapy and Experimental Psychiatry* 34: 73–85.

Ladouceur, R., Dugas, M.J., Freeston, M.H., Leger, E., Gagnon, F. and Thibodeau, N. (2000) Efficacy of a cognitive-behavioural treatment for generalized anxiety disorder: Evaluation in a controlled trial. *Journal of Consulting and Clinical Psychology* 68(6): 957–964.

Ladouceur, R., Gosselin, P. and Dugas, M.J. (2000) Experimental manipulation of intolerance of uncertainty: A study of a theoretical model of worry. *Behaviour Research and Therapy* 38: 933–941.

Lazarus, A.A. (1997). *Brief but Comprehensive Psychotherapy*. New York: Springer.

Leahy, R.L. (2008) The therapeutic relationship in cognitive-behavioural therapy. *Behavioural and Cognitive Psychotherapy*, 36: 769–777.

Leiblum, S.R. (2000) Vaginismus: A most perplexing problem. In: Leiblum S.R. and Rosen R.C. (eds), *Principles and Practice of Sex Therapy* (3rd edn). New York, NY: Guilford Press.

Lewinsohn, P. (1974) A behavioral approach to depression. In: Friedman, R.J (ed.), *Psychology of Depression*. Oxford, UK: Wiley.

Linehan, M.M., Camper, P., Chiles, J.A., Strosahl, K. and Shearin, E. (1987) Interpersonal problem-solving and parasuicide. *Cognitive Therapy and Research* 11: 1–12.

Maes, M., Monteleone, P., Bencivenga, R., Goossens, F., Maj, M., Van West, D., Bosmans, E. and Scharp, S. (2001) Lower serum activity of prolyl endopeptidase in anorexia and bulimia nervosa. *Psychoneuroendocrinology* 26: 17–26.

Maier, S.F. and Seligman, M.E.P. (1976) Learned helplessness: Theory and evidence. *Journal of Experimental Psychology* 105: 3–46.

Maier, W., Gansicke, M., Freyberger, H.J., Linz, M., Heun, R. and Lecrubier, Y. (2000) Generalized anxiety disorder (ICD-10) in primary care from a cross-cultural perspective: a valid diagnostic entity? *Acta Psychiatrica Scandinavica* 101: 29–36.

Malson, H. and Burns M. (2009) *Critical Feminist Approaches to Eating Dis/Orders*. New York, NY : Routledge.

Marks, I.M. (2001) *Living with Fear: Understanding and Coping with Anxiety* (2nd edn). Maidenhead, UK: McGraw-Hill.

Martell, C.R., Addis, M.E. and Jacobson, M.S. (2001) *Depression in Context. Strategies for Guided Action*. New York, NY: Norton.

Martin, D.J., Garske, J.P. and Davis, M.K. (2000) Relation of the therapeutic alliance with outcome and other variables: a meta-analytical review. *Journal of Consulting and Clinical Psychology*, 68: 438–450.

Masters, W.H. and Johnson, V.E. (1966) *Human Sexual Response*. Boston, MA: Little, Brown and Co.

Masters, W.H. and Johnson, V.E. (1970) *Human Sexual Inadequacy*. Boston, MA: Little, Brown and Co.

McGowan, P.O., Sasaki, A., D'Alessio, A.C., Dymov, S., Labonte, B., Szyf, M., Turecki, G. and Meaney, M.J. (2009) Epigenetic regulation of the glucocorticoid receptor in human brain associates with childhood abuse. *Nature Neuroscience* 12(3): 342–348.

McLaughlin, K.A., Behar, E. and Borkovec, T.D. (2008) Family history of psychological problems in generalized anxiety disorder. *Journal of Clinical Psychology* 64(7): 905–918.

Meichenbaum, D.H. (1975) A self-instructional approach to stress management: A proposal for stress inoculation training. In: Spielberger, C.D. and Sarason, I. (eds), *Stress and Anxiety, 2*. New York, NY: Wiley.

Mennin, D.S., Heimburg, R.G., Fresco, D.M. and Ritter, M.R. (2008) Is generalized anxiety disorder an anxiety or mood disorder? Considering multiple factors as we ponder the fate of GAD. *Depression and Anxiety* 25: 289–299.

Meyer, T.J., Miller, M.L., Metzger, R.L. and Borkovec, T.D. (1990) Development and validation of the Penn State Worry Questionnaire. *Behaviour Research and Therapy* 28: 487–495.

Moffit, T.E., Caspi, A., Harrington, H., Milne, B.J., Mechior, M., Goldberg, D. and Poulton, R. (2007) Generalized anxiety disorder and depression: Childhood risk factors in a birth cohort followed to age 32. *Psychological Medicine* 37: 441–452.

Molina, S. and Borkovec, T.D. (1994) The Penn State Worry Questionnaire: Psychometric properties and associated characteristics. In: Davey, G.C.L. and Tallis, F. (eds), *Worrying Perspectives on Theory, Assessment, and Treatment*. New York, NY: Wiley.

Moulding, N. (2009) The anorexic as femme fatale: Reproducing gender through the father/psychiatrist–daughter/patient relationship. In: Malsom H. and Burns M. (eds), *Critical Feminist Approaches to Eating Dis/Orders*. London, UK: Routledge.

Mowrer, O.H. (1960) *Learning Theory and Behavior*. Hoboken, NJ: John Wiley and Sons.

Murakami, K., Achy, T., Washizuka, T., Ikuta, N. and Miyake, Y. (2002) A comparison of purging and non-purging eating disorder patients in co-morbid personality disorders and psychopathology. *Tokai Journal of Experimental Clinical Medicine* 27(1): 9–19.

Murcia, F.M. (2006) Social changes and post-modern personality disorders. *Journal of Psychology (Papeles de Psicologo)* 27(2): 104–115.

Murray, J. and Cartwright-Hatton, S. (2006) NICE guidelines on treatment of depression in childhood and adolescence; Implications from a CBT perspective. *Behavioural and Cognitive Therapy* 34 (2): 129–137.

National Institute for Clinical Excellence (NICE) (2004) *Eating Disorders: Core Interventions in the Treatment and Management of Anorexia Nervosa and Bulimia Nervosa and Related Eating Disorders. Clinical Guideline 9*. London, UK: NICE.

National Institute for Clinical Excellence (NICE) (2005a) *Guidelines on Violence: Recommendations Concerning People with Diverse Backgrounds and Needs, Including Individuals of Black and Minority Groups*. London, UK: NICE.

National Institute for Clinical Excellence (2005b) *The Management of PTSD in Adults and Children in Primary and Secondary Care. Clinical Guideline 26*. London, UK: NICE.

National Institute for Clinical Excellence (NICE) (2005c) *Obsessive Compulsive Disorder: Core Interventions in the Treatment of Obsessive Compulsive Disorder and Body Dysmorphic Disorder. Clinical Guideline 31.* London, UK: NICE.

National Institute for Clinical Excellence (2009) *Depression: Management of Depression in Primary and Secondary Care. Clinical Guideline 23.* London, UK: NICE.

National Institute for Clinical Excellence (NICE) (2011) *Generalised Anxiety Disorder and Panic Disorder (With or Without Agoraphobia) in Adults. Management in Primary, Secondary and Community Care. Clinical Guideline 113.* London, UK: NICE.

Novaco, R.W. (1979) The cognitive regulation of anger and stress. In: Kendall, P.C. and Hollon, S.D. (eds), *Cognitive-behavioural Interventions; Theory, Research and Procedures.* New York, NY: Academic Press.

Novaco, R.W. (2000) Anger. In: Kazdin, A.E. (ed.), *Encyclopaedia of Psychology.* Washington, DC: American Psychological Association.

Office of National Statistics (ONS) (2010) *Focus on Mental Health.* Available at: www. statistics.gov.uk/downloads/theme_compendia/foh2005/2009_MentalHealth.pdf.

O'Sullivan, K. (1979) Observations on vaginismus in Irish women. *Archives of General Psychiatry* 36: 824–826.

Ozer, E.J., Best, S.R., Lipsey, D.L. and Weiss, D.S. (2003) Predictors of posttraumatic stress disorder and symptoms in adults: A meta-analysis. *Psychological Trauma: Theory, Research, Practice, and Policy* 1: 3–36.

Padesky, C. (1988) Schema-focused CT: Comments and questions. *International Cognitive Therapy Newsletter* 4: 1.

Padesky, C. (1993) Socratic questioning: Changing minds or guiding discovery? Keynote address delivered at the European Congress of Behavioural Cognitive Therapies, London, 24 September.

Padesky, C.A. (1996). Developing cognitive therapist competency: Teaching and supervision models. Chapter 13 in Salkvoskis, P.M. (ed.), *Frontiers of Cognitive Therapy.* New York, NY: Guilford Press.

Padesky, C.A. and Mooney, K.A. (1990) Clinical tip: Presenting the cognitive model to clients. *International Cognitive Therapy Newsletter,* 6: 13–14. Available at: http://www.padesky.com/clinicalcorner.htm.

Parkes, R.J., Lawrie, S.M. and Freeman, C.P. (1995) Post-viral onset of anorexia nervosa. *British Journal of Psychiatry* 166: 386–389.

Persons, J.B. (1989) *Cognitive Therapy in Practice – A Case Formulation Approach.* W.W. Norton and Company. New York.

Peters, L., Slade, T. and Andrews, G. (1999) A comparison of ICD-10 and DSM-IV criteria for posttraumatic stress disorder. *Journal of Traumatic Stress* 12: 335–343.

Read, S., King, M. and Watson, J. (1997) Sexual dysfunction in primary medical care: Prevalence, characteristics and detection by the general practitioner. *Journal of Public Health Medicine* 19: 387–391.

Reissing, E.D., Binik, Y.M., Khalife, S., Cohen, D. and Amsel, R. (2004) Vaginal spasm, pain and behaviour: An empirical investigation of the diagnosis of vaginismus. *Archives of Sexual Behaviour* 33: 5–17.

Renshaw, D.C. (1988) Profile of 2,376 patients treated at Loyola Sex Clinic between 1972 and 1987. *Sexual and Marital Therapy* 3: 111–117.

Rescorla, R.A. (1988) Behavioral studies of Pavlovian conditioning. *Annual Review of Neuroscience* 11, 329–352.

Robinson, P. (2009) *Severe and Enduring Eating Disorder (SEED) – Management of Complex Presentations of Anorexia and Bulimia Nervosa.* Chichester, UK: Wiley-Blackwell.

Roos, J. and Weardon, A. (2009 What do we mean by 'Socialisation to the model'? A Delphi study. *Behavioural and Cognitive Psychotherapy,* 37(3): 341–345.

Ryan, V., Malson, H., Clarke, S. Anderson, G. and Kohn, M. (2006) Discursive constructions of 'eating disorders nursing': An analysis of nurses' accounts of nursing eating disorder patients. *European Eating Disorder Review* 14(2): 125–135.

Salkovskis, P.M. (1996). *Frontiers of Cognitive Therapy.* New York: Guilford Press.

Salkovskis, P.M., Richards, H.C. and Forrester, E. (1995) The relationship between intrusive problems and intrusive thoughts. *Behavioural and Cognitive Psychotherapy* 23: 281–299.

Salkovskis, P.M., Wroe, A.L., Gledhill, A., Morrison, N., Forrester, E., Richards, C., Reynolds, M. and Thorpe, S., (2000) Responsibility attitudes and interpretations are characteristic of obsessive compulsive disorder. *Behaviour Research and Therapy* 38: 347–372.

Schmidt, N.B., Zvolensky, M.J. and Maner, J.K. (2006) Anxiety sensitivity: Prospective prediction of panic attacks and Axis I pathology. *Journal of Psychiatric Research* 40: 691–699.

Segal, Z.V., Williams, J.M.G. and Teasdale, J.D. (2002) *Mindfulness-based Cognitive Therapy for Depression: A New Approach to Preventing Relapse.* New York, NY: Guilford Press.

Shankman, S.A. and Klein, D.N. (2002) The impact of comorbid anxiety disorders on the course of dysthymic disorder: A 5-year prospective longitudinal study. *Journal of Affective Disorders* 70(2): 211–217.

Shokrollahi, P., Mirmohamadi, M., Mehrabi, F. and Babaei, G.H. (1999) Prevalence of sexual dysfunction in women seeking services at a family planning center in Tehran. *Journal of Sex and Marital Therapy* 25: 211–215.

Skeem, J.L., Monahan, J. and Mulvey, E.P. (2002) Psychopathy, treatment involvement and subsequent violence amongst civil psychiatric patients. *Law and Human Behaviour* 26(3): 577–603.

Slade, T. and Andrews, G. (2001) DSM-IV and ICD-10 generalized anxiety disorder: discrepant diagnosis and associated disability. *Social Psychiatry and Psychiatric Epidemiology,* 36: 45–51.

Sokol, M.S. (2000) Infection-triggered AN in children: clinical description of four cases. *Journal of Child and Adolescent Psychopharmacology* 10(2): 133–145.

Spence, S.H. (1991) *Psychosexual Therapy: A Cognitive Behavioural Approach.* London, UK: Chapman Hall.

Spitzer, R.L., Kroenke, K. and Williams, J.B. (2006) A brief measure for assessing generalised anxiety disorder: The GAD-7. *Archives of Internal Medicine* 166: 1092–1097.

Stanley, M.A., Beck, J.G., Novy, D.M., Averill, P.M., Swann, A.C., Dienfenbach G.J. and Hopko, D.R. (2003) Cognitive-behavioural treatment of late-life generalized anxiety disorder. *Journal of Consulting and Clinical Psychology* 71(2): 309–319.

Stein, M.B., Fuetsch, M., Muller, N., Hofler, M., Lieb, R. and Wittchen, H.-U. (2001) Social anxiety disorder and the risk of depression. *Archives of General Psychiatry* 58: 251–256.

Stein, M.B., Jang, K.L. and Livesley, W.J. (1999) Heritability of anxiety sensitivity: A twin study. *American Journal of Psychiatry,* 156: 246–251.

Stober, J. and Borkovec, T.D. (2002) Reduced concreteness of worry in generalized anxiety disorder: Findings from a therapy study. *Cognitive Therapy and Research* 26(1): 89–96.

Taylor, S. (2006) *Clinician's Guide to PTSD: A Cognitive-behavioral Approach.* New York, NY: Guilford Press.

Teasdale, J.D., Segal, Z.V., Williams, J.M.G., Ridgeway, V.A., Soulsby, J.M. and Lau, M.A. (2000) Prevention of relapse/recurrence in major depression by mindfulness-based cognitive therapy. *Journal of Consulting and Clinical Psychology* 68: 615–623.

Ter Kuile, M.M., Van Lankveld J.J.,D.,M, Vlietvliland, C., Willekes, C. and Weijemborg, P.Th., M. (2005) Vulvar vestibulitis syndrome: An important factor in the evaluation of lifelong vaginismus? *Journal of Psychosomatic Obstetrics and Gynecology*, 26: 245–249.

Thomas, M. (2000) Existential interventions in eating disorders. Unpublished doctoral dissertation, University of Nottingham, UK.

Thomas, M. (2008). Cognitive behavioural dimensions of the therapeutic relationship. In: Haugh, S and Paul, S. (eds), *The Therapeutic Relationship –Perspectives and Themes*. Ross-on-Wye, UK: PCCS Books. Chapter 8.

Thornton, C. and Russell, J. (1997) OC co-morbidity in the dieting disorders. *International Journal of Eating Disorders* 21(1): 83–87.

Torgerson, S. (1983) Genetic factors in anxiety disorders. *Archives of General Psychiatry* 40: 1085–1089.

Trower, P., Casey, A. and Dryden, W. (1996). *Cognitive Behavioural Counselling in Action*. London, UK: Sage.

Tugrul, C. and Kabakci, E. (1997) Vaginismus and its correlates. *Journal of Sex and Marital Therapy* 12: 23–24.

Van Goozen, S.H. and Fairchild, G. (2006) Neuroendocrine and neurotransmitter correlates in children with anti-social behaviour. *Hormones and Behaviour* 50: 647–654.

Ventegodt, S. (1998) Sex and the quality of life in Denmark. *Archives of Sexual Behaviour* 27: 295–307.

Walsh, B.T. and Cameron, V.L. (2005) *If Your Adolescent has an Eating Disorder*. New York, NY: Oxford University Press.

Weathers, F.W., Keane, T.M. and Davidson, J.R.T. (2001) Clinician administered PTSD Scale – a review of the first ten years of research. *Depression and Anxiety* 13: 132–156.

Weiss, D.S. and Marmar, C.R. (1997) The Impact of Events Scale – Revised. In: Wilson, J.P. and Kean, T.M. (eds), *Assessing Psychological Trauma and PTSD*. New York, NY: Guilford Press.

Wells, A. (1997) *Cognitive Therapy of Anxiety Disorders: A Practice Manual and Conceptual Guide*. Chichester, UK: Wiley.

Wells, A. (1999) A metacognitive model and therapy for generalized anxiety disorder. *Clinical Psychology and Psychotherapy* 6(2): 86–95.

Wells, A. and Clark, D.M. (1997) Social phobia: A cognitive approach. In: Heimberg, R.H., Liebowitz, M., Hope, D.A. and Schneier, F.R. (eds), *Social Phobia: Diagnosis, Assessment and Treatment*. New York, NY: Guilford Press.

Westbrook, D., Kennerley, H. and Kirk, J. (2007) *An Introduction to Cognitive Behavioural Therapy: Skills and Application*. London, UK: Sage.

Westbrook, D., Kennerley, H. and Kirk, J. (2011) *An Introduction to Cognitive Behavioural Therapy: Skills and Application* (2nd edn). London, UK: Sage.

Wetherell, J.L. and Gatz, M. (2005) The Beck Anxiety Inventory in older adults with generalized anxiety disorder. *Journal of Psychopathology and Behavioural Assessment* 27(1): 17–24.

Whiting, A.S. (2008) The client with a personality disorder. In: Antai-Otong D. (ed.), *Psychiatric Nursing: Biological and Behavioural Concepts* (2nd edn). New York, NY: Delmar/Thomson.

Wijma, B. and Wijma, K. (1997) A cognitive behavioural treatment model of vaginismus. *Scandinavian Journal of Behaviour Therapy* 26(4): 147–156.

Williams, C. (2010) *Overcoming Anxiety, Stress and Panic: A Five Areas Approach* (2nd edn). London, UK: Hodder Arnold.

Wilson, G.T. and Fairburn, C.G. (2007) Eating disorders. In: Nathan, P.E. and Gorman, J.M. (eds), *Treatments that Work*. New York, NY: Oxford University Press.

Wittchen, H.-U. (2002) Generalized anxiety disorder: prevalence, burden, and cost to society. *Depression and Anxiety* 16: 162–171.

Wittchen, H.-U., Krause, P., Hoyer, J., Beesdo, K., Jacobi, F., Hofler, M. and Winter S. (2002) Generalized anxiety and depression in primary care: Prevalence, recognition, and management. *Journal of Clinical Psychiatry* 63 (Supplement 8): 24–34.

Wittchen, H.-U., Stein, M.B. and Kessler, R.C. (1999) Social fears and social phobia in a community sample of adolescents and young adults: Prevalence, risk factors and co-morbidity. *Psychological Medicine* 29: 309–323.

Wittchen, H.-U., Zhao, S., Kessler, R.C. and Eaton, W.W. (1994) DSM-III-R generalised anxiety disorder in the National Comorbidity Survey. *Archives of General Psychiatry* 51: 355–364.

Wolpe, J. (1969) *The Practice of Behavioral Therapy*. New York, NY: Pergamon Press.

World Health Organization (WHO) (2007) *Multi-axial Presentation of the ICD-10 (International Statistical Classification of Diseases and Related Health Problems –10th Revision), for Use in Adult Psychiatry*. Cambridge: World Health Organization/ Cambridge University Press.

Young, J. (1987) Schema-focused cognitive therapy for personality disorders. Unpublished manuscript, Cognitive Therapy Centre of New York, NY.

Zarb, J.M. (1992) *Cognitive-behavioural Assessment and Therapy with Adolescents*. New York, NY: Brunner/Mazel.

Zigmond, A.S. (1963) The Hospital Anxiety and Depression scale. *Acta Psychiatrica Scandinavica* 67: 361–370.

Zigmond, A.S. and Snaith, R.P. (1983) The Hospital Anxiety and Depression scale. *Acta Psychiatrica Scandinavica* 67(6): 361–370.

Zimmerman, M.L. (2008) The client with an eating disorder. In: Antai-Otong D. (ed.), *Psychiatric Nursing: Biological and Behavioural Concepts* (2nd edn). New York, NY: Delmar/Thomson.

Index